The Epic in Africa

THE
EPIC
in
AFRICA

Toward a Poetics of the Oral Performance

ISIDORE OKPEWHO

New York   **Columbia University Press**

Columbia University Press

New York   Oxford

Copyright © 1975, 1979 Columbia University Press

All Rights Reserved

Library of Congress Cataloging in Publication Data

Okpewho, Isidore.

The epic in Africa.

Bibliography: p.

Includes index.

1. Epic poetry, African—History and criticism.

2. Folk-songs, African—History and criticism.

3. Oral tradition—Africa.   I. Title.

PL8010.4.038   896   78-12893

ISBN 0-231-04401-1 (pbk.)

Printed in the United States of America

p 10 9 8 7 6 5 4 3 2 1

For my wife,
Obiageli,
and our sons,
Ediru and **Ugo**

CONTENTS

PREFACE

There has been some controversy as to whether the epic, as a genre of traditional oral literature, exists in Africa. Sir Maurice Bowra and (more recently) Ruth Finnegan, working under limitations either of vision or of information, deny that it does. Recent Dutch-Flemish scholars like Knappert and Biebuyck disagree; but they are mainly anthropologists by training and have been unable to address themselves effectively to the literary arguments that are, in my opinion, the key to an essentially literary problem.

Since childhood I have listened to many skilled men singing heroic tales to musical accompaniment; and I have in recent years taken a keen intellectual interest in their art. This long exposure, coupled with my study of various non-African traditions of the genre, has led me to the conviction that the epic is by no means alien to Africa. This book brings together the results of my comparative inquiry.

As the bibliography will show, my primary African sources cover a considerable part of sub-Saharan Africa: from the rich mythic geography of the Mandingo of the western Sudan through the teeming Atlantic south of Nigeria and down across the broad sweep of the Bantu country from Cameroun to Zaire, touching southern Africa lightly. In all, I take roughly one dozen epic tales into account. It should, however, be stressed that the validity of this kind of study does not lie in assembling numerous tales and spinning mostly repetitive logic out of them. I have simply selected representative tales from equally representative areas of the continent and given them as intensive an examination as possible. This approach reduces the urgency to account for the numerous variants of the known classics or for the host of "epiclike" tales from the Bantu country, about which the Dutch-Flemish school have made some overzealous claims.

Something should be said also about the editorial health of our primary sources. A tale like *Lianja* was published in 1949, at the zenith of the European anthropological foray into Africa. The interest then was more in the evidence for traditional social life and thought than in the creative quality of the traditional art; textual issues were given too little attention. Even our Francophone sources of the 1960s have to be used with a certain care in formal analysis; the nationalist zeal of the négritude school, from which some of the editors derive, has not made for firm editorial faith to the original material. In their translation of *Silamaka*, Ba and Kesteloot avow that they have "serré le texte de très près, respectant son rythme et ses images, tout en essayant de faire 'passer' en français le grande souffle épique qui anime la version peule." Fair enough; but the cosmetic touch can hardly be denied. Niane's edition of the Sunjata epic is even less loyal and thus is useful more for content than for issues of structure and style. Not that the old European classics fared much better: our texts of Homer are pretty much a product of long doctoring, one might even say a compromise of brilliant conjectures. Still, from all this we have enough that invites intelligent discussion.

My non-African material consists mainly of the Homeric corpus. For the rest, I have had selective recourse to the traditions of the ancient Near East, Russia and Yugoslavia, and the Medieval European minstrelsy.

The oral provenance of these old, non-African classics may indeed be open to question; but there is little doubt that they reflect the oral traditions of their times or of the immediate antecedents, and are thus of considerable value in our study of observable oral traditions. I have relied on Sandars' Penguin translation of *Gilgamesh;* since I am not using that legend in my major formal discussion, I have not thought it necessary to wade through the heavily lacunose passages of Pritchard's *Ancient Near Eastern Texts.* With regard to Homer, I have made extensive use of Richmond Lattimore's translations of the *Iliad* and *Odyssey,* which by general agreement are as loyal and as sound as can be. Rather than adopt the fashionable expedient of doing my own translations and working them round to suit my arguments, I have stayed with one translator all the way through, if only to demonstrate that my points are not peculiar formulations based on a tendentious reading of Homer. However, I have taken into account various critical issues relating to the original Greek as the occasion arose.

This comparative study of the oral epic does not, of course, embrace all the approaches that have been applied to the examination of traditional lore. I have specifically chosen the oral moment as my main focus of interest because I believe that the contextual approach will yield us a better understanding of the intriguing nature of this kind of art. I have found little of value in scholars like Frobenius and de Vries who, though they have given African heroic myths a kind notice (unlike Bowra), have little more than an ethnological interest in the subject; the introductory chapter of this book will, I hope, demonstrate the limitations of such an approach to an art form in which context makes more than a little difference.

I am even less attracted to theorists of the more abstract kind. The broad taxonomic interest that guides the studies of Lévi-Strauss and Propp inevitably leads to the thesis that—to quote Lévi-Strauss's classic articulation of it—"myths operate in men's minds without their being aware of the fact." This may be true to some extent; indeed, my chapter on form and structure gives considerable attention to some of the ready-made or preverbal resources of the heroic narrative. But to close one's eyes to the peculiar contexts in which this preverbal element—the "deep structure"—of the tale is continually re-created by individual performers is to deny this art form its very life and blood. While granting, therefore, that there are general laws to which these tales are subject, I am continually moved to stress the creative manipulations which the performer is inevitably drawn to make of those laws by the forces operating at the very scene of his act.

This same disinclination toward cold classification has led me away from paths trodden by Freud, Rank, and Jung, or by the various shades of literarists attuned to the more traditional approaches to criticism. Though I am quite sympathetic to all those efforts aimed at identifying "sophisticated" virtues in this kind of epic, I confess myself solidly attached to the more recent tradition of scholarship which sets out primarily to probe the essential orality of the genre.

I would like to thank various persons and institutions without whose help this book might never have been. The book has grown out of my doctoral thesis for the comparative literature program of the University of Denver, which deserves my unreserved gratitude. I am particularly grateful to Professor Leland

Chambers, the director of that program and my supervisor, for his unstinted patience, sincerity, and practical help all through my researches. I also thank Professors Robert Richardson of the English Department and Victor Castellani of Classics, both of Denver, for reassurances and helpful comments at significant stages of my work. I am grateful to Professor Ezekiel Mphahlele, then of Denver and now of the University of Pennsylvania, for his warm encouragement and especially for giving me the benefit of his vast knowledge of African and other studies.

This book has benefited immensely from my discussions with colleagues here at Ibadan. I am grateful to Professor Michael Echeruo of the English Department for his kindness in reading the initial draft of the book, and for his valuable comments and queries. My thanks are also due to Dr. Joseph Egberike of the same department and Dr. Olatunde Olatunji of Linguistics and Nigerian Languages, for generously sharing with me insights from their own folklore researches. I am much beholden to Dr. Abdul Karim Turay, also of Linguistics and Nigerian Languages, for introducing me to Dr. Gordon Innes and for making clear to me certain issues relating to his native Mandingo culture. I have gained much wisdom from students of my oral literature courses in our tutorial discussions, and I feel particularly grateful to those of them—like Paul Akegwure, John Obongha, and John Edemode—who have spent several hours with me on issues arising from their field collections under our program.

The editors of some of my primary sources have been quite helpful. I wish to thank Dr. Gordon Innes of SOAS (School of Oriental and African Studies), London University, for being so responsive and encouraging with regard to *Sunjata: Three Mandinka Versions.* I acknowledge the kindness of Professor John Pepper Clark of the University of Lagos, Nigeria, in letting me look at *The Ozidi Saga* before its final publication. And I thank

Preface

Professors Charles Bird of Indiana University and Daniel Biebuyck of the University of Delaware, editors of *Kambili* and *The Mwindo Epic* respectively, for making certain issues in their texts clear to me.

A portion of the first chapter appeared, in a somewhat different form, in the Spring 1977 issue of the *Journal of Aesthetics and Art Criticism* and is reprinted here with permission.

I am grateful to the following authors and publishers for permission to quote extensively from material copyrighted to them:

Professor Charles Bird, for *The Songs of Seydou Camara,* vol. 1, *Kambili* (Bloomington: Indiana University African Studies Center, 1974)

Professor J. P. Clark, for *The Ozidi Saga* (Ibadan: Ibadan University Press/Oxford University Press, 1977)

Dr. Gordon Innes, for *Sunjata: Three Mandinka Versions* (London: School of Oriental and African Studies, University of London, 1974)

Longman Group Ltd., for D. T. Niane's *Sundiata: An Epic of Old Mali,* translated by G. D. Pickett (London, 1965)

University of California Press, for D. Biebuyck and K. C. Mateene's *The Mwindo Epic* (Berkeley and Los Angeles, 1969)

University of Chicago Press, for R. Lattimore's *The Iliad of Homer* (Chicago, 1951)

My final thanks go to my wife, Mary Obiageli Okpewho. If this book is worth anything, it is because, apart from much else, she has so graciously forborne my frequent stint of company in her anxiety to see me make good my undertaking. She is the ultimate star.

Ibadan University   I. O.
June 1978

VERSIONS
AND
ABBREVIATIONS

VERSIONS

The Mandingo epics used here share many characters'
names, but neither the bards nor their editors have adopted any
standard spellings. Innes is quite at variance with Niane in just
about all the names featuring in the Sunjata legend. I am particularly interested in the two principal figures of the legend, whose
names I have standardized as follows: "Sunjata" for Niane's
"Sundiata" (from Pickett's translation) and Innes' "Sunjata";
and "Sumanguru," which again favors Innes over Niane ("Soumaoro"). Another important figure of the same legend sometimes appears as "Faa Koli" (Innes) and sometimes as "Fakoli"
(Niane; Bird, *Kambili*). I have standardized as "Fakoli." Other
common names in this tradition of tales do not occur so
frequently in this study, and so do not command that much need
for standardization. Quotations will respect names as they appear
in their sources.

I have also had to find a formula for the titles of the four versions of the Sunjata epic treated in this book, which could be re-

ferred to by the name of the editor or of the bard. The formula will be given below.

ABBREVIATIONS

Primary Sources

In obvious cases like the *Iliad* and *Odyssey,* there has been no need to abbreviate. When the full title is too long to stand, an abbreviation has been used. Some of our sources are in verse lines with numbers, in which cases the lines are cited. But other sources are either prose texts or verse texts published in journals that have not bothered to number the lines. "Page," in the following list, thus indicates that the number appearing after the abbreviated title reference (whether in the text or in the footnotes) is a page number. Detailed publishing information on editions and translations used in this study will be given in the Bibliography.

Akoma Mba	"La Guerre d'Akoma Mba contre Abo Mama"
Gilgamesh	*The Epic of Gilgamesh* (page)
Igor	*The Song of Igor's Campaign*
Kambili	*The Songs of Seydou Camara,* vol. 1, *Kambili*
Karta Thiema	"Da Monzon et Karta Thiema" (page)
Lianja	"Nsong'a Lianja: L'Épopée nationale des Nkundo" (page)
Mwindo	*The Mwindo Epic from the Banyanga* (page)
Ozidi	*The Ozidi Saga* (page)
Roland	*The Song of Roland*
SCHS	*Serbocroatian Heroic Songs,* vol. 1 (page)
Silamaka	"Une épopée peule: 'Silamaka' " (page)
Smailagić Meho	*Serbocroatian Heroic Songs,* vol. 3, *The Wedding of Smailagić Meho* (page)
Sunjata I	*Sunjata: Three Mandinka Versions*—version sung by Bamba Suso
Sunjata II	Version sung by Banna Kanute
Sunjata III	Version sung by Dembo Kanute
Sunjata IV	*Sundiata: An Epic of Old Mali*—version yielded by Mamoudou Kouyate (page)

Journals

AJA	*American Journal of Archaeology*
AJP	*American Journal of Philology*
BIFAN	*Bulletin d'Institut Fondamental d'Afrique Noire*
BSOAS	*Bulletin of the School of Oriental and African Studies*
CEA	*Cahiers d'études africaines*
CJ	*Classical Journal*
CP	*Classical Philology*
CQ	*Classical Quarterly*
CR	*Classical Review*
HSCP	*Harvard Studies in Classical Philology*
JAL	*Journal of African Languages*
JFI	*Journal of the Folklore Institute*
JHS	*Journal of Hellenic Studies*
MP	*Modern Philology*
PMLA	*Publication of the Modern Language Association*
TAPA	*Transactions of the American Philological Association*
YCS	*Yale Classical Studies*

The Epic in Africa

Kingdoms and empires are in the likeness of man;
like him they are born, they grow, and disappear.

Djeli Mamoudou Kouyate

As is the generation of leaves, so is that of humanity
The wind scatters the leaves on the ground, but the live timber
burgeons with leaves again in the season of spring returning.

Homer

One

AN INTRODUCTION TO TRADITIONAL AFRICAN ART

Until very recent times, traditional African art of all genres was studied exclusively by anthropologists and art historians. Often, they did not go beyond identifying the art by region of origin or of distribution; otherwise, they made rather inadequate attempts to deduce a community's life and thought from the nature and content of its art. They seldom tried to get to the roots of the aesthetic principles on which the art was executed; as a result, they generally devised blanket theories that had an exotic appeal but were incapable of giving us an insight into the fundamental creative spirit that brought such art to be.

The impressions that these scholars left have not really disappeared. Let us consider one notable example. The prevailing view of traditional African art seems to be that it is executed at the prompting of and in the service of ritual[1]—a view that has made it difficult to see the artist as other than a slave to ritual. Yet there is considerable evidence to the contrary. The proliferation of secular art among the Baule of the Ivory Coast, as well as the long tradition of decorative designs on Nigerian pottery (to name only two cases), clearly indicate that quite often beauty is contemplated for its own intrinsic appeal, not necessarily coerced into religious service. The same is true for the oral arts. The moonlit square has for countless generations been the setting for songs and stories whose primary intent is more to entertain, it would seem, than to edify. A large number of proverbs and quips survive today, and many are outstanding more for style than for content; they impress us more for their technical appeal than as fossils of a complex world-view. And this is not simply because the cultural outlook has changed. It may be argued that among the early races, the needs of religion often outweighed the luxury of beauty, and that the metaphysical concern merely gave way as time went on to a naturalistic sense of charm. Still, it can hardly be contested that beauty has survived as the ultimate irreducible; though we live forever with some form of religion, the urge to create beauty remains a basic impulse whatever the nature or the level of experience we may be involved in.

Those who look for religion or world-view behind all traditional art have often ignored the basic play interest of the artist. Thus nearly every study of traditional African art passes over the numerous pieces of phallic or erotic sculpture found in many African villages that have a lively tradition of plastic art. Where mention is made of such pieces, it is usually in connection with rites of initiation or fertility, which are blithely treated as religious. Nor do we, in the innumerable anthologies glutting the market of African folklore, find very much by way of ribald verse; yet ask any youth in a typical African village to recite his favorite verses, and the chances are the majority of them will have to do with sex.

In fact, in some of the more notable African tales that have anything to do with ritual or religion, the religious element is frequently superseded by the play interest of the narrator, especially in the fervid context of the open performance. A useful illustration of this interest is provided by the *The Ozidi Saga* and *The Mwindo Epic*.[2] Indeed, these tales support those skeptics who have held that there is little connection between myth and religion (or even what Emile Durkheim has called the "collective conscience"). Perhaps we should examine the evidence carefully.

Ozidi's heroic career can be briefly summarized. His father is killed by a number of his fellow townsmen. The hero is born after the murder, develops prodigiously, takes on every single one of the assassins, and (with the supernatural aid of his witch-grandmother, Oreame) destroys them all. Still in the heat of his successes, he is threatened and challenged by various other superhuman characters who try to subdue him, not *really* for the good of society but because they see him as an upstart and consider themselves better qualified for the position of supremacy he occupies. The last of these contenders, the Smallpox King, is, after his initial successes, defeated by the power of the hero's magical alter ego, Oreame; Ozidi recovers fully and cuts the Smallpox King and his retinue to pieces. At the end, he declares himself supreme, gloats over this supremacy, and lays down his conquering sword only because there are no more fights to be fought.

In his introductory essay to the saga, Professor Clark offers certain explanations that are rather open to question. He considers the fights the hero undertakes after avenging his father as a career of excess, pointing to the fight with Odogu the Ugly as one of those unprovoked acts. But there is something about Odogu that logically draws the hero toward taking him on. Odogu's sorceress mother, Agonodi, has received her magical charms from the same source as Oreame—the wizard of the forests, Bouakara-karabiri; so Odogu has all the powers that Ozidi has, including that of summoning a concatenation of weapons from his bowels. It is therefore inevitable that (in the manner of such heroic lore) the two super-powers should face each other to decide who is the stronger in the land. Ozidi, of course, triumphs; and I think it is significant for our estimation of any notions of "excess" that the audience of this particular performance shouts for joy when the hero is revived first (*Ozidi* 305) after he and Odogu have knocked each other unconscious with their deathly blows (303).

Clark also sees the attack of the Smallpox King as "divine visitation," very much I suppose in terms of classic European drama; but I doubt that this reading is justified by the presentation of the myth in this particular performance. Consider the manner of the entry of Anglese (alternatively, Engradon or Okrikpakpa), the Smallpox King. He has heard of Ozidi's formidable feats and decides to take him on. He says to his warring attendants (other diseases):

Oh, out there, there lives a man so powerful that he has executed everybody in town . . . completely laid waste what was once a proud capital city, and now it is said he lives there alone with his mother. I can't but go and see him. Let's go and visit him and see if we too are for him to murder. So fit a boat immediately.

So, off they go in a gunboat, and bombard the hero with pockmarks of smallpox that lay him out. But his sorceress grandmother eventually overcomes these with potent herbs (381ff.)—not, as Clark says, with ordinary fresh water. The hero surmounts the temporary setback, then summons his weapons in the normal way to the final onslaught. The Smallpox King and his band do not go off "in a huff," as Clark says. They are thrown into panic at seeing that the hero has recovered; in their attempt to escape, they are set upon by Ozidi and cut to pieces, boat and all (386).

There is therefore little support for the view of the Smallpox King as divine retribution. In the first place, he has not been sent to Ozidi by the supreme deity, Tamara, who does feature in the tale; he is simply a self-appointed rival to the hero who fails summarily. Second, he is introduced in a manner not unlike that of such earlier rivals as Tebekawene (321), who have simply heard of Ozidi's reputation and cannot accept it. Indeed, the bumbling portrait of the Smallpox King that emerges overall seems to indicate that he is slated for destruction just like the others. As in earlier cases, first the king lays Ozidi out with his deadly weapons, and there is the initial confusion in the family and search for an antidote. Oreame scours the bushes for potent herbs and charms to set the hero on his feet again (and is there any reason but mythic drama why herbs meant for yaws should put Smallpox in disarray?). As in earlier cases, the recovered hero destroys the Smallpox King in their final confrontation.

Furthermore, the Smallpox King can hardly be any more a divine visitation than the evil figures with whom Ozidi has earlier contended: Ogueren the Giant of Twenty Limbs, Engbesibeowei the Scrotum King, Tebesonoma of the Seven Heads, Tebekawene the Head-Walking Ogre, and various other figures who set cauldrons on the boil in which they try to cook the hero and his family. These eerie figures are all outcasts from human society who live in the "evil bush" at the peripheries of town (just as the Smallpox King does). Ozidi could hardly be guilty of excess in eliminating them, even though he has executed his filial duty by avenging his father of his assassins. Not only does their fall rid the land of evils; but so long as they are around, they constitute a threat to the supremacy of the hero—which has to be established at all cost in a system of values in which might, more than much else, is right.

The only figure in the tale who seems to qualify as the victim of Ozidi's "excess" is the unredeemable idiot uncle, Temugedege. But it is hard to see how he deserves our sympathies. In a world of powerful sorcerers and strongmen, he seems all too readily slated for elimination. He cowers at every turn and serves only to put the hero's insuperable might in harsh relief. Killing him does look like a cruel joke (the joke is indeed pressed to the very end, for the old man still has a soft spot in the middle of his head) (375); but if Oreame can survive the final trials of that world, then it seems clear that weaklings like Temugedege have no place in it. It is too much a world for the unusually strong. This is as far as we can see from the *myth*.

I emphasize the word because I think that in our reading of folklore we strain too hard for ulterior meanings (rather in the style of criticism of written literature) and listen too little for the peculiar but immediate strains of oral myth. Yet no attempt is being made here to ignore the metaphorical import, such as there is, of the figure of the Smallpox King. True, in traditional African societies, disease is sometimes seen as punishment for past evil; in that case, there may be sense in drawing some sociological or ritualistic meaning from the Smallpox figure. But this inference must be severely qualified by two considerations. First, the moment of purification (if such it is) of the hero would be the washing of his malady with herbs, followed by the withdrawal of Smallpox ("in a huff," if you like) and his return to the supreme deity who may have sent him as an agent of retribution. Instead, the hero recovers and kills him and his cohorts and continues to brag that he remains unbeaten in all the land; there are no more contests to win, so he turns in his weapons. Second, what purpose would purification serve? That the hero be cleansed and be received once more into the society of men? But the Society of the tale is not exactly of men such as men are; moreover, the hero has killed everybody off and survives alone in Orua with his family of equally highly endowed figures. If there is any metaphor to be sought, it is obviously in the heightened and idealistic portrait of the strong-man-fighter who transcends all the threats and limitations attendant upon mortal life, destroying all the evil men (the assassins) and evil forces (the monsters and the diseases) in his search for a

6

pure, unperturbed existence. He is driven by a mad, uncontrollable rage to assert himself, but such alone are the terms of his heroism (310); peace comes for him only when there is nothing left that threatens his supremacy. Such is the fantasy in which the heroic ideal of strength is cloaked. Though the bard may strain to express certain societal values, the peculiar outlook of the ideal and the more mundane picture of reality inevitably diverge. Yet the ideal has its own immediate interest, its own direct and uncomplicated imagery.

A somewhat similar disalignment occurs in *The Mwindo Epic*. Mwindo's pursuit of his errant father takes him mostly through the Underworld regions, and his quest is obstructed by two hostile divinities, Muisa and Sheburungu; the latter, as the editor of the epic tells us, is "one of the epithets under which the supreme divinity of fire, Nyamurairi, is known" (*Mwindo* 27n). These are no inconsequential figures of a vague pantheon, but deities with their full appurtenances of worship. They are grouped along with some other gods in the Nyanga cult system, and of them we are told:

All these divinities, together with the ancestors, are known under the generic term *bashumbu*. Shrines are made and plantains are grown for them, women are dedicated and married to them, sheep and hunting dogs are consecrated to them, prayers are said to them, and distinctive cultural paraphernalia for each of them are kept by their adepts. They manifest themselves in dreams and oracles and are responsible for good and evil in Nyanga life. (*Mwindo* 4f.)

It would thus normally be considered sacrilegious for any human (and Mwindo certainly is not divine) to be portrayed as contending against and overcoming the gods of the pantheon. But Mwindo gets into a severe physical confrontation with Muisa. In the first round, Muisa levels Mwindo with his magic belt (*karemba*); Mwindo recovers, and with the aid of his own magic *conga*-scepter smashes Muisa to the ground (later he does so again). With She-burungu there is only a battle of wits—the *wiki* game. The god wins against Mwindo; but the hero, finding that ordinary human wits are no use against a divinity, throws his magic *conga*-scepter into the bargain and wins.

For a character to fight and win against a deity is far from the spirit in which a society's religious life is conducted. Even when Mwindo is translated into the sky by the lightning-god Nkuba and warned against further heroic excesses, the warning is uncon-nected with his fights and victories against Muisa and Sheburungu; Nkuba himself had helped Mwindo part of the way in those con-frontations. Let us look closely at Nkuba's conduct in this connec-tion. Early in the story he takes sides with the enemies of Mwindo, but the hero always wins nevertheless. Then Nkuba turns around and becomes an ally of the hero in his struggles with some of his other enemies, including Muisa and Sheburungu. But the final showdown with Nkuba comes when Mwindo angers Nkuba by kill-ing a dragon that is sacred to the god. Though the denouement of the story tries to set the hero up as an overreacher, it is evident that the case for this rests only on his offense against Nkuba and does not at all include his earlier acts of ostensible "impiety." The explanation offered by the editors—that "there was an excuse for the hero as long as he was the victim of his father's unjust deci-sions and actions" (145n)—is inadequate. Sheburungu, over whom the hero had earlier triumphed, is, as the same editors tell us (106n), the supreme creator-god as well as god of fire; and there is nothing either in the tale or in the editorial notes that tells us that Nkuba occupies a superior position to that of Sheburungu in the Nyanga cult system.

The implications here are quite obvious, particularly if we take into consideration (as we should) the live context of the heroic song. In the live, bubbling atmosphere in which the Mwindo legend has been performed, what was normally a matter of serious concern for the community has become subject to the peculiar demands of the play instincts of the artist. We may not go so far as Lévi-Strauss in maintaining that "myths operate in men's minds without their being aware of the fact," for those obtrusive "religious" details and strophic comments that punctuate the song argue a certain presence of mind. But it is quite clear that in this mythopoeic context both the bard and his audience have been drawn into an experience not altogether germane to the spirit of worship or ritual. The figures of the cult belief have been subjected to patterns of behavior that tend sometimes to detract from the awe in which they are traditionally held, especially in a tale like *Mwindo* whose dramatic resources are evidently as much comical as serious. An audience treated to such songs will in no way consider their pious instincts offended by the bard's strange picture, particularly when they reflect that the human beings with whom the gods are fabled to be contending are not exactly like their next-door neighbors. Of course, they believe that the gods are responsible for evil as well as good, and indeed the whimsical nature of the gods revealed by these songs may well mirror some of their convictions. But they are unaccustomed, in their sober theological thinking, to conceive of divinity in the peculiar dramatic circumstances in which the mythmaker puts it and are well content to overlook the strange content and outlook of a heartwarming evening's performance. Clearly, the artistic play drive has got the better of the religious instinct.[3]

II

Perhaps the most fundamental element in this inquiry involves what one might define as the traditional African world-view. In this respect, one cannot accept without qualification some of the phrases that have constantly been bandied about.[4] When they have approached clarity, they have often implied a tendency among members of the traditional society to respect the unlimited scheme of things and like helpless romantics to preserve unmolested the sanctity of a complex universe.

Let us examine how that picture accords with the historical facts. The old "Bushman" of the south finally devised a way of mastering his environment: not content with his crude weapons, he drew realistic pictures of animals on the walls of his rock dwelling so that he could keep them constantly before his mind's eye. To this day the "Bushman," who has been a little reluctant to give up the old ways, hunts the ostrich most effectively by tucking his neat little frame into a stuffed effigy of the bird and penetrating the unsuspecting herd. In the area of religion, we find the same remarkable sense of the practical and the real. It makes little difference whether religion grew out of man's primary feeling of terror at the unknown or the overwhelming presence, or whether he buckled to his knees after he had failed to master his world by his artful ways.[5] What seems reasonably certain is that on the African continent, as men evolved a systematic theology, they sought to bring their ideas as close to home as possible. They infused their pantheon with their own ancestors. Though they could not see the spirits with their eyes, they tried to portray them in the most vivid images. Tutelary spirits or genii were represented in the images of beings within their areas of authority; if, for instance, the same genius was seen to guard over man and the realms of his livelihood, the same totemic figure was employed to signify this composite weal[6]—and that, under the circumstances, was the nature of the spirit. The Supreme God they could still not reduce in plastic terms, but they forced him into human reference with names and attributes taken from human experience: thus *Mawuyo* ("God is Kind") of the Ewe, the Yoruba *Olorun su* or the Ibo *Chi ejieela* ("God [i.e., the sky] is overcast"), or the Urhobo name *Oghener-*

huele ("God repairs"). In all, as E. B. Idowu puts it, "The world invisible is viewed, the world intangible touched, the world unknown known, and the world inapprehensible clutched."[7]

I stress this idea of the dynamic, creative temper because it would appear to be the source of true aesthetic worth. Art came to the service of religion only after the craftsman had attained a creditable sureness of hand; only then was he recognized as the repository of a certain measure of beauty and thus enlisted as a trustee of communal truth. Statements like the following by Elsy Leuzinger appear somewhat misleading and indeed ill conceived:

It must be emphasized once again that for the negro art serves first and foremost a religious purpose; he feels it would be presumptuous of him to fashion a sculpture in human form. It is only in the field of secular art, when rendering heroes and godlike kings, that he grapples with a subject in an effort to reproduce its natural elements and proportions in a manner true to life.[8]

Leuzinger seems to misunderstand the mimetic principle under which the traditional artist operates and, much more seriously, fails to recognize that art has a primarily secular impulse. True art has hardly flourished in the hands of medicine men or fetishists (as Leuzinger indeed conceives elsewhere)[9] because they have more religion than skill, and no amount of inspirational glow can kindle creative torches where nature has been grudging. But where there is due progression from native talent through conscious practice and apprenticeship, the result is often truly ennobling art, the kind that would "inspirit" the clan—to use Arnold's fine word.[10] Only then is the sweet union realized between private talent and public truth. In the old monarchical societies of Africa, only the best of a highly competitive crowd attained the royal patronage;[11] the works of the rest, the unhappy majority, have been lost to history because they crumbled with their makers' homesteads.

Much the same pattern is noticeable in the oral arts. We need hardly mention that in traditional festivals, where bards perform in competition with one another, the highest acclaim is normally reserved for the most accomplished in delivery. What Babalola says of the career of the *ijala* artist is sufficiently illuminating. Though it is initially conceded that "every ijala artist is merely Ogun's mouthpiece," we are in the end left in no doubt that "the best ijala-chanter, at a social gathering where several master ijala artists perform in turn, is the one whose repertoire is the most extensive and accurate, the best balanced in themes ... and the best chanted."[12]

Of course, religion or ritual is important in the evolution of African art; but it is not always the starting point. In those areas where truly imaginative art flourished in the environment of ritual, that ritual was merely the culminating point of the creative will. The artist had previously been carving tools and ordering his homestead. The people, liking what they saw, enlisted the artist to arrest for them in a concrete and harmonized manner the myriad forms around which their daily life and thought revolved. There was first the private creative will, which was then harnessed to give concrete meaning to the sacred communal weal; art in fact brought ritual into being. In the verbal arts, talent certainly comes first, as Babalola notes:

It is only those who have a natural flair for ijala-chanting who successfully go through their period of apprenticeship. Failures are not uncommon among these apprentices. No ijala pupil-artist embarks on this course of training merely because he is ordered to do so by his father or mother or other superior. It is generally assumed that compulsion will merely ensure the failure of a pupil learning ijala-chanting. Over and over again the ijala artists interviewed by the author came out with the declaration ... "It was because I longed to be able to chant ijala beautifully that I voluntarily went to a master ijala-artist and requested him to take me on as a pupil."[13]

To appreciate this concept of the primacy of skill, we must look beyond the all-too-fashionable distinction between secular and religious art. If we can transcend this rather evasive distinction, we shall have gone a long way in exploring how the traditional creative mind works, whatever the environment. We shall be able to tell who is a good artist and who is not, even among those who have put art at the service of religion. And we shall recognize that beneath even the most intense sacral motive is an underlying sense of form, which hitherto has been too often disregarded.

Some will probably object that the traditional African artist-divine feels no divisive stresses: his art finds a happy gestation in his ritual and vice versa. That may be so. But if there are degrees of aesthetic merit in traditional art—and no one to my knowledge has shown that this merit bears any direct ratio to the quality of ritual—then art must depend on principles other than religion for its just and proper growth.[14] If we don't, then we may be ignoring the fact that religion itself, as a system of organized worship, with a pantheon and a hierarchy of figures neatly conceived, is a product of man's creative intellect. That intellect progressed from a primarily secular sense of wonder, casting about for forms and names, until it succeeded in erecting a system to which it then lent the support of its creative energy.

If our task is to inquire into the aesthetic world of traditional African art, then clearly an examination even of several vaguely identical cult images from the past—since they bear no names, we can hardly establish their authorship, whether individual or collective—will yield us no small insight into the underlying creative ego beneath the (obtrusive, might we say?) veneer of rite. One has in mind the kind of diligence that in Ife art has isolated "the master of the aquiline forms" from the rest of the kindred crowd.

We shall save this question of authorship for the next section. For now it will suffice simply to observe that the student of the traditional aesthetics is severely handicapped in his quest for valid interpretations, especially when confronted with art that has survived from the past. His vision is considerably dulled by the fog of time and the vagaries of experience, among other things. In the plastic arts, too much has been lost (not only to the elements but to the secrecy of shrines and to the art thief's cupboard) that could have given us a fuller picture. In oral literature the problem is even more complex. Some quite sensitive oral art is shrouded in the secrecy of the cult; commenting on the initial problems of collecting *Ifa* and *Iwi* verse, Wande Abimbola reports, "Unless a man is . . . initiated into the secret societies that possess these forms of literature, it may be difficult or even impossible for him to collect anything."[15] Part of the difficulty also derives from the very nature of nonliterate art. It might be true that the traditional bard had no need of writing, but there is more to the issue than the apologists have been willing to admit. Traditional oral literature is largely performed, and performance is often rewarded with material gifts—many artists still live partly by their performances. It therefore seems a fair guess that if the lure of material rewards had not overtaken the quest for literacy, we would be in far less want of documentation than we are today.

III

In this section we shall be looking at the working artist, examing briefly some of the dynamic principles and atmosphere determining his productivity. We are too far removed from the roots of that art to attempt to be exhaustive, but certain views can nonetheless be advanced.

The Mimetic Principle

In hypothesizing about the creative outlook of the traditional African artist, we must consider his society's view of reality. Does reality exist out there in a kind of "circumambient air" (to borrow from Hulme), and does the artist place his creative powers at the mercy of a formless infinitude, an intangible world of abstractions? Or does reality exist in the realm of human experience, whereby the artist could seek to explain the nature of the unknown? In view of what I have identified as the traditional society's pressing sense of the real, the desire to have "the world inapprehensible clutched," it seems logical to suggest that experience is its fundamental frame of reference. For art this will mean that, though he accepts and respects a metaphysical order, the artist reduces the abstractions to recognizable form in due proportions. The traditional African artist is thus first and foremost a realist artist. But he operates on two levels of realism.

The first level relates to objects of the visible, physical world treated in their just features and characteristics. In this category can be classified much portrait art such as Ife and Benin lavishly offer—kings, queens, queen mothers, and so forth. Portrait art is also known elsewhere in Africa: among the Bakuba of Zaire and the Baule of the Ivory Coast,[16] for example. There are also other shades of experience covered by this category of direct realism: for instance, the funeral heads among the Ashanti.[17] Benin once again offers us naturalistic portraits of horse-soldiers, hunters, and the like.[18] We need hardly emphasize the overwhelming sense of realism that Benin and Ife reflect: the care taken over the facial marks, beads and bangles by their numbers, the insignia of office, coats of mail, stoles in their proper lengths—no metaphysical qualms here; just plain reality in its striking outlines.

But the artist has a further level of realism for what has been called the "spirit-regarding order." Art critics have repeatedly and erroneously called this style of art "abstract." Not only do the components of the artistic statement not fool our recognition, as so many of the mind-boggling travesties in Greenwich Village quite often do, the simple fact is that in this category of art the tradition-al artist is addressing himself not to ideas as such, or abstractions, but to spirits and deities vividly conceived. The distinction is worth emphasizing, because abstraction properly belongs to an age that has lost considerable faith in the perceptible real—an age, as it were, of disbelief. Those horrendous shapes that feature in both the folk myth and the plastic arts are as real as the forests and the sequestered shrines that they inhabit. The *chi wara* of the Bamba-ra is not simply "fecundity" as an abstract idea; it was a spirit sent down by the Creator to promote fecundity. But although you can-not accurately portray a spirit, the Bambara have too vivid a sense of the real to be lost in imprecisions. So they portray the *chi wara* in the stylized form of a denizen of the fecund environment, the antelope, worn as a mask during their ritual dances.

A figure is not abstract simply because it combines selective images in a composite form and is stylized. Such figures are vivid elements of a people's living myth. The classical Allecto, with ser-pents for her hair, is not an abstract idea of fury: she is *a* Fury. The same applies to our ceremonial masks. They are the artist's vivid portrait of an ancestral or a genial presence—the figures, as Sen-ghor tells us in his "Prayer to Masks," *through whom the spirit breathes.* But since the artist cannot claim knowledge of the exact outlines of a spirit's physiognomy, he endeavors to strike a just balance between his limitations and his pressing sense of the real; those masks are a just biomorphic response to the various forms and natures of the spirits concerned. It is remarkable how close these portraits of spirits can aim to be sometimes. Margaret Tro-well has observed about the *Sakapu* society among the Ijo of southern Nigeria:

The members performed a most elaborate system of plays in hon-our of the Owu or water spirits. After sacrifices, with feasting and dancing, the Owu are asked to come forth from their home under the sea and to be present at the rites. The head-dresses are said to represent the Owu when they were last seen.[19]

Surely, to label such an effort as "abstract" is to misunderstand the tremendous closeness and empathy the traditional artist feels with his subject. Abstraction is a withdrawal, a disengagement—Eliot has the right phrase in "dissociation of sensibility"—whereas the traditional artist puts little distance between himself and the vivid throng of presences that he feels around him. "Abstract," it is true, is only a formal label; but when applied to traditonal art it fails to take due account of the attitude that gives birth to such art.[20]

Much the same pattern of realism is observable in oral literature. On the one hand, it offers a vivid naturalistic portrait of the animal world whose livelihood is so closely tied to man's. There is a typically anthropomorphic touch to these portraits, especially in the dialogues. But overall a remarkable pattern of verisimilitude is maintained. The smart tortoise overplays his hand but has the last laugh on his captors anyway: swearing he loves nothing better than to be dropped in boiling oil, he wails that a cool stream would be the death of him. He is dropped into a cool stream and escapes. A misguided sense of kindness brings upon the billy goat the rag of stench and folly originally intended for the tortoise. The dog's habit of dillydallying on his way is given a tragic turn when he fails man on a mission of immortality. The catalogue of such tales is endless. The subjects may be nonhuman, but they are treated with such interest and intimacy that the line of distinction virtually disappears.

Man is also observed in his own integral circumstances; his successes and failures are seen in terms either of his admirable courage or of his moral shortcomings. Stories of conflicts between communities abound. Few metaphysical or theological implications underlay the details; there is simply an interest in man's grim confrontation with his not-so-gracious kind. Daniel Kunene bears witness to this category of realism in his study of the poetry relating to the legendary world of Moshoeshoe:

The heroes are not superior beings except in so far as their earthly deeds make them so, least of all are they gods or descendants of gods. They do not possess supernatural powers, or do battle against other-worldly creatures such as monsters and demons. They do not go on adventures to worlds beyond that of man. Nor are they wont to provide lavish feasts in palatial mansions. In short, they are ordinary human beings engaged in ordinary human activities. Not seldom, however, the poet, in the vividness of his imagination, uses metaphor, imagery, and symbolism which transport these ordinary activities to a level of extraordinariness, and the hero is often described as fighting against monsters, or as being himself a monster or other terrible creature destroying his opponents. But this is never meant to be more than figurative.[21]

However, a good deal of the traditional literature of Africa—at least the bulk of it in which one might recognize a truly imaginative touch—explores this very idea of "adventure to worlds beyond that of man." We need not linger over the ease with which the artist conceives his setting and peoples it with all manner of shapes, nor the easy spatial links that he establishes between the worlds of spirits and of man. What has been said of the plastic arts holds true here: those myriad wraiths and trolls are as germane to the artist's sense of concrete presences as the thicket in the backyard. But perhaps the most significant aspect of the realism in this connection is the tremendous empathy the bard establishes between himself and the subjects of his tale, particularly the hero. For instance, in the various sub-Saharan epics, one is struck by a pattern of narration in which the pronouns seem happily confused. No doubt for the bard the only way of coercing the supernatural world to an acceptable human reference is by a performance in which, according to Biebuyck and Mateene, "The singer associates himself with his subject and his heroes so intimately that he seems to identify himself with them."[22] Rather unlike Homer, he immerses himself in the story with an empathy that Plato would have condemned as ignoble frenzy. This device is particularly noticeable in *The Mwindo Epic*. The career of Mwindo takes place in a largely supernatural milieu; but from both the bard's identification with him and the rather careful epilogue[23] we are made to feel that we have a stake in the fortunes of the hero. This is realism at its most sublime.

The Ecology of Art

"Hunter," said Gnankouman Doua (griot to Maghan Kon Fata, Sunjata's father), "your words are obscure. Make your speech comprehensible to us, speak in the language of your savanna" (*Sunjata* IV:5).[24]

There is a subtle but discernible link between art and the landscape out of which it grows. If we concede that the earliest art was a response to the immediate pressures of man's living conditions—whether these pressures took the form of hunger, self-defense, or any other form—then we can see clearly why the environment would make a difference to the forms or the quality of art. And it would appear that much of the aesthetic nourishment of traditional African art derived from the nature of the surrounding landscape and the concomitant throb of animate company within it.

The griot of Old Mali therefore spoke well within aesthetic reason when he made a connection between the uncomplicated clarity of his native speech and the lean vegetation of the surrounding savanna. In a rather subtle way, the legends from the savanna country reflect this leanness. For one thing, the scope of heroism seems a little more restricted—as witness the idea of entry into the other world. We come pretty close to it in *Sunjata* IV, when the

19

hero pursues the vanquished Sumanguru until the the latter disappears into a "black cavern" in Mount Koulikoro—and there the pursuit ends, as we watch Sunjata gaping helplessly at the mouth of the cave! There is much greater bravado in the forest country. One could safely conjecture that there Sunjata would have been made to carry the fight with Sumanguru into the underworld. There are hardly any restraints on the hero in the forest country, as shown by the extraterrestrial exploits of Fagunwa's Akara-Ogun, Tutuola's Drinkard, and Rureke's Mwindo.

There is also a correspondingly greater belief in life in forest than in savanna myth. The *Kambili* epic[25] is a good case in point. One is struck by a certain haunting and elliptical effect to the whole narrative, an oppressive sense of loss, decline, and death. The same effect is noticeable in northern Nigerian tales as compared with corresponding pieces from the south of the country. There are *jinns*, of course, but nothing to compare in extravagance, variety, and ebullience with the figures in, say, Yoruba mythology. Besides, the tales from the forest country tend to explore a victory over death as over its forces and on the whole reflect the throb, lushness and elan of the organic life and fellowship around them: a veritable song of life. It is perhaps no accident of detail that whereas in *Kambili* the dominant sentiment is, "All things that stand eventually lie down," in *Mwindo* it is, "Whatever sleeps shall wake."

It may be said that the savanna regions I have referred to are places where Islam has succeeded considerably in suppressing the vigor of traditional life and myth (though *Kambili* here and there reveals a vigorous opposition to the Islamic faith). However, what Biebuyck and Mateene tell us of the oral arts in the Congo country seems particularly relevant here. In reviewing the Hunde songs of the Nyanga bard, Mr. Sherungu, within the context of the Hunde society of the savanna, they comment: "the recorded text is, in many respects, interesting and significant. It represents a chanted text rather long for this region of Africa where the majority of songs have dwindled to a simple proverb."[26] The Hunde, like the Nyanga, are Bantu-speaking, and were grouped by the Belgian authorities into administrative districts very similar to those of the Nyanga. Biebuyck and Mateene recognize in Sherungu the roving bon vivant; but it is evident also that among the Hunde the creative imagination has not found the kind of organic environment that has been the signal blessing of the Nyanga of the neighboring rain forests. The myth, as well as the language, has consequently suffered.

The point is that the forest country is the crowded region. The persistent rainfall gives rise to thick vegetation, wildlife in myriad shapes and numbers. The intervening spaces allow for throbbing population densities; luxuriance of life stimulates a corresponding luxuriance in communication, and buxom mirth attends the teeming camaraderie. Where else but in a forest of merry ghosts could we find the mythical figures of Drum, Song, and Dance, as in Amos Tutuola's *Palm Wine Drinkard*?[27]

Roughly the same pattern is found in the plastic arts. There is a certain elegance in those proportionally long and slender antelope figures, masks, and even ancestral figures that dominate the art of the Bambara and the Dogon of the arid western Sudan; here again the landscape seems an influential factor. The vegetation is thin and low, and the animal as well as human forms stand out in slender relief against the background of scanty bush. This is, arguably, the underlying principle behind those lean, long horns and headwear; the stylization only heightens the effect. Besides, there is little in the savanna flora that would supply the kind of stout, lusty wooden material necessary for rotund figures. But it is interesting what happens as the vegetation begins to thicken. The next major group south of the Bambara are the Senufo, and their representative pieces are somewhat fleshier than those of their northern neighbors. The rotundity becomes complete as we get to the Ngere-Wobe, south toward the Atlantic coast.[28] Ecology thus adds further dimensions to the realism of traditional African Art; which is perhaps another reason why we should be careful in using labels like "abstract" in describing the career of artists for whom matter and manner are starkly unified.

Tradition and Originality

The problem of tradition and the individual talent has engaged several generations of critics, though we have not often drawn the right distinctions between the literate and the unlettered artists' views of tradition. It may be, of course, that scholars have today agreed to understand tradition as a pattern of growth rather than as a rigid invariable. But though we can reasonably trace the historical origins of literate art, we cannot safely do the same for the unlettered kind. Thus it is difficult to establish the relationship that the traditional artist's talent bears to works that his community has come to accept as standards of artistic performance. We can perhaps trace the artistic portraits of Julius Caesar's life to records in ancient Roman literature. But since we cannot accurately date the origins of the myths of the *chi wara* of the Bambara, or the ibeji of the Yoruba,[29] it becomes something of an academic exercise for us to talk of standards in examining various plastic representations of these myths, however old some might happen to be; and how do we tell one version of a tortoise-tale from another, if neither contains any historically datable details?

The difficulty of judgment is particularly acute for the plastic arts. In an examination of the art surviving from the past, we have no artists' signatures to guide us in making the right distinctions between independent creations and those inspired by a "school" of creative thinking. It was noted above that artists whose work enjoyed no patronage or adoption were doomed to oblivion, as their pieces crumbled with their homesteads. This situation has led art historians and critics to consider those pieces housed in a shrine or a palace, or excavated in their vicinities, as the definitive output of the community, forgetting that much more that did not conform to the fashionable styles of the "schools" might have been done. It would further appear that the exotic interest shown by foreign collectors of African art—going as far back perhaps as the early trading forays of the fifteenth century—has led to a weakening of the old creative integrity. As a result, we can note the growth of a prosperous tourist industry catering to foreign wonder; where once there was an honest creative genius giving due imaginative expression to the intimate forms of a community's life, there has flourished a cheap, mercenary interest characterized by an unreflective haste to churn out mere photographic copies of chosen models. The collectors themselves hardly give any or at least honest dates to these works, because they are anxious that an aura of antiquity or exoticism should attach to their winnings. So we seem forever condemned to bestow false halos on a multitude of figures that are neither truly old nor an honest reflection of a people's creative spirit. In his search for the truth, the judge of traditional art is thus confronted with a sore question: is the traditional African artist primarily a slave to model, or does he, like the truly imaginative leader of his people, seek first and foremost to give vitality and meaning to the community's life and myth with the aid of his creative vigor?[30]

It is possible to draw some conclusions from the careers of traditional artists surviving from past generations, since we cannot have full faith in the silent pieces that deck the museum shelves. In his *Contemporary Art in Africa*,[31] Ulli Beier gives an account of two artists who grew up in the old tradition, one in the service of ritual and the other under the patronage of the royal court. Yemi Bisiri of Oshogbo carves figures for the *Ogboni* society of the Yoruba, like his father before him. Yet he has the courage to make an almost total break from the legacy of his father's days not only in material (he works with brass instead of wood) but also in style (an almost Gothic ornamentation as against the simplicity of the older figures). In Benin, Ovia Idah has made a considerable break from the old ways, using strange materials like ebony and cement instead of the traditional bronze and ivory and exploring new forms that some of his fellows find disturbing.

It is interesting that Idah's revolution has not been tolerated as calmly as Bisiri's. The reason for this difference may be sought in the economic life of Benin, which depends considerably on the tourist industry; visitors will be familiar with the stereotypes of the "Benin head" or the "antique jewelry" which the government has herded into lucrative curiosity shops! The Benin guild of carvers to which Idah belongs, and the community that benefits so much from their kind of work, are naturally worried that Idah's apostasy might harm the tourist economy. Nevertheless, the careers of such representative artists lead us to wonder about the generations before them. If it is true that society changes (as a result of war, migrations, and so on), would not the pattern of its myth change? In that case, would it not be natural for the artist to give the new forms due expression, counting on his genius to strike the right balance between the new elements and the ancestral legacy? Coming as they do from the old school, Bisiri and Idah attest once again to the restless, creative temper of the traditional artist, who has a distaste for unintelligent copying.

The problem of respecting tradition without stifling the individual talent is no easier in the oral arts. But if it is recalled that the folk literature is delivered largely in performance, then we can understand why tradition in this regard faces an even more likely risk of change than in the plastic arts. Of course no artist is applauded for a brutal violation of the essential legacy, or what Albert Lord has called "the historic truth,"[32] of traditional song. Given the fluidity of his medium and the unpredictable nature of his audiences, however, the dominant challenge of his art lies in the peculiar stylistic twists and turns that he works on the original material. Put differently, the aesthetic principle in the oral arts involves a slight tilt of the balance in favor of beauty over truth.[33]

Even in tales having to do with history, it is remarkable how much the truth is tinkered with, in spite of the singer's claims to the contrary. In his version of the Sunjata legend, for instance, Djeli Mamoudou Kouyate tells us he received the legend "free from all untruth." Now, the highlight of the story is the defeat of Sumanguru and his disappearance into a cave in Mount Koulikoro. Niane tells us in his notes of numerous versions of Sumanguru's end. Bowra, quoting Lord, recalls one such tradition that claims that Sumanguru remained unconquerable to the end, becoming the hero of an epic of "about ten thousand lines" in which "a special group of singers, old men called Djale, sing the glory of Sumanguru, the hero of the Fetichists, to the accompaniment of a native violin."[34] Besides, Niane tells us in his preface that "each princely family had its griot appointed to preserve tradition." It seems arguable that such a griot would feel inclined now and then to bend the truth somewhat in favor of the family,[35] since he earned his keep singing their praises.

Nothing perhaps is more eloquent of the variability of the griot's oral art than the following observation by Ba and Kesteloot:

It is well known to experts of African oral tradition, that the griot always composes on a fixed scheme and develops his episodes in accordance with his mood and the audience before him; if on the same day you were to make a narrator repeat the same account, you would hear a different version each time. In short, the griot is disinclined to tell the story two successive times in identical terms. He is, first and foremost, a literary man; the variety of his language is a token of his good taste as well as proof of his talent and his expertise.[36]

Music, to which the words are frequently sung, may be partly responsible for this element of variability, since music generates different moods under different circumstances. "Music," says Djeli Kouyate (*Sunjata* IV:39), "is the griot's soul." And music, especially as an expression of the will to please, would seem that much more of a threat to the duty to leave the "truth" unadjusted.

We can thus imagine what liberties are taken in the area of purely imaginative literature, or at least literature that is considerably free from the tyranny of historical fact. *The Mwindo Epic* is again a good case in point. The editors tell us they have five other versions of the epic, the longest only half the length of the present one. On the whole, the Rureke version is a thoroughly personal performance; within the very fabric of the song, the poor transcribers, Biebuyck and Mateene, are challenged to speed by repeated, rather formulaic commands of, "Scribe, move on." One is left with an overwhelming sense of immediacy, which perhaps vindicates Lord's observation that "an oral poem is not composed *for* but *in* performance."[37]

I am not denying the traditional African artist's regard for tradition, assuming tradition to be a hallowed kernel of truth that has to be constantly kept alive by memory. But it seems clear that in an art form supported largely by the challenge of ready delivery and the encouragement of ready rewards, the artist is generally forced to rely more on his own creative (i.e., manipulative, among other things) energy than on the shaky prop of memory. And dynamism works to the advantage of the tradition, as Babalola has noted of the Yoruba *ijala* artists: "Studied or spontaneous improvisation on traditional themes is what the ijala-chanters regard as their individual contribution to the repertoire of ijala-chants.[38]

IV

We have tried to identify the traditional African artist as a man with a very pressing sense of real and concrete presences, enjoying the closest intimacy with the physical and metaphysical environment. By means of his dynamic sense of form, he tries in all sorts of combinations, with linguistic as well as plastic resources, to give tangible meaning to those visible and spiritual presences that give context to his daily life and thought. And as the truly guiding sensibility of his community, he continually leads the way in re-creating the progressive forms of the communal myth.

I have often referred to the artist as the "imaginative leader" or the "guiding sensibility" of his community. In a society where the means of disseminating ideas are rather limited, the artist is usually responsible for giving a firm foundation to new cultural influences that might otherwise have been treated as passing fancies and have been allowed to die. Take the example of the traditional hairdresser in Nigeria (see p. 246). The officials who come to conduct the census probably spend only a day or two in the village. But their strange hairstyles make a deep impression on the local hairdresser. She reproduces them on the heads of her local customers, and those styles survive the brief sojourn of the census takers who have introduced them. This, needless to say, is the major means of infiltration of various life-styles into most traditional societies. Or take the case of the village carver. Most Nigerian villages have no airfields, but every day planes fly above the heads of their citizens. Because he trades in strange modes and novelties, and because he knows that he attracts attention in that way, the carver endeavors to translate his vague impressions of the planes in sculptures which he either sells to curious clients or decorates his shop with. He has succeeded in bringing closer to his community what was at best a distant reality.

It is therefore clear that I have chosen to see the traditional African artist as an active mind operating within a dynamic context. Indeed, it seems to me that we must reexamine the role of religion and world-view in his work. The well-known Keatsian principle—"Beauty is truth, truth beauty"—is acceptable only insofar as it illustrates that the artist manipulates tradition and its values, giving them fresh relevance, fresh meaning, fresh being.

But who supervises this protean exercise and ensures the authenticity of the new forms? In his discussion of traditional art, Macebuh states, "except on those occasions when expert opinion was called for, the farmer, the hunter, and the wine-tapper could be relied upon to muster a sufficiently meaningful response to art, and this merely as part of their general awareness as citizens of a community of beings."[39] This pious portrait of social cohesion is admirable, but it seems a slightly inadequate guide to understanding the *growth* of art in its context. There is little doubt that this "meaningful response"—if it means, as it should, a critical support for the evolution of valid aesthetic standards—can be supplied only by those who by virtue either of native skill or (more usefully) of longstanding connection with the career are qualified to offer intelligent views, not only on the "historic truth" but indeed on the acceptable ingredients of "beauty." In the plastic arts, despite the corrupting influence of tourist demand, only a fellow artist or a man closely connected with the practice of traditional art can meaningfully criticize a piece of craft. In an oral performance, the mob at large is hardly the best judge of excellence; very often the performer is at the mercy of certain partisan interests or at least the menacing comments of spectators who try to force him to be slavishly loyal—against his better instincts—to the "historic truth."[40] Of course, such distractions may teach the artist skillful ways of negotiating his lines around their interests; which is, in one sense, a dynamic gain to his art. But such accidental benefits play only a limited part in the actual growth of his art. For true technical excellence, he generally depends on the knowledgeable comments of fellow bards and skilled judges who can tell whether or not his work is any improvement on the classic performances of more recent memory. For them, such improvement is the best insurance of tradition.

V

In conclusion, it seems necessary to defend the broad cultural geography within which I have chosen to explore the traditional art of Africa. First, in the above introductory survey, I have tended to treat Africa as a unit, an attitude that may raise a number of disturbing questions: How valid is it to assume a pan-African culture? Are we not perhaps bowing to a habit of political thinking that is only a few decades old? Is Africa not too diverse in geography, race, and language patterns to be subjected to such ready paradigms, even with the best of intentions?

These are pertinent questions, but it would be outside the scope of this study to attempt a detailed justification. Ethnologists and political scientists have treated the question of the African personality times without number, and I hardly intend to duplicate their conclusions. Quite apart from the idea of skin color, however, there is one point which should perhaps be obvious: as an integral land mass affording considerable mobility and contact between one group and another—whether by war, displacement, commerce, or ordinary migration—Africa has an ancient pattern of interchange of myths and modes. Beyond that assumption I have not been inclined to go without jeopardizing the unity and clarity of this inquiry.

Second, the succeeding discussion of the oral epic in Africa will be based principally on the published texts of heroic narratives from those sections of sub-Saharan Africa that ethnologists have designated the Congo-Niger family; my broad-based assumptions are therefore justified on ethnological grounds at least. However, I shall have frequent recourse to other areas of the continent for useful points of illustration: sometimes the similarities will be too close to be accidental, and I shall not hesitate to reach for necessary clarification beyond these narrow limits.

Lastly, the following study of the epic in Africa will be made with comparative illustrations from the Homeric, Slavic, and other worlds. This study is principally about the epic in Africa—phrases like "the bard" or "the hero" have meaning chiefly within the African context—but considerable work has been done on oral epics from other societies, which does have tremendous relevance to this particular study. As a result, the temptation to extrapolate is very strong indeed. But if now and then I am moved to use some African evidence in suggesting useful ways of looking at Homer or the Yugoslav material, I have not forgotten that I am dealing with different cultures. Perhaps the approach is based on the simple faith that different peoples, placed under roughly the same circumstances, would behave in roughly the same ways or have similar goals and expectations. The warning given by G. S. Kirk about such comparative ventures does ring with deafening truth: "It is, indeed, important to remember that different cultures *are* different—that the different preoccupations of mankind . . . do not express themselves in the same way or the same proportions from culture to culture. General theories of myth . . . are no simple matter."[41] If the world was divided between those who search for agreements and those who are not particularly interested in them—and in a comparative study of such widely differing cultures as Africa and Greece or Yugoslavia there is a real temptation to see those as the basic polarities—one would be willing to risk the charge of näivete by lending a discreet support to the former group. But the choices are not so simple; and while I shall maintain a clear awareness of the differences in background, there seems every reason to believe that the comparative approach can suggest fruitful ways of appreciating the art of the oral epic as an independent subject unsubordinated to the critical attitudes traditionally applied to literate art.

Two

THE RESOURCES
OF THE ORAL EPIC

The major problem in discussing the oral epic involves nomenclature. I have expressed a belief in the integrity of the *oral* art
as a subject distinct from the *literate* variety, with an idiom of its
own. A qualification of this belief is, I think, necessary. I do not
mean that there is no common ground whatsoever between the
two kinds of art. On the contrary, it is clear that, since they both
aim to please through the medium of the word and the images
that words, aptly combined, can create, they share certain archi-
techtonic tendencies and effects: the fitting description, the portraiture of a character that is true to life or at least to the peculiar
ideals of the world within which the character operates, and various other creative tricks and devices. In such respects, admittedly,
the distinction between oral and literary art is hard to make. But
the fundamental difference is in the process by which the work of
art comes to be, the context within which it is created. It is in this
regard that the *word* is subject to behaviors that make it acceptable for one category of art and unsuitable for another.

For instance, a statement may be apt; but if the poet is so
thoroughly overjoyed by its aptness that he is moved to repeat that

statement many times over, then the text is very likely to be the product of an oral performance in which the poet perhaps used a musical instrument to support the lyrical feeling engendered by that happy statement; for no writer, however pleased he is with a statement, will feel inclined to belabor it over several successive lines just for the sheer joy that he finds in its aptness. Faced therefore with the text of such a statement, we are moved not simply to admire its verbal excellence but indeed to glean the circumstances that led to its being repeated so many times. That is the logic of an independent poetics for the oral performance: much more than literary criticism ever cares to do, oral criticism asks questions about the context or process during which a piece of poetry is created.[1]

A second problem in studying the oral epic is painting a balanced picture of the tradition as we see it now and what it was several ages ago, in the preliterate days. We have much cause to believe that in those days the bard did not encounter the kinds of curiosity he finds in the modern audience. Then, he sang simply as part of a social process before familiar clansmen, or on the road before strangers to whom he was a familiar phenomenon. Today, cornered into a recording studio, made to perform before strange equipment and without the regular audience, asked questions about his art to which he had never given much of a thought, he watches with a certain distraction as his interrogator studiously scribbles down his statements. Clearly, we are dealing with two generations of the oral epic; standard pictures of the bard cannot be easily painted. In his preface to *Sunjata* IV, Niane observes that the career of the contemporary griot (the bard among the Mandingo of the West African Sudan) "was not always so in ancient Africa." Then, they counseled kings and cheered them with songs of noble deeds; today, they play and sing for curious and not so kingly audiences and are congealed into record by scholars like

Niane. From his experience in Yugoslavia, Albert Lord tells us of the practice of "seeking a normal ten-syllable line" from the Serbian guslars whose songs are recorded; as a result of this practice, "the dictated version tends to be more perfect metrically than the sung version."[2] We ought to be grateful to the scholar who has taken the trouble to catch something of a great tradition before it is completely swept away by the relentless tide of progress. But it seems only honest to admit that the bard whom we meet in our recorded songs is not quite the archetypal singer of a distant age. He may be the worse for being put into an unfamiliar environment, or he may be the better for the new challenge that the scholar's expectations set for him. In either case, he is a bit different and thus we should be cautious in making connections between the past and the present.

Finally, something should be said about the terms "oral" or "traditional" epic and "bard," which will be used many times in this study. Lord has definitively analyzed the difficulties attending the nomenclature of this genre of art;[3] it would be superfluous for me to try to stretch the arguments any further. An oral epic is fundamentally a tale about the fantastic deeds of a person or persons endowed with something more than human might and operating in something larger than the normal human context and it is of significance in portraying some stage of the cultural or political development of a people. It is usually narrated or performed to the background of music by an unlettered singer working alone or with some assistance from a group of accompanists. To avoid monotony, terms like "traditional epic," "heroic song," or "narrative" will be used in its place, but the nature of the art remains the same.

It is convenient to see the bard exclusively within the context of the oral epic, since that is the subject of this study; however, a full appreciation will often reveal that his competence embraces other kinds of songs. In Africa, the singer of heroic tales sometimes finds himself obliged to sing ordinary lyric songs that he has in his repertoire and is happy to garner a varied patronage by demonstrating this versatility.[4] In fact, there is little difference in training between the "epic" bard and any other kind of performer in song.[5] Admittedly, the structural nuances of the heroic narrative song and the touch of grandeur that characterizes its content make it somewhat different from, say, the ordinary lyric song. But our bard is a performer just like the others, and shares with them both the training in the creative use of memory and the overall sense of public image. He becomes typecast by the heroic narrative because he sings it more often either by request or by choice; quite often he can also sing many other kinds of song, but may just not feel inclined to dabble in those other areas.[6]

II

We shall start our discussion by examining the very title of bard, which has often been extended, with varying degrees of defensibility, to anyone with a modicum of skill in song. The chances for this confusion are particularly great in studies of African musicianship. We have often been told that the African, because of his early exposure to musical situations, has a built-in capacity for music. Says J. H. K. Nketia of the Akan child in Ghana:

His experience, even at this early age, is not confined to children's songs. Like other African peoples, Akan mothers often carry their children on their backs to public arenas. Sometimes they even enter the dancing ring with their children on their backs. Later when the children are old enough, they are even encouraged to take part in the dancing. By the time a child reaches adolescence, his musical experience has widened considerably.[7]

This is an impressive picture, but we must draw the line somewhere between exposure and interest, between contact and career.

The pertinent question in our search for the right definition of the bard should perhaps be: in his scale of occupations, what position does his interest in song take? The question is important because our search for the traditional bard has often taken us—no doubt with good reason sometimes—to characters in our texts who have in one way or another been associated with music. Under this category comes much of the poetic self-praise done by many African chiefs.[8] In the Sunjata epic we have the interesting case of the king Sumanguru who periodically sang his own praises to the accompaniment of a charmed harp (IV:39). Even the hero-child Lianja—still called "gamin" at this stage of his career—plays the harp (Lianja 53). A similar case occurs in the Iliad. When the Achaean peace party visits Achilles in his tent, they find him with a lyre in his hand, with which he "gladdened his heart and sang the feats of men" (9:189). If we take Beowulf 2105ff. as referring to Hrothgar, as some editors seem to do, then the old warrior-king must have made an impression on the Geat party with the "glee-wood," fetching back old-time feats both "true" and "wonderful."[9] Tempting as these references are, we must place the expertise of our bard considerably above that of the rest of the population, even when it can be shown that "the art is enjoyed by a whole society."[10] The seminal qualification for the bard must therefore be that he has a specialist's interest in the art. The warrior-ruler would care far less for the craft than the bard would.

Yet, in spite of this criterion, we are not necessarily justified in crediting the bard with professional excellence in the modern sense of the phrase. Put differently: even when singing is what the man excels in doing, we may not really call it his "profession" in terms of a sole or major source of sustenance and thus of a steady concern for self-improvement.

In fact, very few bards, in the traditional (rural) context, actually sustain themselves and their families primarily by their songs. Of the Akan bard-musician Nketia says:

In the past he could live on the bounty of the chief if it was his duty to perform on state occasions, but this was a privilege enjoyed by all servants of the State. In ordinary life he is like everybody else—a farmer, trader, carver, or fisherman who depends more on these for his living than on his music.[11]

Of the Bala in the Congo country, Alan Merriam says:

Among the Bala, no musician is a complete economic specialist. Even the *ngombe*, who is a wandering musician, keeps his ties to the land, which he cultivates himself when possible or leaves to the care of members of his family. All informants are agreed on this matter; all say that it is impossible to make one's complete living from music, though some will argue the question as a theoretical point . . . .[12]

Merriam adds that, in spite of this situation, such a minstrel can sometimes earn almost a third of the average income in his community in one festival week.

Babalola comments on the *ijala* or heroic hunters' chants among the Yoruba of Nigeria:

Ijala-chanting is rarely a full-time occupation for any of the artists. Although some members of the public spoil the reputation of the ijala-chanters by calling them *onraye, ole, koninkanise*, etc., meaning that they are lazy drones seeking an easy life, investigation reveals that in actual fact many an ijala artist takes to ijala-chanting only as a hobby or a side-line, and that he is primarily a hunter, a farmer, a sawyer, or a diviner-physician.[13]

The bard of *The Mwindo Epic,* Mr. Shekarisi Rurede, is a maker of baskets and mats, among other occupations (*Mwindo* 15ff.).

So far, we have been talking about bards of a more or less independent status, who owe no allegiance to a steady patron. It seems clear that though they enjoy public acclaim for their excellence, they still have to support themselves and their families by having a regular job, which means they cannot devote undivided attention to their songs. There are parallel cases among the Yugoslav guslars of the Parry-Lord collections. Salih Ugljanin farmed livestock in his native Ugao; at Novi Pazar he kept a coffeehouse, until he became too old and made his living as hired help (or consultant). Sulejman Fortić found life "hard in the village," and preferred life as "a waiter in the coffeehouse" at Novi Pazar. Demail Zogić also kept a coffeehouse there. Sulejman Makić was a cattle farmer from Senica, and Alija Fjuljanin a country farmer from Stavica.[14] In classical Greece, Hesiod is apparently the only acclaimed bard of independent status we know of, and he was a shepherd in the valley of Mount Helicon (*Theogony* 23).

The situation of the bard with a steady patron, like the court minstrel, is not radically different. In *Sunjata* IV, we have the case of Gnankouman Doua, griot to Nare Maghan, the hero's father. Doua is a gleeman and sings Maghan's praises. But he is also a seer, sorcerer, and the king's counselor and closest confidante, sharing with him his cares of state; Doua's son, Balla Fasseke, inherits the same functions when Sunjata comes of age. This all-purpose role of the griot is vividly portrayed in one tale of origin that Hugo Zemp records from the Dan of the Ivory Coast. From the words of his informant, Zemp is able to conclude: "The account of the old man from Dan underlines the time-honoured function of the court musician: to swell the prestige of the chief. The text also indicates the peculiar position of the griot: he serves as messenger."[15]

In many such court situations in Africa—as in the emir's palaces of northern Nigeria—the bard is a multipurpose palace hand, performing duties that are often far from glamorous. We are reminded in Homer of the singer whom Agamemnon is said to have left behind in Argos with full instructions to spy on Klytaimnestra (*Odyssey* 3.267ff.); in a similar vein, in the Ozidi epic, the witch Oreame strikes the earth, and a drummer and hornblower issue forth, charged specifically with protecting the boy-hero against intrigue (*Ozidi* 48).

The concept of professionalism may seem to be different with regard to bards who today receive quite generous patronage from radio and television networks, or from rich businessmen, and may therefore not bother to seek other work. But in real terms, and as far as the performance of extended texts of heroic tales are concerned, there is hardly any difference between the city-based bard and his rustic counterpart. Seldom does either sit down and carefully chisel out his lines so as to achieve anything like a flawless text. Almost invariably, songs are performed for patrons on short order or "as occasion requires,"[16] and in such spontaneous moments textual purity is beyond the capacity of the bard, even with the best of a formular device or mnemonic skill. He may indeed, never be inclined to achieve the kind of verbal and structural uniformity that we may hope to find. Since the song is composed "in" and not "for" a performance, he is likely to be content that the other ingredients of his craft (music, dramatization, and so on) will make up adequately for the incidental mud along the way. That mud is of the very nature of the oral performance, and we may be doing the bard a disservice by endowing his work with a transparency or "purity" that he never intended.

Even from the training of the bard, it is possible to glean something of the background to this happily informal character of traditional minstrelsy. This does not imply that the mode of learning is any less conscientious. Rureke, the bard of *Mwindo*, started his training as a youth by becoming "a helper of Kenyangara of Bese, who was such an expert narrator of the Mwindo epic;" such an apprenticeship requires that one cultivate a thorough presence of mind so as to be able, for instance, to "repeat a whole sentence during each short pause made by the bard" and indeed help him "find the thread of his story" now and then (*Mwindo* 13, 17). But the very unfixed nature of the text makes it clear that the apprentice is being trained not in the rigid use of memory but in the flexible technique of improvisation. From early youth, as Babalola tells us of the apprentice *ijala* bard, the pupil learns his trade assiduously. But he also soon develops "a strong sense of competence and self-reliance," which come through in his response to charges of historical inaccuracy in his performance: "*K'onikaluku o maa ba poro opo 'e lo*" (Let each animal follow the smooth stretch of its own road).[17]

Other than the mode of attachment discussed above, the bard's training can be quite informal, though the learner remains dedicated to his goal.[18] But the most interesting aspect of the training of the singer is the practice of acquiring an extensive repertoire. It seems to be almost universally accepted as a sure means of sharpening the bardic skill. Among the Nyanga, as the editors of *The Mwindo Epic* tell us, "the expert narrators and singers may know a fairly large number of texts" (*Mwindo* 6). Among the Yoruba, Babalola says, "the best ijala-chanter" is "the one whose repertoire is the most extensive,"[19] among other criteria. Ames tells us that among the Hausa the process of musical training "often entails learning a host of songs."[20] And the editors of *Kambili* write of the repertoire of the bard:

A typical evening's performance will include songs for amusement and dancing, ritual songs which can be danced only by those who have performed certain deeds and, at the close of the evening, an epic song of one of the many hunter heroes. We have recorded twelve epic performances of Seydou Camara and well over fifty of his songs. (p. ix)

We could compare this with the situation elsewhere. The foundations of the formular technique may indeed lie partly in the fact that the bard has a vast number of tales or lays from which he could draw some easily deployable phrases and themes. Homer has been credited with quite a few songs. Aristotle ascribes the satirical *Margites* to him; Callinus of Ephesus, according to Pausanias (x.9.5), attributed a *Thebaid* to him; and the Herodotean life of Homer reports that on the day of the new moon, the bard went about the homes of rich men singing, in the company of children, a short song called *eiresione*. Within the *Odyssey* we have an indication of the minstrel's varied repertoire. Demodokos sings of the Trojan experience of the Achaeans and draws tears from Odysseus. But he also has some lighter and even danceable lays, like the one on the luckless adultery of Ares and Aphrodite. In an earlier parallel, in book 1, Phemios has been singing of the Achaeans' grievous homecoming and moves Penelope to tears with his tunes. Thereupon she pleads with him:

Phemios, since you know many other actions of mortals
and gods, which can charm men's hearts and which the singers celebrate,
sit before them and sing one of these and let them in silence
go on drinking their wine, but leave off singing this sad
song, which always afflicts the dear heart deep inside me,
since the unforgettable sorrow comes to me, beyond others,
so dear a head do I long for whenever I am reminded
of my husband, whose fame goes wide through Hellas and midmost Argos.
(1.337-44)

The Chadwicks also discuss the tradition of Irish minstrelsy, in which training involved "learning a large number of sagas each year."[21] And the Yugoslav guslar Sulejman Fortic tells us that, in the course of learning to be a minstrel, "the best thing is for us to know as many songs as we can" (*SCHS* 225).[22]

In view of this large fund of songs and themes, an interchange, whether we call it interpolation or interflow, frequently occurs. For the bard who knows his craft well, the incidental mud, as I have said, can only add a touch of color to the overall flow of the delivery. A good case in point is furnished by the *Kambili* epic. The warrior Kanji is unable to have a child, and several soothsayers are invited to solve the problem and name who among his wives will bear the child (the hero Kambili). If a soothsayer fails in the task, he is immediately beheaded by the order of Samory Toure, Kanji's general and ruler of the land. Now, one of these soothsayers is Nerikoro, a head of the powerful Komo (blacksmith cult-group) which is the ultimate mystical power in traditional Mande society. Beheading such a man would be unthinkable; so though Nerikoro fails to solve the child problem, he goes scot-free. Here is how the bard introduces the character Nerikoro into the story:

Nerikoro, the Komo man has come!
Fakoli was a smith, Samory!
If an insult is made to a smith, pleasure will sour.
The world's first child was a smith,
An insult to a smith, pleasure is ruined.
Ah! Smith! Samory!
If you insult a smith . . .

(536-42)

The significant reference in this piece is "Fakoli." He does not feature at all in the Kambili epic as a character, but is very much one—and a force to reckon with—in the Sunjata legend. According to his editors, the bard Seydou Camara has a version of this legend, yet to be transcribed. But most other versions feature Fakoli, leader of the powerful blacksmith caste. In both the Innes and Niane editions, Fakoli is nephew to Sumanguru, the sorcerer-king of the Susu and archenemy of the hero, Sunjata. In the great war between these two, Fakoli takes Sunjata's side against his uncle

Sumanguru, who has offended him by taking his wife from him (*Sunjata* IV.43). And part of the reason that Sumanguru comes to grief in that war is that he has alienated the powerful smith caste who venerate Fakoli.

An "insult" to a smith, such as Fakoli has experienced, is therefore fraught with serious consequences. In the relevant context in *Kambili*, the detail serves a cautionary purpose and explains why the bard does not subject Nerikoro to a treatment he ordinarily deserves. Thus a detail or line from one song is deployed, with functional ease, in another song in such a way that it bestows on its new context a bold associative or metaphorical flavor. Perhaps this, other than prosody, is the effect intended when Homer calls the swineherd Eumaios "foremost of men" or says that Telemachos' sneeze "clashed horribly," or even makes Eumaios' pigsty[23] look very much like Priam's palace in layout, as Monro has observed. This may be mud, but it does give the flood a touch of genuineness—and epic song is hardly a clear, mellifluous stream.

Now, what does the bard look like as a person, and what does he think of himself and his craft? In many cases, apparently, he would like to draw public attention to himself by the materials that he wears. Otherwise, something marks him out (when he leads a group) other than the musical instrument that he holds. This could take the form of the representative paraphernalia of his craft. The photograph on the cover of the text of *Kambili* shows Seydou Camara decked all over with charms—amulets, cowries, and whatnot—like the hero-hunter of his song. Likewise, the cover photo to the *The Mwindo Epic* has Rureke holding the musical calabash-rattle in the right hand, and in the left a "*conga*-scepter," the main instrument of power continually wielded by the hero in the story. For the Ozidi affair, the narrator will hold in one hand a fan (as constantly used for magical effect by Oreame in the tale) and in the other a sword (the hero's regular weapon) (*Ozidi* xxiv). In the

43

Sunjata story, perhaps of the same order is the picture of Gnan-kouman Doua, griot to Nare Maghan Kon Fatta, as he responds to "the grave music of the 'bolon'" during the celebrations of the king's marriage to Sogolon Kedjou: "Doua, standing amid the eminent guests, held his great spear in his hand and sang the anthem of the Mandingo kings" (*Sunjata* IV.10).[24]

Alternatively, these outward effects are largely a mark of the gleeman's love of display, evidence of his public image. This is apparent from David Ames's observation about the Hausa musician:

The musician often wears gowns made of brightly colored and richly patterned cloth. The items of clothing seldom match since they have been received as payment from different clients and patrons.[25]

"The Mongo bards," in Daniel Biebuyck's useful catalogue, "wearing a feather hat, adorn their bodies and face with various geometrical designs, and carry a ceremonial knife or spear. Among the Fang, the bards wear a feather hat, a mane-like coiffure, a fiber skirt, a multitude of wild animal skins that hang from their arms and waist, and anklet bells."[26]

A similar picture emerges from Salih Ugljanin's description of the legendary Yugoslav guslar, Cor Huso Husović, from whom Salih claims to have learned some of his songs. Asked what Huso did for a living, Salih says: "Nothing, he had no trade, nothing but his horse and his arms, and he went about the world. He was blind in one eye and his clothes and arms were of the finest. And he went thus from town to town and sang to everybody to the gusle" (*SCHS* 61). Although the singers of the Parry-Lord collections are not particularly well dressed, Salih's observation of Huso perhaps indicates that the glamorous get-up is something of an ideal among this tradition of singers.[27]

We may also usefully compare the Homeric scene. Homer says nothing of the bard's outward appearance, but some scholars have understood the "wand" or the "rod" as a later or post-Homeric substitute for the *phorminx* or *kitharis* in the accompaniment of heroic song. This is only half the truth, however. The earliest reference to the wand is from Hesiod, who tells us that the muses "plucked off and gave to me a rod, a twig of sturdy laurel, an admirable thing: and they inspired me with a divine voice to celebrate things that are to be and things that have been" (*Theogony* 30ff.). The next authority, Pindar, gives us the picture of a "rhapsodic" Homer in words that faintly echo Hesiod. Pindar is talking about Homer's glorification of Ajax:

But Homer has done him
Honour among men; for he set straight
All his prowess, and to his wand of celestial words
Told of it, to the delight of men to come.

(Isthmian 4.37-40)

It seems clear that the rod (*skeptron*) that Hesiod claims to have received is nothing more than a recognition of his bardic eminence by the muses (he finds another occasion, in *Works* 657, to mention this eminence). Of Pindar's remark there are many possible interpretations. Perhaps the most plausible is that the rod—on the authority of Hesiod, at least—came to represent for later generations a symbol of excellence in "divine" or "celestial" song. The rhapsode thus held the rod as he recited his lines (an example is the vase figure of the Kleophrades Painter's rhapsode), more to demonstrate his claims to authority in celestial song than as "an aid to rhetorical emphasis in recitation"[28] or a substitute for a lyre.

Evidently, the concern for image or external effect is a traditional feature of the bard's craft. Bards are also generally very outspoken about their merits. They have a rather competitive spirit—

especially when a number of them operate in the same community—and are usually jealous about each other's claims and capacities. It is possible that Djeli Mamoudou Kouyate, the bard of Niane's edition of the Sunjata epic, saw the transcribing scholar as a threat to his trade and was thus moved to condemn the culture of "dumb books" as inferior to "the warmth of the human voice" which he represented in the transmission of history (*Sunjata* IV.41). In his version of the same epic, Bamba Suso proudly announces that he comes from a distinguished line of griots who have told the tale, starting from his grandfather Koriyang Musa, who received his harp-lute from the spirits:

> He met the *jinns*, and brought back a *Kora*.
> The very first *Kora*
> Was like a *simbingo*
> The Kora came from the *jinns*.
>
> (*Sunjata* I.13-16)

In yet another version, the griot Banna Kanute, apparently on observing that the host is not particularly impressed by his performance, tells him with a certain touch of pique, "Don't you know/That an ordinary narrator and an expert singer are not the same?" (*Sunjata* II.1265f.). Of the Hausa singers, Ames observes that "they commonly view themselves as outstanding musicians but neglect others."[29] Merriam notes that among the Bala of the Congo, "the individual musician . . . invariably names himself as the outstanding musician of the village."[30] And Seydou Camara has several lines in his song touting his abilities—for example:

> Ah! It's the voice of Seydou!
> The thing is not easy for all.
> It's the sound of the harp-playing Seydou from Kabaya.
>
> (*Kambili* 51-54)

There are several parallels from the European world. Hesiod's mention of his excellence in song, as I have observed, is clearly of this order; and it is possible, as some have pointed out, that he sets the "truth" of his song against the "fiction" of the Homeric School (*Theogony* 27f). The blind bard of "rocky Chios," who sings the hymn to Delian Apollo, is anxious that he should be judged "the sweetest singer" to visit Delos.[31] Among the Slavs, the bard of *The Song of Igor's Campaign* would seem to be setting his standards against those of a legendary Boyan, not only in terms of style but also of the honesty of his sentiments (*Igor* 10ff.). At Novi Pazar, on being told that Salih Ugljanin claims he knows a hundred songs, the reaction of Sulejman Makic is an immediate denial: "He lies!" (*SCHS* 265). And Milman Parry quotes the following from Matija Murko's record of his experiences in collecting folk songs:

The singers are artists, as is well demonstrated by the fact that they seem extremely jealous of one another. One day, at Sarajevo, after I had recorded three singers, I paid all three of them the same amount. One of them refused to take his payment. It struck me at once that I had behaved rather badly. The people there did, indeed, intimate to me that the man regarded himself as a much better singer than the other two.[32]

But we may well ask: If it is true that the bard has such a bold view of his merits, then why does he attribute his creative powers to a divine source and lay his merits at the feet, so to speak, of divinity? For this appears to be the pattern among many societies, and anthropologists generally seize upon it as a proof of the religious uses of art. Among the Yoruba, the *ijala* artist claims to be the "mouthpiece" of Ogun,[33] the god of blood and iron, of war and the deadly hunt. The Mandingo griot traditionally traces the source of his art to a certain Sourakata, reputedly the closest companion and aide of the Prophet Mohammed.[34] Among the Nyanga, the god Karisi is said to impart the skill of singing the Mwindo legend and could reveal himself in a dream to whoever he blesses with this skill (*Mwindo* 12,14). The dream element also

47

appears in the origins that John Pepper Clark has traced for the Ozidi Saga:

Tradition holds that many years ago the High Priest of Orua in Tarakiri clan fell asleep at the foot of the clan's big shrine. In that sleep came the vision of Azudu, or Ozidi as he is sometimes called. And so compulsive was the urge to tell it the man woke up never to have a moment's rest again, moving from town to town through one clan into another down the hundred odd creeks and islands of the Niger Delta. The story took him seven nights in telling, and on each occasion, however far away from Orua, he had always to return home to the foot of the shrine to intone the last line there or die on the spot of telling in a strange land.[35]

In their several ways these claims tend to reinforce the bard's tremendous self-esteem and sense of uniqueness; like Hesiod, every bard considers himself, and none other, the chosen one in his craft, commissioned by the supernatural powers to deliver the *truth* in song. It is possible that Homer's appeal to the muse ("Sing, goddess . . . ") is of this order. If the very daughters of almighty Zeus chose to speak through the mouth of the poet, what greater proof could there be of excellence and veracity?

It is not clear what the reason is for this self-esteem, especially in view of the variety of circumstances in which the bard is to be found. In monarchical societies, the bard often holds a revered place in the king's court; perhaps the attitude is principally an effort to justify this reverence. The society of ancient Mali is generally reputed to have its origins in Mecca,[36] and the griot who shared the counsels of his lord naturally saw himself in the same position that Sourakata held with Mohammed. Among the Akan of Ghana, the court musician also saw himself as occupying this time-honored position, as is clear from the following drum message:

When the creator created things,
When the manifold creator created things;

What did he create?
He created the court crier,
He created the Drummer,
He created the Principal State Executioner.[37]

In some societies, republican as well as monarchial, the bard may not be held in much regard. People may like his music for the joy that it brings, but they do not consider him indispensable. In such a situation, self-esteem might simply be a reaction against injured pride. Among the Dan of the Ivory Coast, as Hugo Zemp tells us, the griot is today considered inferior, and nobody would allow his daughter to marry one of these musicians; so it is significant that it was from among them that Zemp collected the legend that when Zra (God) created the first chief he gave him a griot as a close companion.[38] In the emirates of northern Nigeria, as Ames reports, the situation is very much the same as in the Ivory Coast; the musicians, thus painfully underestimated, are reduced to ranking one another on the basis of patronage.[39] And the idea of the dream/vision may be just as plausible a means of self-justification as the above cases; as Bowra has observed:

Dream may well give a man the confidence and impulse which he needs to start poetical composition. He will regard them with great awe as coming from the gods and remember them clearly, and, what is more, he will feel that the gods have chosen him for a task, and this will give him a special sense of his own importance and ability.[40]

The implication of all this seems clear. The flights of song will be beyond the compass of a bard who cannot summon the presumption for such an exercise. In the more communalistic world of the olden days, the attitude probably helped the bard to demonstrate that his efforts were just as germane to the common good as those of other craftsmen, like the prophet, the physician, or the woodworker—a fact succinctly stated by Eumaios in *Odyssey* 17.328–185. In today's more competitive milieu, quite possibly the bard is anxious to avoid being done out of the scheme of things. Among the Bala of the Congo, as Merriam reports, musical talent is regarded as "a matter arranged by Efile Mukulu (God)"; yet Chite, the most acknowledged musician in the clan, owned he took up musical training "because I thought of all the money I would make!"[41]

III

We may best look at the bard from the point of view of his performance. In this connection, it cannot be stressed often enough that in evaluating the live medium of art we should try to abandon those impressions that our familiarity with literate art has bred in us. Chief among them is what we have constantly under-stood "poetry" to mean.

Conditioned as we are to the *fixity* of the recorded detail, we are much more interested in the independent merits of the finished work of art than in the raw human and contextual resources out of which it has been put together. The high-water mark of this cul-tural attitude is the concept of the "biographical" or "intentional fallacy"; and with good reason. The portrait of a landscape or description of an experience may be so effective as to surpass anything that we can find in nature; but who can say whether the portrait is the product of a calm and contented mind, or whether it represents the last, bold attempt by an isolated and tormented genius to reach contact with an elusive reality?

To be sure, some critics have urged—as I. A. Richards of Wordsworth's "Westminster Bridge"—that we try to put ourselves in the imagined circumstances and frame of mind of the artist as a way of capturing the moment of creation of his work. But one of the principal features of literacy is that the artist looks ahead to some finished form of his work. He is aware that, once it is published, his disembodied voice will be left at the mercy of the cold impersonality of the page, from which it can hardly be recalled: *nescit vox missa reverti*, as Horace has so succinctly put it (*Ars Poetica* 390). So he endeavors to chisel out his lines at every opportunity he gets, each time in a different mood and a different environment, which seldom leave their marks on the chosen focus of the work. Under these circumstances, would it not be just as mechanical for us to appraise the work on the basis of a putative creative personality as not to assume any personality at all?

But the antithesis of fixity is *process*. For the bard this means the routine of the act, whether programmed or spontaneous, supported by the knowledge that he will live to play another day. The excellence of a song is not determined by the results of a single performance; rather, it is influenced by the audience atmosphere (rapport, indifference, hostility) within which it is performed at any one time.[42] And though the bard may remember that on one happy day he was moved to surpass himself, he is certain that he will do so again if he is lucky enough to find a similar motivation. Adam Parry once asked a very pertinent question with regard to the monumental excellence of the *Iliad*: "Did he [Homer] say on some occasion: 'I'll never do it better than that: reproduce *that* version!'?"[43] Such a picture would best fit a jazz artist listening to a brilliant first take of his recording in a Manhattan sound studio but would be grossly unrepresentative of an artist who felt most at home in the open yard—whether of his village or of a patron.

Since, therefore, excellence in traditional minstrelsy is not defined in terms of the isolated performance that has become a standard or a classic, but rather in terms of the overall context of each performance, we should emphasize the living process by which performance is continually actualized. In this form of art, the means is more worthy of our attention than the end, for poetry here implies more the moment and process of creation than the finished product itself.

A close examination, therefore, of many a recorded text will reveal a debt to the fervid atmosphere of the open performance.

What is the nature of this performance? The reports of scholars who have collected songs from the African field often indicate a tremendous fullness of effect justifying redefinition of the word "poetry." Something of this is reflected in J. P. Clark's comment on the performance of the Ozidi epic:

> not just the tape recorder or bound volume which records the sound alone, but perhaps a full-length color film appears to be the one medium that can catch and convey something of the complete, complex and magnificent texture that is the [Ozidi] epic.[44]

A similar observation has been made by Smith and Dale of the Zimbabwe: "It would need a combination of phonograph and kinematograph to reproduce a tale as it is told. . . . Every muscle of face and body spoke, a swift gesture often supplying the place of a whole sentence."[45] Poetry, in a context of this nature, moves beyond a simple order of words and lines, or even the subtle flavor of a phrase, and involves the totality of the moment of making: which is what *poiesis* is.

If therefore the tale is performed, as is mostly the case in Africa, clearly there will be a considerable reduction of emphasis on the narrative element and an accompanying accentuation of the other elements that give the performance its dominant flavor, such as drama and music. It would hardly do here to say, as Lord has said of Yugoslavia, that "the tale's the thing."[46] This may well be true of plain dictation, the kind that has yielded many of the Slavic songs of the Parry collection. It may even be true of recitatives in certain African communities, in situations where the reciter is far less of a performer than a disinterested transmitter, where even the response of the audience is sternly discouraged, as Coupez and Kamanzi have observed of historical recitations among the Ruanda of Central Africa:

Unlike the amateur, who makes gestures with body as with voice, the professional reciter adopts an impervious attitude, with a rapid and unaccented style of delivery. If his audience reacts with admiration [for the recitation], the reciter holds back his voice with detachment, until silence is restored.[47]

But where the bard sees himself primarily as a public performer, challenged to acquit himself admirably (especially in a traditional context, among his fellows), the circumstances of their delivery matter more than the words themselves.

Perhaps the most prominent of these circumstances is the drama of the moment: the medium of dance, gesticulation, and histrionics. We have seen some of this in *Sunjata* IV: the picture of the griot Gnankouman Doua holding aloft a spear as he "sang the anthem of the Mandingo kings." In *The Mwindo Epic*, the narrator dances pointedly as he sings the various chants in the tale, and also uses gesticulation to indicate, for instance, an effect of numbers (*Mwindo* 71, 133). Among the Akan of Ghana, heroic resitations are frequently done to good dramatic effect, as Nketia has reported: "The delivery of the poems is very dramatic and expressive. . . . The person reciting the poem half covers his mouth with his left hand as he points the sword which he holds in his right hand to the chief in front of whom he stands to perform. This heightens the dramatic effect."[48]

One of the great dramatic moments of *Akoma Mba* occurs when the bard assumes the roles of two characters quarreling over the broken pieces of a drum (1225ff.). The exchanges are fast, and the menace comes through in the words to which the performing bard no doubt gave the benefit of expressive facial and body movements. J. P. Clark's comments concerning the histrionic aspect of a performance of *The Ozidi Saga* are especially interesting:

Finally, there are the imitative and highly stylized dances representing specific actions. The *aro* dance, for example, depicts the progress of a war-canoe like that used by the Smallpox King to invest Ozidi. A good number of others represent attack and defence motions of battles recurrent in the saga. The take-off of witches is simulated by flying movements, and the hand-over-head dance, *avinvin se*, is symbolic of great grief as when Ozidi is struck down by deadly disease.

Side by side with all this is the unfailing use of face expression, limb movement, and general gestures to mime segments of the action. The ambush and bludgeoning to death of the older Ozidi, though done to pantomime and grunts, comes across in all its fierceness and horror—and it is only one of several instances where movement of muscles alone arouses just the right degree of meaning.

A great amount of improvisation and personal resourcefulness goes into this pantomime but many of the motions and gestures . . . spring from the common stock of expressions that the community has drawn upon for generations. The widowed Orea, beating flies off her mutilated husband, the boy-hero, playing games of tops and target-shooting with agemates who taunt him for not knowing his father, the magician-seer Bouakarakabiri conjuring up his master-charm of mortar-and-cauldrons for the hero, and the Awka blacksmith, forging a sword for the hero in a confused forge—each of these characters employs motions and gestures that express for the audience definite moods and emotions. (*Ozidi* xxxi)

In some tales histrionics serve to reinforce certain onomatopoeic ideophones used especially in describing the actions and movements, often to humorous effect. For instance, in *Kambili*, it is conceivable that the bard would employ such a device as he described the cumbersome motions of the two villainous women in the story—"galump, galump, galump" (1404) and "gwiligigwo-logo" (1475). There are numerous such situations in *The Ozidi Saga* and *Akoma Mba*—the ideophones are so forceful that only dramatization can give them meaning. Hardly any of these effects can be transferred into the frigid form of the text of the heroic song. But it seems clear that a new definition should be sought if we are to do justice to the poetic moment of an oral performance; as Ruth Finnegan has aptly put it, "The bare words can *not* be left to speak for themselves."[49] Forceful though it is, even the concept of the "speaking picture" of art (as understood by Mazzoni and others) fails to convey the warmth of the live moment of *poiesis*.

The situation may very well be different elsewhere. If indeed "the tale's the thing" for the Yugoslav guslars, then among them the performance element may be very weak—perhaps because in that tradition of heroic singing, there grew a considerable interest in accuracy of detail, which is more easily achieved in a recitative than in a performance situation. Furthermore, with the publication of traditional epic songs in Yugoslavia, and thus the emergence of "standard versions" to which guslars felt attached and against which their individual performances were regularly measured,[50] it would appear that the singer became leery of any technique that might impair his efforts to follow the established paths of his story. Much may be due also to the nature of the musical instrument. The singer normally holds the gusle across his knees; since he must be seated, it becomes difficult to do much but tell the story. In Africa, the singer is not often saddled with a musical instrument that completely eliminates the potential for histrionic movements. There are stringed instruments, rattles, drums, and gongs, but the bard, all too aware of his role as a performer, generally manages to "speak" with his body as often as the need arises. Even the elaborate accompaniment to the *mvet* epic of the Fang (a stringed wooden bar to which are attached about three to five half-calabashes serving as resonators) does not prevent the bard from realizing his multiple role as a musician-dancer-raconteur who gives full play to the dramatic potential of his tale.[51]

The histrionic resources of the Homeric songs are functionally unknown to us, largely because our texts are the products of several generations of careful doctoring; they leave an impression of a tradition of rigid narration without the complication of other devices. But certain references make one wonder if the whole act was as sedate as it now seems. Bowra's view that "heroic poetry is sung by a single bard and has no dance"[52]—assuming this to refer to the Homeric bard alone—may be true only to an extent. That the bard did not himself dance may well be granted, but there is so much talk of dancing to the songs of the bards in Homer that we may well wonder what form it took or what exactly gave rise to it.

We may quickly dismiss the rather confused and unruly scene at Ithaka. In *Odyssey* 1.32f. Phemios sings as the audience listens in silence. The song hurts Penelope, and she comes down to the hall and pleads that Phemios change the subject. Telemachos intervenes and asks her to take it all gamely. She withdraws into the house once again, and later,

The others, turning to the dance and the delightful
song, took their pleasure and awaited the coming of evening,
and the black evening came on as they were taking their pleasure.

(421-23)

Obviously Phemios, out of courtesy, does not return to the sort of theme that has saddened Penelope. The new theme, although lighter in spirit that the "grievous homecoming of the Achaeans," may well belong to the same heroic repertoire: to argue that the subject is not heroic simply because it is light in spirit would be like saying that the Deceit of the *Iliad* is not heroic material. This brings us to Demodokos' love theme of *Odyssey* 8. "Alternative entertainment" it may well be, as Lord has described it,[53] but it belongs very much to the broad heroic world around which these tales have been constructed; in fact Plutarch's interlocutor, no doubt confusing the title of the story, groups it along with other heroic tales of war such as were later set to music and performed in contests by Terpander.[54] However, the important thing about Demodokos' story is that it is accompanied by a dance performed by "young men in the first of their youth, well trained in dancing." What kind of dancing the young men do is not clear. Merry suggests, "The dance was probably so arranged as to interpret the spirit of Demodokos' song by the dancers' gestures."[55] The bard probably never danced; but there may well have been a tradition of "heroic dancing" that did some justice to the histrionic potential of the tales. In Africa, such potential is generally explored to the fullest.[56]

But nothing makes the difference, in an open performance of the heroic tale in Africa, quite so much as the music. A full consideration of the relative roles of music and narration would no doubt reveal that they constitute the two arms of the balance in a performance.[57] This means that the more the music is emphasized, the less likely it is that verbal exactitude and a faultless narrative order will be observed. Alternatively, the neater the narrative and verbal patterns of a heroic song, the more certain we can be that the musical accompaniment to the text was sternly subdued or nonfunctional, or indeed that the text is the product of straightforward dictation or of normalization.

I do not mean to underestimate the importance of words in the heroic song; without them, there is no "song." Indeed, the incidence of "talking" drums in West Africa, to take a significant example, clearly demonstrates that in African music words are by no means taken lightly. Ames makes an important point in his discussion of Hausa music when he reports: "The paramount importance of the lyrics of songs to the Hausa was succinctly put by an elderly man who said, 'What would be the use of it?' when I remarked that much of Western music is purely instrumental."[58] J. P. Clark makes the same point somewhat differently but no less effectively: "While action . . . is described as well as demonstrated, it is the responsibility of the story-teller to conjure up by word the beauty and pity pregnant in the situation" (*Ozidi* xxviii). But, delivered in the context of music, words behave in a way that reveals the tremendous influence exerted by the music.

It is not easy to trace the roots of this influence. Music has meant all kinds of things to all manner of peoples at different stages of their cultural history. To some, as Plutarch notes, it represented "an act of piety and a primary concern of mankind to sing hymns to the gods, who have blessed them alone with articulate speech."[59] To others—in Plato's view of ancient Egypt—music was one of the means traditionally employed by society in habituating its youth to forms and strains of virtue.[60] To yet others, it is an indispensable element in man's desire to activate his vital forces, as Zemp has discovered among the Dan of the Ivory Coast (West Africa):

The encouragement yielded by singing and music plays an eminent role in Dan society. . . . We are not talking here simply of the ordinary encouragement given by flattering phrases, but of a genuine infusion of force by music.[61]

In tales traditionally told to the accompaniment of music, it is interesting how much influence music exerts on the narrative element. Once the music is removed, something strange begins to happen to the words of the tale—if the remarks of field researchers on this subject are any guide. For instance, Bruno Nettl has reported from his recordings in Africa how seldom could the "native singers ordinarily give either text or music alone without difficulty."[62] Similarly, from his work among bards in the modern Grecian world, Notopoulos confirms that "singers . . . find it difficult to dictate their versions without the aid of the music."[63] Among Yugoslav guslars, the musical element is evidently equally important: under interrogation from Nikola Vujnović, Milman Parry's field assistant, the guslar Sulejman Makic acknowledges that the principal mark of a good singer is his ability in playing the gusle (SCHS 265).[64] In his field notes, Parry reports how difficult it was for Vujnović, on one occasion, to go beyond the first twelve lines of a poem in the absence of accompaniment on the gusle.[65]

In Africa at least, then, we cannot easily accept the claim that "the tale's the thing" if we give due consideration to the role of music in an oral performance. The traditional bard is to a large extent a music man (and one should here distinguish the "traditional" context from the recording studio); side by side with his responsibility to keep faith with words is his desire to deliver a good musical performance. To be sure, it would be disastrous for the bard to lose track of his tale completely. But many a time music has come to the rescue of a straying imagination; when the details of the tale become entangled or uncontrollable, the bard can count on the music to sustain the performance while the loose ends are being tied together.

Music, therefore, is "the thing" in traditional African song; as the old Mandingo griot puts it, "Music is the griot's soul" (Sunjata IV.39). The performance will simply not come alive if the musical support is either defective or oppressive, if the right sort of warmth has not been generated.

The stabilizing role of music can be seen in The Mwindo Epic. When the hero, Mwindo, approaches to be identified by his aunt Iyangura in her subaquatic abode, he breaks into a song (70). At this point the bard loses the thread of the story and begins to fill in the time with several chanted remarks and reflections. Evidently, the music intensifies, and so too his dancing, as he loses no time in pointing out to the audience:

Kasengeri is dancing [wagging his] tail . . .
If I am at a loss for words in the great song,
If it dies out, may it not die out for me there,

with the last line implying that the bard cannot afford to fail the audience in dance the way he has done in his narration! The random sayings continue, to the throb of the music, until (72) the bard is able to pick up the story once again. Usually, the audience is inclined to take the loss and recovery in good grace, and indeed would applaud a well-contrived recovery in which the excitement of the performance is undiminished. As the editors say, "What counts here is the singing, the dancing, the rhythm, and the music, not the verbalizations; the aim is not to convey ideas, but to enjoy sound and rhythm."[66]

The question might well be asked: if a bard knew his story well and attained the local prominence that many of our recorded artists apparently enjoy, what would make his mind stray in the middle of his story? Perhaps only a bard could explain why this occurs. A good deal may depend on the flow of musical accompaniment and the overall level of excitement. "Without the right rhythm," in the words of Professor Biebuyck, "the narrator simply seems to lose the thread of his inspiration."[67]

This is what happens occasionally in the *Kambili* epic. The performance is punctuated with Seydou Camara's comments on the music and his warnings to the accompanists. Earlier in the story, he is happy to be getting the right rhythmic backing and duly observes that things are moving well:

Ah! Allah has been good to harp-playing Seydou.
Playing before the European is not easy for all.
The strings have been good to the Kabaya Smith

(279-81)

As the performance progresses, it would seem that the accompanists feel the excitement themselves and let their fingers run away. Seydou does not hesitate to call this to their attention:

If you speed up the strings,
I am not able to speak

(333-34)

In time, the exertion begins to wear out the music men, and their support falters. The bard, feeling the effect of this on his song, warns: "*Ah! Harpist, you're slowing down my words!*" (2065). The music gains once more in momentum, somewhat beyond the bard's needs, thereby upsetting the balance of the performance. Seydou lets the offender know it:

Ah! Rhythm man, rhythm man!
Slow down a little!
Speaking is not easy; not being able to speak is not easy.

(2104-6)

Sometimes the notice can take the form of a rather harsh chastisement:

"*Sleep has made your eyes heavy! Pay attention to the rhythm.*"

After this the performance would appear to be moving on smoothly to the end. We can thus see how much the bard depends on music for the success of his performance; to concentrate all interest on the bare words of the tale would be to underestimate the importance of music in such a tradition.[68]

What is the nature of this musical element in African heroic song? A full discussion of African music is beyond the scope of this study; but one fundamental aspect, its polyrhythmic nature, is relevant here. The different instruments in the musical accompaniment may be so tuned as to achieve a harmonic balance and provide an apt support to the song. Quite often, however, each instrument pursues its own rhythmic pace, creating a certain complexity of effect. Polyrhythms in African music vary as one moves from east to west of the continent, with West Africa as the region of the greatest complexity, as Bruno Nettl has observed: "West African rhythmic material is differentiated from East African by greater rhythmic complexity and more heterometric tendencies."[69] On the whole, however, in any one performance, the narrative élan is balanced by a corresponding instrumental excitement. Add to all this a full histrionic touch, and it will become clear what an open performance of a heroic tale in Africa can be like.

We can now understand why in such a context the role of words is considerably modified or controlled. I shall be discussing the question of the structural balance of the heroic song in a later chapter; for now it will be partially clear that such balance as we have learned to recognize in a written poem has very little relevance to this art form. Indeed, the music can be remarkably suggestive, thereby drastically reducing even the need for words. In those areas of West Africa where the "talking drum" is used as an accompaniment to poetry, as among the Yoruba of Nigeria and Akan of Ghana, numerous phrases may well be delivered on it. The bard thus spends that much less time on actual narration, since he finds his efforts adequately supplemented. Sometimes an entire historical recitative is done on the drum![70] In Africa, the potential for musical accompaniment to the song is limitless.

The difference between Africa and the European societies in this regard will emerge when we compare the musical accompaniments to the song. *The Mwindo Epic*, we are told, is generally done by a bard who

accompanies himself with a rattle. He may also hold a representation of one of the favorite symbols of the hero, such as the *conga-scepter*, which, in the Mwindo epic of the Nyanga, is the major magical device the hero possesses. The singing bard is accompanied by a percussion stick, which is placed on the ground and is beaten with small drumsticks by three or four young men.... These young men, together with people in the crowd, also hum while the bard sings.... At all times during the singing of an episode the percussionists keep up with the rhythm and humming and singing, enhancing the sound and sometimes speeding up the rhythm when the bard pauses.[71]

Kambili has a six-stringed harp-lute as well as a "ridged metal pipe which is scraped by an iron rod"—not to mention the complex rhythmic support given by the bard's voice as well as by a group of accompanists, as the editors have pointed out in their introduction. The basic musical accompaniment of the *mvet* epic of the Fang is a stringed wooden bar (sometimes curved into a bow) to which is attached an assembly of three to five semicalabashes used as resonators; the bard is himself usually accompanied by other back-up musicians playing the same kind of instrument and other rhythmic types like bells and wooden gongs.[72] In Homer, however, the bard accompanies his song only on the lyre.[73] The lay in *Beowulf* 2107 is played to a harp. And the Yugoslav singer has just a gusle, which is a simple one-stringed violin. In most of these European cases, the singer is not accompanied by any other musician.

The rhythmic complexity of the African song consequently imposes a looseness on its prosody. In many cases where, for instance, the singing is done on the basis of breath groups, the bard may set himself the challenge of getting in as many words within each group as possible; the rhythmic pattern does not change, he simply has to speed up the pace of his delivery. Alternatively, if gravity is required, the pace may be considerably slowed down, with fewer words occupying the breath groups or "rhythm segments." The same flexibility is noticeable in the accentuation; accents are distributed more often to achieve emotional emphasis than on a fixed quantitative basis. Again, the rhythmic background against which this is done does not change; the words of the song, accentually as well as syllabically, are distributed on a free basis to allow the best vocal and histrionic effect to the performance.[74]

Such problems tempt one to wonder what the relationship could have been between the harp and the words in the Homeric epos. The hexameter (whatever its original components) may have come to stay as the basic pattern of composition. But what becomes of the music when, for instance, an ordinarily short vowel suddenly becomes long simply because it is succeeded by two consonants, or because it is the first of three successive shorts, or some such complex technical situation? To achieve a prosodic consistency, the bard may well have had recourse to a linguistic potpourri such as Notopoulos has pointed out: "We must get used to the notion that the literary dialects in Greek literature are for the most part mixed and artificial and do not correspond to the spoken dialects or the mature dialect of the author."[75] But this tells us nothing about what part (if any) a lyre or harp could have played in achieving that consistency. That the songs of Homer are indebted to the oral tradition is abundantly clear from both their structural character and the outlook they reveal; but it is hard to believe that a bard who accompanied himself on a musical instrument would not often tend to modify the complex prosodic pattern (not such simple systems as the syllable count of the Yugoslav songs) that our texts reveal. One is thus tempted to conclude that such technical loyalty could only come from a normalization of the dictated text (as Whitman believes), or from a performance in which the bard struck the strings only at the end of single, unenjambed lines (in Kirk's view),[76] or from a performance by a bard who did not himself play any instrument. The introduction of writing, and subsequently the standardization of the text of the epic song for purposes of festival recitations by professional singers or rhapsodes, would seem to provide a good opportunity for attempting such consistency as we have in our texts of Homer. In any case, writing must have had a good deal to do with the results.[77]

The relation of words to music in a performance is by no means an easy matter to resolve. Some scholars take rather categorical positions on this question, though their impressions have been based on very limited evidence; for instance, Bowra has mostly the Slavic world in mind when he says: "Heroic poetry puts the words first and subordinates the music to them."[78] Other scholars have chosen to be on the safe side of the debate; there is surely good sense in the noncommittal attitude of a musicologist like Bruno Nettl, who observes: "In many cases, linguistic features are violated when words are combined wth music. It is impossible to say now that in any particular culture the music is definitely subordinate to the language or vice versa."[79] Still, as far as one can see of the situation in Africa, music is indispensable, as Seydou Camara's warning to his rhythm man amply demonstrates:

Man, pay attention to the rhythm!
Don't miss the rhythm whatever you do!

(*Kambili* 2002-3)

We have talked mostly about prosody, assuming that a heroic song must necessarily be in verse. That view has been categorically expressed by Bowra, Parry, and Lord,[80] and verse appears to be one major criterion on which Finnegan denies that the epic as an art form exists in Africa.[81] I shall be taking up the issues of prosody and structure more fully in a later chapter; meanwhile I urge that, as far as the oral performance is concerned, some of our present understanding of the nature of verse should be reexamined. It may well be, as Lord has observed, that "prose would be the easiest and most natural way to tell a story."[82] But prose placed in the rather complex musical and histrionic environment such as we can see of *Mwindo* and *Ozidi* is not simply prose. It is prose propelled by the force of music, and the aesthetic results are bound to be different from those of an unaccompanied narration. The story thus told is a song, and its poetry consists more in the fervid process of making than in any qualities we may recognize when the hands are resting and the voice is still.

IV

We may conclude with a brief look at the milieu of the heroic song—the heroic world in which the mind of the bard operates. That world has too often been described with phrases of dubious import like "heroic age." Believers in a heroic age have usually put more than necessary faith on traceable history in the content of a heroic tale, forgetting that the oral artist's concept of history or fact is in many ways different from ours. We have, in the previous chapter, described the traditional African artist as a man with a very pressing sense of real and concrete presence, enjoying the closest intimacy with an environment that is both physical and metaphysical. Such an artist would feel too attached to his metaphysical material to give it a lesser position of importance in his scheme of thought; he would be just as inclined to consider as fact what to us would be merely a mental construct, or fancy.

History for the unlettered artist is both what has actually happened and what is fabled to have happened. For him myth has considerable historical value; because it has been told all too often, it bears the stamp of truth. Such claims to truth are frequently employed by the bard as a way of seeking approbation for his craft; he makes every effort to convince us that what he says is generally accepted or true and should therefore be taken seriously. Of the story of Sunjata the griot Mamoudou Kouyate says: "My word is pure and free of all untruth; it is the word of my father; it is the word of my father's father. I will give you my father's words

66

just as I received them; royal griots do not know what lying is . . . "
(*Sunjata* IV.1); this "pure" word includes an account of Sunjata
and Sumanguru hurling threats at each other through their owls
shortly before the battle of Krina. "Ah! Comrades! I don't tell lies,"
exclaims Seydou Camara (*Kambili* 665); in his song a child pulls a
buffalo home effortlessly with a rope, and a man turns into a lion.
A similar quest for approbation is made by the *Mwindo* bard Rureke when he says in a chant:

We are telling the story
That the Babuya have told [long ago]

(60)

Because the story is old, it should be taken seriously.

Claims to truth as a plea for approbation are probably no different in other societies. The poet of *Igor* rejects the romantic fancy
of the ancient diction as exemplified by Boyan in favor of what he
considers a realistic approach:

Let us, however,
begin this song
in keeping with the happenings
of these times
and not with the contriving of Boyan.

(6-10)

Yet he has his Igor settling upon the water like a white duck and
flying up to the mists "like a falcon"! "Thus I heard the tale and
thus I have told it to you": that is the formula frequently used by
the guslars to end their songs, and Sulejman Makic states categorically, "One must sing what one has heard and exactly as it
happened. It isn't good to change or to add." (*SCHS* 226). But we
also have the following observation by Albert Lord in his portrait of
Avdo Mededović, so far the most outstanding of these south Slavic

67

bards: "His technique, and that of his fellows, was expansion from within by the addition of detail and fullness of narrative. Catalogues are extended and also amplified by description of men and horses."[83] If we question Avdo about his brilliant details, he is quite likely to affirm that it was all "exactly as it happened," even though his amplifications of an old tale are based largely on his own experience.

Claims to truth were also made by poets in ancient Greece and the Near East. An interesting example occurs in *The Epic of Gilgamesh*, in the lines with which the poet begins and ends the life of the hero:

He was wise, he saw mysteries and knew secret things, he brought us a tale of the days before the flood. He went on a long journey, was weary, worn-out with labor, returning he rested, he engraved on a stone the whole story. (61, 117)

The story, whether of the Flood or of the exploits of Gilgamesh, is more authoritative if it is a replica of the one originally engraved on a stone by the hero himself. Hesiod makes the muses draw a distinction between "fake" and "true" utterances (*Theogony* 27f.) in a way that would award him the benefit of truth over the so-called romantic school as represented by Homer.

In spite of this characteristic concern for approbation, the very nature of the oral epic marks it out as unreliable history. In the first place, because the heroic song is an ever-living event, the bard is continually obliged to use contemporary material and so frequently adulterates the basic antiquity of the song. Although he is working with old, traditional material, he is so eager to make an impression on the contemporary audience that he is led to rework some of that material. Often he is unaware of this violation of his ancient trust; what counts for him is more the continued relevance and appeal of his song.

The text of an old song is thus often dotted with anachronisms and references that are clearly reflective of the period during which the song is performed. Part of this tendency is what we might designate the journalistic temper of minstrelsy, in the sense that certain elements of the song—perhaps even the overall flavor of it—are good only for the day or for the peculiar occasion of the performance. These elements are sometimes easy to identify, for they stand out either as excrescences or as cosmetic touches to the basic material of the song, which goes to prove that the bard responds actively to fresh environments of "truth." His creative impulses are ever alert; he is no slave to a fossilized tradition.

The journalistic temper reveals itself in many ways. It may happen that the bard, either moved by the magnitude of a recent event or anxious to win the approbation of a new patron, would come up with a new song on the basis of or with the aid of traditional formulas. When Sumanguru surprises Balla Fasseke in his fetish chamber, the griot is forced to improvise a song in honor of the villain king; the improvised tune, we are told, delighted Sumanguru (Sunjata IV.40). In such a situation, Balla Fasseke would simply try to fit the name and attributes of Sumanguru into the appropriate places in a familiar heroic lay, just to keep the king happy. Nketia makes roughly the same point in his discussion of the solo musician, among the Akan of Ghana, who is invited to perform at special occasions. Such a bard will take care to make an impression, partly by readjusting the original material of his song: "On arrival it would be a matter of etiquette for him to mention his host in his songs, and if the occasion is a funeral, to include suitable references to the deceased and the bereaved."[84]

Some interesting examples of this deference to patronage are provided by the versions of the Sunjata stories collected by Gordon Innes. The performance and recording of Banna Kanute's version was sponsored by a certain Bakari Sidibe, as we are told.

69

At several points in the text, the bard pays homage to Sidibe and his lineage (*Sunjata* II.390-403; 573-79; 1254-63). These asides are restricted to the recitative sections of the performance and do not interfere unduly with the telling of the tale (though a less careful transcription would have left room for much confusion in this regard). But a more intrinsic interpolation occurs in the version of the tale by Dembo Kanute. The host on this occasion, a government official by the name of Seni Darbo, gets more than ordinary credit in the text. Not only does the bard, as Innes tells us in the notes (p. 312f.), "mention the names of his various patrons who have treated him generously in the past, as well as mentioning the name of Seni Darbo, in whose honor the performance is being given"; the bard drags an ancestor of Darbo into the Sunjata legend and indeed makes him the star of that famous incident in which Sunjata chases Sumanguru, who has taken to flight in a battle between them. The ancestral Darbo is made the leader of the chase, over even Sunjata himself! (*Sunjata* III. 956ff.)

This tendency may not be as strong in other cultures. But there is evidently some element of the journalistic in that scene at Heorot where "Beowulf's prowess was praised in song" and his recent deeds skillfully woven into the fabric of old lays:

Time and again a gleeman chanted,
A minstrel mindful of saga and lay.
He wove his words in a winsome pattern,
Hymning the burden of Beowulf's feat,
Clothing the story in skillful verse.

(867-71)

Some scholars have identified this sort of temperament as "panegyric," as distinct from "epic," which has a broader compass; but the distinction is hardly justified in this case. Whether he sings panegyric or epic, the bard is moved to celebrate a great event or to do a patron proud, and every time he sings the song in a different context he tends to readjust the material. In so doing he imposes on a later generation, all too eager to establish the exact historicity of his material, the rather unenviable task of unraveling fact from embellishment. This, for instance, is why it has remained difficult, in Homeric research, to identify locales like the paradisiac island, Scheria. Alkinoos may simply have been a contemporary king who was celebrated in Homeric verse because he has treated the poet well. Vivante has put the matter quite fittingly: "Scheria is like an Ionian city, and the wonder of Alcinous' garden is conveyed by nothing else but its exuberance which, though extraordinary in the rhythm of its growth, is such as the earth might produce in a happy climate."[85] Archaeology may eventually locate Scheria, but it is unlikely to establish what segment of its history we can with certainty fit into the fabric of the story of the grievous homecoming of the Achaeans from Troy. That segment was quite possibly a product of the bard's alert genius operating on the spur of one happy moment; the result is a song that violates the canons of history as we understand it.

The journalistic temper may also reveal itself in brief digressions woven into the song. It will usually be clear that such remarks are alien to the original material, thrown in either to fill in the time or to achieve a special effect during the performance. In *Kambili*, Seydou Camara's salutes to his apprentices and audience (55ff.) are of this order. But such remarks may not always stand out clearly. Babalola points to a style of digressions among the *ijala* bards of Yorubaland, which "stems from the chanter's whim when he happens to focus his eyes on a particular member of the audience during his chanting performance. He may interpose impromptu a few utterances in salute to that person before returning to his proper theme."[86] A printed text of such a performance could be misleading to a reader in a later generation, especially if it was unaccompanied by explanatory notes. Considering that the *oriki* or heroic praise verses that these *ijala* bards sing usually trace the family tree of their subject, the reader may not realize that the digressive salute to one of the bard's audience is not in the original chant.

Many violations of historical fact are motivated by political interest. A notable example in African heroic song is the Sunjata legend. Scholars of western Sudanese history have often warned that the oral evidence provided by the griots' songs should be taken with a grain of salt.[87] In the heroic "world" that these bards celebrate, truth is equatable with glory. So long as the parochial or political interests of the group are upheld (and in the caste societies of the Western Sudan the idea of "group" is taken quite seriously),[88] the bard does not worry about sticking to the facts.

In the Sunjata story, a good example is provided by the bard's treatment of the fortunes of Balla Fasseke, griot to the hero. Djeli Mamoudou Kouyate tells us at the beginning of his story that "since time immemorial the Kouyates have been in the service of the Keita princes of Mali"—which means that the bard is a descendant of the long line of griots who have served the family of Sunjata. Naturally he exploits every opportunity to do his family proud. Such an opportunity arises in the successive appropriations of Balla Fasseke, first by Dankaran Touman (Sunjata's half brother) and then by Sumanguru. This is how the bard sums up the immediate cause of the war between Sunjata and Sumanguru:

Thus Balla Fasseke, whom king Nare Maghan had given to his son Sundiata, was stolen from the latter by Dankaran Touman; now it was the king of Sosso, Soumaoro Kante, who, in turn, stole the precious griot from the son of Sassouma Berete. In this way war between Sundiata and Soumaoro became inevitable. (*Sunjata* IV.40)

To the objective historian this would be a ridiculous pretext for war. In spite of the importance of the griot in the career of a king, Sunjata had more cause to be fighting the menace of Sumanguru's territorial ambitions than to be desperate over the loss of his griot. But a bard who claimed descent from Balla Fasseke could scarcely have it otherwise: a classic demonstration of what the transcriber of the tale, Professor Niane, has himself called "a concern for truth aimed solely at glorifying the griots' caste."[89]

A slightly different shade of political interest is revealed by Dembo Kanute's version of the Sunjata legend. In that same pursuit of Sumanguru by Sunjata and his men, this Gambian griot mentions a certain "Sitafa Jawara" (Sunjata III.976) as a member of the pursuing party. Quite usefully, the editor explains, "Sitafa Jawara is not a traditional character in the Sunjata epic, but seems to have been introduced into it here by Dembo, presumably out of deference to the then Prime Minister of The Gambia, Sir Dauda Jawara." Political concern may not be all that easy to establish; but a bard who sings mostly to please will sell his craft in any field of social life, including politics.

Such a concern is not easily traceable in the songs of Homer, perhaps because we do not know the political interests of Homer or of the numerous rhapsodes who recited his songs. But scholars even of this largely unitarian age of Homeric criticism are willing to concede that the material does show signs of tampering, and a Peisistratid manipulation of the text of the songs has often been alleged.[90]

Political manipulation is the least of the things that can happen to songs that have enjoyed ages of popularity among peoples. Invariably, they show signs of the ages and cultures with which they have had contact. Thus, in the Sunjata epic, the king Nare Maghan is shown to have "taken up his usual position under the silk-cotton

tree" (*Sunjata* IV.4). Nare Maghan was reputedly a thirteenth-century figure, and the silk-cotton was introduced to West Africa by
Portuguese traders in the fourteenth or fifteenth century; the detail
about the tree must therefore have come from a later version of
the legend. In his version of the same epic, Banna Kanute makes
Sunjata fire at Sumanguru with a double-barreled gun loaded with
a cockspur (*Sunjata* II.1937-38)—a clearly anachronistic variant of
the more popular version in which the hero shoots at Sumanguru
with an arrow tipped with cockspur. In the old Fang epic, the king
summons his secretary and dictates to him a letter calling all his
district heads to a meeting (*Akoma Mba* 33ff.). The hero, Mengono Mba, gives a feast to the entire nation "in the manner of the
white man": tables laid out with everything from glasses to silver-
ware (1819ff.). In the Ozidi story, the old witch, Oreame, is said to
be wearing a "Lagos blouse" (343)—not surprisingly, as the bard
lives in Ibadan, much nearer Lagos than his ancestral home in
Tarakari (in the Niger Delta, deep in the south of Nigeria). In *The
Mwindo Epic* we have the case of a possible survival of detail from
a truly old version. The village of Tubondo is resuscitated after its
annihilation by Mwindo, and among the animals brought in to
replenish it are cattle. Cattle are unknown to the Nyanga of the
rain forests of the modern Congo, and the editors suggest that
"this part of the text may have preserved a tradition known by the
ancestors of the Nyanga before they migrated from the East African grassland into the Congo rain forest" (119n).

In Homer, too, ages or transmission have left their marks on the
old material. Thus when Achilles emerges from his tent and roars
across the trench to frighten off the Trojans, his shout is likened to
the sound of a trumpet, an object unknown to the Mycenaean
world:

As loud as comes the voice that is screamed out by a trumpet
by murderous attackers who beleaguer a city,
so then high and clear went up the voice of Aiakides.

(Iliad 18.219-21)

A helpful scholiast comments here that though the poet knows of the trumpet, its use is alien to his heroes![91] Similarly, in the Yugoslav collections of Parry and Lord, the imperial "firman" of the Ottoman days is replaced now and then by the very modern telegraph, "and impressive houses and palaces of many stories appear in places and times when even the best of dwellings had no more than three stories."[92]

It is therefore clear that if we recognize the oral epic as a living and not a fossilized tradition, we should emphasize the historical resources of the song less than the context of its re-creation and the mythopoeic temper of the singer. The material of the song may have come from far back in the past, but for the bard that material reflects an ever-living potential or an ideal worth keeping alive. Where there is lament of the past, it is because the bard regrets that the present society is in danger of turning its back on an ideal of behavior that is its living heritage. The concept of a "heroic age" is relevant only to an interest in history conceived as a rigid entity, which is alien to the mythmaking genius of the bard. To him history is truth eternally re-created with the power of song, "not as a dry record of the past, but as a vital memory of the past as exhortation to present action."[93] The *Kambili* epic celebrates the legendary world of Samory Toure, the late-nineteenth-century ruler of the Segu Tukulor Empire. But from the thirteenth-century world of Sunjata the bard drags in the hero Fakoli (*Kambili* 537), and from the twentieth century he gives his salute to the "Parisian man of the hour" (335), meaning Charles de Gaulle! In heroic song the *klea andron* are a timeless ideal of living, as valid for the

world of the bard as they have been for the distant age that gave
birth to his song. For Djeli Mamoudou, Sunjata "left his mark on
Mali for all time and his taboos still guide men in their conduct. . . . Go to Krina near Ka-ba," he challenges the unbelieving,
"and you will see the bird that foretold the end to Soumaoro"
(*Sunjata* IV.83). You may not see the actual bird of the thirteenth
century; but so long as the species survives and Krina remains, the
traditional artist, with his peculiar sense of the real, summons
them as timeless witnesses to the glory of an indestructible spirit.
The interest of the traditional bard is in the timeless seen through
the eyes of the present.

What then is this heroic world around which the bard builds his
song? The arguments for a heroic age are particularly weak when
tested on Seydou Camara, the bard of *Kambili*. If he finds it so
easy to illustrate his image of valor with three different generations
of heroic figures—the thirteenth-century world of Fakoli, the nine-
teenth-century world of Samory Toure, and the twentieth-century
world of Charles de Gaulle (who is not even a Mandingo!), then
obviously he is celebrating an ideal that transcends a specific age.
His interest is not in history but in the things that history yields:
values, ideals, and the dangers attendant on these. He merely
illustrates these elements with concrete examples; he keeps as
close as possible to the facts but seizes every opportunity to use
contemporary examples so long as they are, in his peculiar reck-
oning, apt. There will always be a heroic age as long as great and
fearful things are done and traditional bards exist to weave them
into the tested motifs of their art. Living men, if they will but bestir
themselves, have every chance of being as great and as memorable as the men of bygone days. Thus Dembo Kanute tells the host
of his performace:

My minds goes to
Many, many great men besides.
Don't you know that the Marena woman's Seku
   Alifa Jaaju is dead.
Seni Daabo, do something, sir;
Life consists of doing something.

(Sunjata III.64-68)[94]

Deeds that move the spirit are the material of the bard's song. His art is built on the affective element, and the heroic characters who people the world of his song simply serve to provide an agency for those deeds (otherwise de Gaulle has no place in an old Mandingo myth).

The heroic narrative also presents a somewhat dualistic portrait of the heroic society, reflecting perhaps the Aristotelian idea of just proportions, or perhaps the play of an unschooled imagination. The hero is frequently formidable, self-centered, and disruptive; but he also has moments in which he feels love and concern for his fellows. The bard is moved to celebrate the bravado and the destructive energy of the hero; but he also endeavors to represent certain elements without which the society in which the hero lives will cease to exist. This balancing factor may consist of love, loyalty, or friendship. Ozidi is as capable of tenderness and consideration (252-53) as he is of reckless bloodletting. Mwindo levels everything that stands in his way—men, monsters, gods—but he also shows a concern for harmony and accord. Kambili is the formidable and "invincible" hero, but he is also the "hope of the group," and the salvation of the community is ensured by his marriage to Kumba. Achilles is insufferably proud and selfish; but as his friends fall one after the other and gloom hangs over the Achaean host, he laments:

77

I was no light of safety to Patroklos, nor to my other
companions, who in their numbers went down before glorious Hektor,
but sit here beside my ships, a useless weight on the good land.

(*Iliad* 18.102-4)

At the celebrations in Heorot marking Beowulf's victory over Grendel, Hrothgar's wife, Wealtheow, sketches for the Geatish hero a
portrait of the communal spirit that has kept the Danish heroic
tempers under control:

Here each hero is true to other,
Gentle of spirit, loyal to Lord,
Friendly thanes and a folk united,
Wine-cheered warriors who do my will.

(*Beowulf* 1228-31)

Love, loyalty, accord: these maintain sanity and balance in the
fearful world of the brave. It is also necessary to ensure that the all-
powerful ruler is benevolent and does not grow too far out of
reach of his community. "Lo!" the councillors of Tubondo exclaim,
"if the chief cannot be disagreed with, then it is too great foolish-
ness" (*Mwindo* 126). The first thing that Mwindo does after he
destroys the Dragon is to allocate land to his little subjects who
have been rescued from the insides of the ravaging beast (134).
"The generosity of kings makes griots eloquent," Djeli Mamoudou
tells us (*Sunjata* IV.14); and the portraits of Maghon Kon Fatta
and his son Sunjata are etched with generosity[95] and prudence.
Similarly, Agamemnon, who at other times demonstrates a phenomenal lack of judgment, rewards Ajax handsomely for his stout
career on the field of battle (*Iliad* 7.322). And the courtly circles of
Beowulf and *Maldon* are particularly notable for the honor and
kindness shown by the king, "the gold-friend of men."[96]

It may be argued that the events portrayed in these songs can,
given time and diligence, be located historically. But love, accord,

and generosity are not history. The bard has woven select historical and mythical threads into a fitting pattern of sentiments and
emotions and has introduced this pattern into his song. Lilyan
Kestleoot's portrait of the training of the griot shows clearly why, in
heroic song, the facts of history are so linked to the values and
ideals of the bard and his community:

The same apprentice will go in the morning to farm his master's
land, and in the evening will be initiated into the secrets of a mystic
tale or a king-list. . . The education that the young African received
in these workshops was thus a full and balanced education, aimed
at a perfect integration of the individual into his group. . . a simple
method of farming, or design in weaving, could give the master an
opportunity to expound a myth of origin; similarly the epic of
Sunjata, for example, will he interrupted for a lesson in social
psychology on the plight of a crippled man, or a lesson in botany
on the use of baobab leaves; every subject of conversation or of
observation is an opportunity for a digression, and every digression is an opportunity for an instruction.[97]

The history of Sunjata generously spiced with digressions on
contemporary life is history oriented toward group psychology,
quite distinct from a confining interest in specific moments vaguely
recalled. This sense of the timeless, this concern for broad cultural
values[98]—such is the material of heroic song, such is the framework
on which the bard builds his portrait of the world of the brave,
albeit by means of artistic symbols which have an interest all their
own.

Three

THE HERO:
HIS IMAGE AND HIS
RELEVANCE

There has been a long tradition in Western scholarship of seeing the portrait of the hero in an oral epic as a neat linear or organic design, very much as we see a character in literate fiction. The roots of this tendency, exemplified in Homeric criticism, go back to the organicist outlook of classical Athens. Plato was perhaps the first to articulate the idea of the organic nature of a literary composition when he made Socrates say, in his dialogue with Phaedrus:

Well, there is one point at least which I think you will admit, namely that any discourse ought to be constructed like a living creature, with its own body, as it were; it must not lack either head or feet; it must have a middle and extremities so composed as to suit each other and the whole work. (*Phaedrus* 264c).

It was, however, at the hands of Aristotle that the organicist theory achieved a truly authorative illustration. Preferring the dramatic unity of Homer to the episodic ragbag of other epic poets, he states that while only one or two tragedies can be gleaned from Homer's poems, the poem of the epic cycle could yield numerous tragedies (*Poetics* 1459b). On the organic unity of epic poetry, he writes:

Besides, it is necessary that the parts of the plot be put together in such a manner that, if any one part is transposed or removed, the whole will be disorganized and disjointed. For that whose presence or absence has no visible effect is no part of the whole. (1451a)

These are no doubt the origins of the unitarian tendency of tracing a straight line of progression in Homer's conception and development of his themes and characters. Perhaps the most notable example in recent years is Cedric Whitman's discussion of the "evolution" of the character of Achilles.[1] It is a quite ingenious study, deserving the respect of even the most unsympathetic critics. But the student of oral, traditional song must have reservations about a system of analysis that, inspired by Aristotelian canons, sees the Homeric epic purely in terms of the conscious draftsmanship of literate art. Aristotle and his circle had little interest in oral literature and its peculiarities;[2] in fact, they represent that attitude in classical culture that was responsible for "the gradual tidying-up," according to G. S. Kirk, "to which Greeks down to the time of Aristarchus subjected the *Iliad* and *Odyssey*."[3] Any criticism that fails to take account of the peculiarities of the performance—the empathy or hostility of the audience, the lack of sufficient time to sing all of one story, the failure of memory, and so on—will naturally have recourse to those well-worn criteria.

Against this literate attitude may be set the concept of *parataxis* as enunciated by Notopoulos.[4] The virtue of Notopoulos' theory is that it keeps a keen eye on the demands of the live performance and the peculiar pressures put upon the bard by his audience. He is continually forced to take account of the numerous elements, visual as well as mental, that continually confront him as he performs; he therefore operates more on the spur of the moment than according to a preconceived plan. This makes all the difference between the inspired play of the bard's mind and the meticulous techniques of literate art. As Notopoulos says, "Inspiration and logic are frames of minds which do not readily mix and so inspired poetry, shaped by the mood of the moment, the psychological union of the poet and his audience, leads to digression."[5]

This dominant interest in moods[6]—or what I. A. Richards elsewhere calls "attitudes"—largely determines not only the structure of the oral heroic tale but indeed the portraits of its heroic figures. For an oral Homer, the defiant will of Achilles has as much of an affective appeal as his *communis sensus*, and the bard has no hesitation in building a tandem career for both sentiments. He may tax our credibility here and there, but no matter; he will count on his music and everything else he does to make up for his lapses, so long as he is sure that in the end he will have given his partons a heartwarming evening. If there is one danger inherent in the organicist judgment of the heroic song, it is the tendency to overlook those moods and sentiments for which the bard never intended anything like a subordinate role.

There may, however, be a compromise between the positions represented by Whitman and by Notopoulos, that will help us understand the various idiosyncratic techniques possible in an oral atmosphere. If the organicist approach demands a too rigid concern for schematic order on the part of the bard, there is in the paratactic a danger of seeing him as incapable of holding a story together. We may, therefore, wish to see the heroic song as a narrative collage of affective moments and moods. The principal emphasis in the song is on the *moments* of its subject's life, and the narrative sequence (in terms of time, the order of events, and so on) is simply a superstructure that may be altered at will by the bard and is by no means rigid; as field collectors invariably observe, a tale is never sung the same way twice. We should thus be open to the possibility that characterization, insofar as it involves careful development, can have little relevance for the bard of the traditional heroic song.

Indeed, by one of those paradoxes that mark traditional lore, the bard combines a sense of spontaneity with selectivity. The idea of selectivity must seem strange to anyone familar with the boring pile-up of detail characteristic of heroic song. But the bard knows the sentiments or moods that appeal to him and to his audience, and concentrates on these with a seemingly endless accumulation of illustrative or reinforcing detail. For instance, in *The Mwindo Epic* the occasions on which the bard is jolted into a chant can be easily broken down into only four heroic moments: when the hero challenges his opponents ("You are impotent against Mwindo" [65]); when he summons the aid of his magical powers ("The cattle that Shemwindo possesses,/May they join Mwindo" [82]); when he glorifies his victories ("He who went to sleep wakes up" [118]); and when eventually he establishes his authority over his subjects ("He who will go beyond what Mwindo has said,/He will die from seven lightnings" [141]). In the *Iliad*, the majority of the extended speeches and episodes are centered around a few affective moments—involving valor (as in the numerous *aristeiai*; the fearful taunts between Agamemnon and Achilles; the games in honor of Patroklos; and even Nestor's endless reminiscences of his warlike youth); fellow feeling (as in the meeting of Achilles and Priam, and the accord of Diomedes and Glaukos); or heaviness of the heart (as in the funeral of Hektor, and even the valedictory moment between him and his wife, Andromache). The heroic song is a narrative collage of such moments and moods and concentrates its interest on events that elicit immediate audience response.

Perhaps we should explore this concept of the narrative collage a little further. Collectors of African epic tales have consistently observed that an entire epic is seen in largely episodic terms: either each episode is first sung and then narrated and dramatized, or the entire tale is punctuated with songs that bring together neatly the major incidents involved in the various segments of the narration.[7] The song mode is thus a distillation, an attempt to encompass in a lyrically convenient capsule the major moments of the hero's career. The narrative mode is more or less an explication of the neat package of incidents reflected in the songs. It is, in fact, arguable that a mere handful of songs can summarize all that would have taken a whole evening to narrate. Thus in the Ozidi story, rather than go through the gamut of details about the fight between the hero and Badoba, the bard simply sings Ozidi's "slaughter song" (152), eloquently demonstrating that all the narrative that might have been is only a fleshing out. In such a tradition, the portraiture of character is based more on an assemblage of these independent accents than on a neat alignment of homogeneous details. Consequently, in our examination of the heroic image, we should concentrate on those elements that have an affective appeal for the bard. The heroic character is simply a sum total of these affective elements.

II

We might best approach the hero from his origins, to see if there is anything in his lineage that promises a noble career and provides material for glorification in song. An examination of a wide range of epic songs in Africa would reveal that many of them dealt with the ruling or noble houses of the community, perhaps because, historically, these houses bore the brunt of martial action, which is one of the most popular subjects of epic song. Mythically speaking, we may look to some of those tales of origin in which minstrelsy is said to have originated in the court. We have seen one such tale from among the Dan of the Ivory Coast, which says that when God (Zra) first created the chief he gave him a griot.[8] A similar idea occurs in Greek myth, which makes Calliope, the muse of epic poetry, an attendant of venerable princes.[9] Economics also play a part in this emphasis: it may simply be that the traditional minstrel received his most generous patronage from the ruling houses who controlled the economy of the community. The societies that gave rise to heroic songs were generally aristocratic, so the singer put his mouth where the money was.

Whatever the case may be, the hero of the song usually has the advantages of birth that set him above the rank and file. Sunjata is the son of a king and later himself a *mansa* (emperor). His mother, Sogolon (Sukulung), is the "buffalo woman" and thus brings to the hero all the mystic force of her totemic personality. In another version of the same epic, his archenemy, Sumanguru, was born of a human mother but of a spirit father (*Sunjata* I.737ff). Silamaka of the *Silamaka* epic is the son of the chief of Macina. Ozidi is of the ruling house of Orua—his father is killed by fellow townsmen, and his entire career builds up to his absolute sovereignty. The hero of the *Kambili* epic is the son of Kanji, a general of the emperor Samory Toure to whom he seems to be particularly close. Mwindo of *The Mwindo Epic* is the son of the king of Tubondo.

Simularly, Achilles is a Myrmidon prince, son of King Peleus and the goddess Thetis, a sea nymph. Hektor on the other side is not so highly privileged but has a divinely descended king for a father. Gilgamesh is King of Uruk, two-thirds god and one-third man. In the *Song of Igor's Campaign*, the Kievans are led by the princely brothers Igor and Vsevolod. And Beowulf makes his origins known to the Danish coast guard in no mistaken terms:

My father was famous in many a folk-land,
A leader noble, Ecgtheow his name.

(*Beowulf* 262-63)

Often, too, there is something in the birth and early youth of the hero that sets him apart from the natural course of life and inspires awe and veneration. In the African myths, it is indeed at this stage of the hero's life that the foundations of his formidable career are laid; the heroic song, which is in many ways a tale of terror, is immeasurably nourished by a concentration on the image of the *Wunderkind*.

The advent of the hero in the world is marked by some awe or mystery; some portentous event. The coming of Sunjata is prophesied by a hunter who visits the king his father from the unknown and enjoins him to marry the strange "buffalo woman" from Do. She is ugly, warns the sorcerer-hunter, she is revolting to look at, "but, mystery of mysteries, this is the woman you must marry, sire, for she will be the mother of him who will make the name of Mali immortal forever. The child will be the seventh star, the seventh conqueror of the earth. He will be more mighty than Alexander." (*Sunjata* IV.6).[10] The unborn hero stayed seven years in his mother's womb (*Sunjata* I.49f); when he is finally born, there is an unusual sign in the heavens:

Suddenly the sky darkened and great clouds coming from the east hid the sun, although it was still the dry season. Thunder began to rumble and swift lightning rent the clouds; a few large drops of rain began to fall while a strong wind blew up. A flash of lightning accompanied by a dull rattle of thunder burst out of the east and lit up the whole sky as far as the west. Then the rain stopped and the sun appeared and it was at this very moment that a midwife came out of Sogolon's house, ran to the antechamber and announced to Nare Maghan that he was the father of a boy. (*Sunjata* IV.13)

After his delivery the king's griot bursts into song, rejoicing that "the child is born whom the world awaited." Another version of the legend also tells of the warning Sumanguru had received from his soothsayers: "Your conquerer will be born in Mali."[11]

There is the same sense of foreboding in the birth of Kambili. To begin with, he is the subject of a painful trial of skill in which several soothsayers lose their heads because, though their magic symbols describe the coming of a male child, they are unable to name which of his father's nine wives will be the mother (378ff). Still, all the soothsayers agree that the coming child will be "a vicious hunter," the "hope of the group," and "invincible." His career in the womb of his mother, Dugo, is itself portentous:

And after nightfall around about midnight;
Dugo's Kambili would get up and walk about.
As the dawn was lightening,
He would come back
And throw himself down on his mother's mat
as if nothing happened.
"Mother!" she cried, "Mother!
During the day, here I am Dugo pregnant.
During the night, here I am Dugo with empty stomach.
I can do no more with this thing inside me, Mother."

(1527-35)

Mwindo performs in a simular fashion in his mother's womb. He even has the luxury of deciding what will be the means of his delivery, and he chooses a unique mode—delivery though the middle finger:

Where the child was dwelling in the womb of its mother, it meditated to itself in the womb, saying that it could not come out of the underpart of the body of its mother, so that they might not make fun of it saying that it was the child of a woman; neither did it want to come out from the mouth of its mother, so that they might not make fun of it saying that it had been vomited like a bat . . . . Where the child was dwelling in the womb, it climbed up in the belly, it descended the limb, and it went [and] came out through the medius. (54)

Other African heroes follow an equally portentous path to delivery. In the Fang epic cycle of Akoma Mba, the subject is born after a pregnancy lasting one hundred and fifty years; still in the womb, he lets his mother know that he cannot come out of an organ that serves a urinary purpose, then tears up the mother's stomach and jumps out![12] The "twin" children who aid him in his struggle to rescue the lost race of the Ekang are born after only a day's pregnancy; somewhat like Mwindo, they emerge fully armed, not from the womb but through the big toe! (*Akoma Mba* 817-1086). Lianja's birth is preceded by the emergence, from his mother's womb, of ants, birds, and men of various ethnic groups. He too elects his own mode of delivery, through the leg; he is born with a very pretty twin sister, Nsongo, and, like the above others, is fully armed at birth (46-47). A great storm begins to rage as soon as Ozidi's mother falls into labor; the hero is born at the end of seven days of turmoil (12f.).

There would appear to be a greater tendency in African than in other cultural epics to pursue the career of the hero from his very conception right to his death (or at least to the consummation of a chosen purpose). However, many of the foreign epics that have survived to our times represent only a segment of the larger cycle of tales involving the hero; the content of the surviving material has commanded overwhelming interest with successive generations of narrators, and the earlier segments (involving the birth of the hero, and so on), not being re-created often enough, have simply dropped out of the canon.[13] It may also be that editors have consistently treated as extraneous material, and so carefully expunged, all those portions of the tale in which the poet pursued the odd detail about the hero's origins into an extended narration: one can, for instance, see how a bard would be tempted to expand Eurpylos' mention of Achilles' pharmacological training under Cheiron (*Iliad* 11.831). In ancient Indo-European heroic narrative, however, the poet occasionally explores the birth of the heroic figure. The Homeric *Hymn to Athene*, which sets the fantastic birth amid meteorological turmoil of the type that we have seen in some African epics, is a good example:

From his awful head wise Zeus himself bore her arrayed in warlike arms of flashing gold, and awe seized all the gods as they gazed. But Athena sprang quickly from the immortal head and stood before Zeus who holds the aegis, shaking a sharp spear: great Olympus began to reel horribly at the might of the bright-eyed goddess, and earth round about cried fearfully, and the sea was moved and tossed with dark waves, while foam burst forth suddenly: the bright Son of Hyperion stopped his swift-footed horses a long while, until the maiden Pallas Athene had stripped the heavenly armour from her immortal shoulders. (4-16)[14]

The growth and development of the epic hero is also generally extraordinary. He would hardly be a fit subject for glorification if the progress of his career were no different from the norm. In Africa, the heroic career starts right from infancy. As a baby, Silamaka does not blink when a gadfly sucks blood from his face; the fly, gorged, falls and dies (10). In his very first day of life, Lianja kills his father's assassin (49). Ozidi has a string of heroic credits to his childhood. When he is "only a couple of days" old, he picks up and dashes to death children far older than himself (13); he frightens off a leopard (which he calls a cat), carries a whole iroko tree home as wood for his mother, then chops it up with ease (22-23); a little later, he cuts down a silk-cotton tree with the sword newly forged for him (47).

Sunjata's youthful career is somewhat like Ozidi's. As a three-year-old child, he has no affinity of interest whatsoever with children of his age; he is dead serious when they are cheerful and smashes the brains of any one of them that comes near him (Sunjata IV.15). At seven he finally begins to walk. He asks that his father's smiths make him "the heaviest possible iron rod." When this has been made and toted up to him, he picks it up with one hand and bends it in "the form of a bow" the next minute. His mother had suffered a humiliation when she asked her co-wife Sassouma Berete for a few baobab leaves to season her stew. Sassouma had mocked the inability of Sunjata (who had not yet walked) to pluck baobab leaves for his mother. To correct the insult, Sunjata tears up the entire giant tree from its roots and sets it right in front of his mother's hut. From then on his greatness progresses "from day to day," and before he is ten years old "he received the title of Simbon, or master hunter, which is only reserved for great hunters who have proved themselves" (19ff).

A like pattern of development is seen in *Kambili*. When the hero has just begun to walk, he is already fighting with chickens and ducklings. He grows prodigiously "from one day to the next" and, while still a little lad armed only with "young boy's arrows," grapples with a leopard and her cubs:

He went out one morning.
He and the young boys went off,
Saying they were off to look for lizards.
There was a leopard down in the forest.
A leopard had given birth down in the forest.
Her two babies were down in the forest.
He put them both in his bag.
Ah! And then the mother leopard came.
She was coming to save her babies.
He pulled out his young boy's arrows,
And put one into her nose,
And put another into her eye.
The beast cried in pain.
The beast started to run off.
Kambili went on home
And took out the spotted beast's babies,

And gave them to his true father.
"Father, your mother cat gave birth in the forest.
I have taken her two babies."[15]

(1814-32)

To the infant prodigy the leopard is only a pussycat! He moves on from leopards to buffalos, antelopes, bushbucks, and "all the kinds of game in the bush" (1844-85).

A simular prodigious development is followed by mythic heroes from other cultures. One good example is Herakles, who saves himself and his twin brother, Iphikles, from the venomous ill will of Hera (angry at Zeus's intercourse with their mother, Alkmene). Pindar records the legend as follows (no doubt after an oral tradition):

The Queen of the gods was angry at heart
And at once sent snakes,
Which passed through the open doors
Into the chamber's wide space,
Eager to writhe their quick jaws
Around the children. But *he*
Lifted his head on high and made first trial of battle.
In two unescapable hands
He seized the two serpents by their necks:
He strangled them, and his grip
Squeezed the life out of their unspeakable frames.

(*Nemean* 1.37-47)

In the youths of Odysseus and Achilles we see something of the marvel and distinction by which the hero prepares for the climax of his career. Odysseus seems to have been quite young when he killed the boar on Mount Parnassos (*Odyssey* 19.393-454); though he is said to have a "thick hand" (a simple formulaic epithet given to even the lady Athene in the Theomachy), his "beautiful shining eyes" which his grandmother Amphithea kisses are no doubt a sign of adolescence. And Achilles' apprenticeship under the centaur Cheiron, which Homer mentions only in passing, is told in considerable detail by Pindar in language that recalls the myths of Ozidi, Sunjata, and Kambili:

Brown-haired Achilles stayed in Philyra's home,
A child whose play was mighty exploits.
Often his hands threw
The short iron javelin to rival the winds;
He dealt death in battle to ravening lions
And boars were his prey. Their panting bodies
He brought to the Centaur, Kronos' son,
In his sixth year at first, then through all his days.
Artemis marvelled at him, and bold Athena,
That he killed deer without hounds or treacherous traps.
By his feet he defeated them. (What I tell
Was spoken by men of old.)

(Nemean 3.43-54)

Likewise, Beowulf was a mere boy when he killed a sea monster during his swimming contest with Breca (549ff).[16]

Thus, by his parental origins, his birth, and his early development, the hero gives promise of an unusual career. The awe all this arouses works to the advantage of the bard, whose song is traditionally a glorification of deeds of terror and of wonder.

III

What follows here is a discussion of the image of the hero as he assumes his full potential; but this does not necessarily mean that in these epic tales, there is always a careful progression from the childhood to the adulthood of the hero. Niane's edition of the Sunjata story shows a certain careful progression, but this may reflect Niane's editorial efforts; the other versions in the Innes edition are not nearly so systematic. Ozidi continues to be treated as a boy by his opponents to the very end; in fact, when Smallpox attacks him, he is washed by his mother as a little boy attacked by yaws. Mwindo also remains diminutive right to the end. Kambili is only a young, newly circumcised boy (1878) when he pulls home some rather fearful animals on the leash; shortly after, he is married and fighting the menace that threatens the whole community, the "lion-man" Cekura. In all such cases, it would appear that the bard does not set much store by meticulous chronology. The affective purposes of his art are better served by a swift leap across time; the hero is all the more heroic if he accomplishes the most impossible feats prematurely.

Thus in discussing the image of the hero, we should beware once again of presenting a too unified portrait of the heroic personality. We have described the heroic song as a narrative collage of affective moments and moods and have pointed out that the emphasis is on the affective element. Those who put the emphasis on the narrative element—the "tale"—will naturally be persuaded, quite erroneously, of the inferiority of the traditions of heroic singing in which performance supersedes the simple narration. To be sure, it would be bad art in any tradition for the story to break down completely. A performer who loses the trend of his story and is unable to contrive a way to continue is likely to be laughed out. A good oral performance depends on the maintenance of a healthy balance between the tale, the music, the histrionics, and everything else to which the performer lends his genius in a live context. But one of the interesting differences between a performance and a simple narration is this. A narration, devoid of emotional accents and usually unaccompanied by music, is apt to pursue the line of the story in a logical and undeviating order to the end. But in an oral performance the singer, observing the effect that a detail has on his audience or on his own spirits, tends to linger on that detail and exploit its affective value to the fullest (consider the amount of inflation that happens in the different chants in *Kambili* and *Mwindo*). A system of this kind, which puts so much premium on the affective, is that much less likely to be subject to a neat alignment of facts—nor is the audience any more likely to cavil at the logic—than is necessary. Thus inconsistencies are likely to occur here and there, and in many cases the character of a hero that emerges is more the sum of the affective details of action that the singer credits him with—and details often differ between versions of the same tale by the same singer—than a consistent, carefully developed portrait.

Perhaps the most noticeable feature of the hero's image is his preeminence among his fellows. This sometimes takes the form of outstanding good looks or sheer force of personality. At ten years of age, for instance, Sunjata's "arms had the strength of ten and his biceps inspired fear in his companions. He had already that authoritative way of speaking which belongs to those who are destined to command" (IV.23). This image becomes significant when later he and his family are driven into exile and obliged to seek asylum with neighboring rulers. At the court of Soumaba Cisse, king of Wagadou, during the plea for asylum by the hero's mother, "the king and his brother had not taken their eyes off Sundiata for an instant. Any other child of eleven would have been disconcerted by the eyes of adults, but Sundiata kept cool." King Soumaba is forced to observe, "There's one that will make a great king . . . . If he has a kingdom one day everything will obey him because he knows how to command" (34). Later, at the court of King Moussa Tounkara of Mema, he makes the same impression. Here, at age eighteen, "he was a tall young man with a fat neck and a powerful chest. Nobody else could bend his bow. Everyone bowed before him and he was greatly loved. Those who did not love him feared him and his voice carried great authority" (37).[17]

Homer himself also glorifies the looks of his heroes. Priam asks his daughter-in-law, Helen, about Agamemnon:

Who is this Achaean man of power and stature?
Though in truth there are many others taller by a head than he is,
yet these eyes have never yet looked on a man so splendid
nor so lordly as this: such a man might well be royal.

(*Iliad* 3.167-70)

Telamonian Ajax is evidently the most imposing of the figures on the Achaean side—in Priam's words, an "Achaean of power and stature/towering above the Argives by head and broad shoulders;" and Helen agrees that he is the "wall of the Achaeans." Yet the truly superlative treatment is reserved for Achilles. He is simply "perfect," "faultless" (*Iliad* 2.674) in physique.[18] In the same vein, when the Danish coast guard notices Beowulf among the Geat party, it is the hero's good looks that attract attention:

I have never laid eyes upon earl on earth
More stalwart or sturdy than one of your troop,
A hero in armor; no hall-thane he
Tricked out with weapons, unless looks belie him
And noble bearing.

(*Beowulf* 247-51)

This physical force is frequently matched by strength of mind. The traditional hero is in most cases either a leader of his group or one destined to lead it shortly. It is therefore important that he should be capable of good counsel or shrewdness, either in organizing his people, or in evaluating moments of danger and deciding on the right time to act.

The Sunjata story portrays the hero's intellectual aptitude for his role as leader. The foundations for this trait are laid very early in

his youth, even before he turns ten, by a mother anxious to incul-
cate in her child the ways of wisdom. We are told:

Every evening Sogolon Kedjou would gather [Sundiata] and his
companions outside her hut. She would tell them stories about the
beasts of the bush, the dumb brothers of man. [Sundiata] learnt to
distinguish between the animals; he knew why the buffalo was his
mother's wraith and also why the lion was the protector of his
father's family. He also listened to the history of the kings which
Balla Fasseke told him; enraptured by the story of Alexander the
Great, the mighty king of gold and silver, whose sun shone over
quite half the world. Sogolon initiated her son into certain secrets
and revealed to him the names of the medicinal plants which every
hunter should know. Thus, between his mother and his griot, the
child got to know all that needed to be known. (*Sunjata* IV.23)

The first subtle proof of Sunjata's mental powers is shown in his
use of proverbs. "Men's wisdom is contained in proverbs," the
bard tells us, "and when children wield proverbs it is a sign that
they have profited from adult company" (29). Such wisdom is
amply demonstrated by the following brief conversation between
Sunjata and his half brother, Manding Bory:

"Mother is calling us," said Sunjata, who was standing at one side.
"Come, Manding Bory. If I am not mistaken, you are fond of that
daughter of Mansa Konkon's."
    "Yes brother, but I would have you know that to drive a cow into
the stable it is necessary to take the calf in."
    "Of course, the cow will follow the kidnapper. But take care, for
if the cow is in a rage so much the worse for the kidnapper."
(*ibid.*)[19]

It is no wonder, therefore, that when he comes well into his own,
Sunjata is able to handle his affairs and risks deftly and to impress
his fellows "by the lucidity of his mind" (37). His administration of
the war with Sumanguru, and his politic division of the new empire
of Mali, attest to his mental strength.

One interesting way of demonstrating mental alacrity is by winning games that test shrewdness. Ozidi is unbeaten in the game of tops. Sunjata excels in *wori*, a checkers-type game that he plays with the murderous Mansa Konkon at the risk of his life (IV.30f.). A similar game, called *wiki*, is played in the *The Mwindo Epic* by the hero and the god Sheburungu; Mwindo wins in the end by the magic power of his *conga*-scepter (108f.). The game of wits is clearly one way of putting the hero through an intellectual test. That Mwindo can use his mind quite shrewdly is demonstrated by the trick he employs in overcoming Musoka's barrier to his passage, during Mwindo's pursuit of his father (67).

The *wori* and the *wiki* are roughly of the same order as the game of "knuckle-bone," which comes up once in Homer in connection with Patroklos' homicidal past (*Iliad* 23.88). Of course, in the military world of the Homeric *Iliad*, valor takes precedence over every other quality; but wisdom and mental alertness are also highly regarded. Thus, in *Iliad* 1, Achilles, the man of utmost might, is seen—to Cedric Whitman's wonderment—"turning stones to achieve the [Greek] army's safety"[20] from Apollo's wrath. Of the paternal wisdom and discreet caution we have many an example in the characters of Nestor, Phoinix, and Polydamas. Odysseus, however, remains the supreme example of the lively mind. He is a combination of courage and wits, as Diomedes observes (*Iliad* 10.232, 247); and it is possible that, in the *Odyssey*, Homer achieves that final balance of the two virtues which is a rather hard proposition in the oppressively bellicose world of the *Iliad*.[21] Such a balance we see, in somewhat unequivocal terms, in the characters of Gilgamesh and Beowulf.[22]

The hero of the song therefore is eminent in bearing, might, and mind. What is more, he *knows* his superiority and lets it be known, in word as in deed, that he is the greatest. "Modesty," as Djeli

Mamoudou tells us, "is the portion of the average man, but superior men are ignorant of humility" (*Sunjata* IV.34).

Being proud, the hero does not take an insult lightly; society is expected to respect even his most unbecoming behavior. Thus, when Mengono Mba is chided by his wife for being so frivolous as to ask for delicacies, his pride is deeply hurt and his heart sore; he packs his belongings and swears never to return home until he has accomplished that to which nothing can be compared (*Akoma Mba* 1398ff.).

Moreover, the hero has an exaggerated notion of his worth. He claims precedence above everyone else, his elders included, and expects others to recognize his greatness. On learning that Da Monzon has sent fifty warriors against him, Silamaka feels insulted by the paltry figure and asks his army to take a holiday while he and his friend Puluru dispose of the Segu pack; he even smokes a pipe as he takes them on! (25). Lianja now and then lets it be known that he is "the fearless one." In his fight against Sausau, he asks the latter, who is much older than he, to make several throws of his spear before he replies; Sausau agrees, and Lianja makes a mock of every throw from the older man (53). A similar arrogance is demonstrated by Sunjata, who lets the older Sumanguru make the first throw of the spear in their confrontation (*Sunjata* II.1892ff.). But the supreme show of self-esteem appears in Mamoudou Kouyate's version of the epic. In one of the most poetic climaxes of the story, the two heroes, shortly before the decisive battle of Krina, hurl threats at one another through their magical owls. Sumanguru begins:

"Know, then, that I am the wild yam of the rocks; nothing will make me leave Mali."

"Know also that I have in my camp seven master smiths who will shatter the rocks. Then, yam, I will eat you."

"I am the poisonous mushroom that makes the fearless vomit."

"As for me, I am the ravenous cock, the poison does not matter to me."

"Behave yourself, little boy, or you will burn your foot, for I am the red-hot cinder."

"But me, I am the rain that extinguishes the cinder; I am the boisterous torrent that will carry you off."

"I am the mighty silk-cotton tree that looks from on high on the tops of other trees."

"And I, I am the strangling creeper that climbs to the top of the forest giant."

(*Sunjata* IV.60)

A veritable song of terror: at the moment of the hero's recognition and proclamation of his powers the poetic fancy of the bard is jolted into full play. A similar moment comes in *Kambili*. During the celebrations of the wedding between the hero, Kambili, and his bride, Kumba, the hero is told of the bloody rampage of the lion-man Cekura. He responds that the lion-man is a pushover:

They had thus finished the wedding procession.
The wedding speeches had been given, Allah!
When the message had been given to Kambili,
It was none but the hunter Kambili's voice:
"This man-eating lion, Allah!
If the man-eating lion, is going to die, . . .
Ah! If the man-eating lion is going to die in Jimini,
The lion is going to die with one shot in Jimini!"

(2109-17)

This is just a little show of bravado, but it is enough to inspire a flight of gnomic lines in which the bard laments the cooling of the heroic temper among the men of his days (2118ff.).[23] *The Mwindo Epic* contains numerous chants in which the hero warns his opponents that they are "impotent against" his powers or brags that he

99

has accomplished the impossible. But nothing in the story demonstrates his superlative self-esteem quite as much as the ever-present formula, with which he confronts friend and foe alike, that he is the "Little-one-just-born-he-walked." The egocentricity in the story is overwhelming.

A similar egocentricity can be seen in the heroic society of Homer's songs; Achilles is perhaps Homer's ideal of heroic self-love. No doubt self-love is the logical attitude in a society where everyone thinks it his duty "to be the best and to surpass all others"; indeed, long after Homer, we have it on the authority of Aristotle that self-love (*philautia*) is a seminal ingredient of human excellence.[24] This excellence, at least in the curious aristocratic world of the Homeric poems, is measured not merely in terms of what a man is actually worth but what he is seen to be worth. A tremendous premium is placed on the public eye in a world where everyone strives to lift his head above all others; but first the individual has to convince himself that he is equal to the competition.[25] Thus Achilles vaunts over a beaten Lykaon, who begs that his life be spared:

Do you not see what a man I am, how huge, how splendid
and born of a great father, and the mother who bore me immortal?[26]

(Iliad 21.108-9)

The same is true of Hektor. The son of mere mortals, permitted to shine only for as long as Achilles is sulking, he is a stronger candidate for our sympathies than Achilles. But he is no less a symbol of the strange heroic outlook that Homer sketches in his story. That he feels a like self-esteem is evident from his hopes for his little son Skamandrios, as demonstrated by his following prayer on the boy's head:

Zeus, and you other imortals, grant that this boy, who is my son,
may be as I am, pre-eminent among the Trojans,
great in strength, as I am, and rule strongly over Ilion.[27]

(6.476-78)

And yet, this self-love of the hero's is nothing like the passive, morose self-gaze of a Narcissus; rather than being consumed in silence, the hero furiously craves for an opportunity to put his estimation of himself to the proof. Love of danger is thus a frequent corollary of self-esteem. The hero may not always die from the risks that he takes; in fact, his survival is proof of his invincibility or durability. But shoud he die, his death is not the pitiable or despicable one of a Narcissus, but rather an awe-inspiring one, because of the circumstances in which the life is hazarded.[28]

Love of danger and of martial action frequently reaches hysterical, even pathological proportions among several heroes of the African epic. So compulsive is Abo Mama's urge to fight that his mother asks him, "Does the prospect of sure death intoxicate you like wine?" (*Akoma Mba* 339). Nor can Ozidi rest any easier, as he knocks off one adversary after another: "He hated sitting down idle. His desire . . . was for war" (274). When Da Monzon finally sends a cavalry of five hundred against him, Silamaka laughs and says, "Da Monzon has at last begun to move!" (27). In another epic from the same cycle, Da Monzon finds himself grappling with the rebel leader Karta Thiema. At the least intimation by Da Monzon of war against the rebel, the famed Bambara warlord, Saro Sogolon, jumps up and declares that the affair is "like a well-cooked meal," promising havoc on Karta (*Karta Thiema* 191). Of Karta himself we are told, "It is always with laughter that he severs the chain of life of his enemy" (*ibid.* 195).

The compulsive love of action is especially well protrayed in Sunjata's advance with his army against Sumanguru. At one point during the march, his passage is blocked by the forces of Sosso Balla, son of Sumanguru and commander of a division of his army. Sunjata's men are quite unprepared for his reaction to the situation:

When [Sunjata] saw the layout of Sosso Balla's men he turned to his generals laughing.

"Why are you laughing, brother, you can see that the road is blocked."

"Yes, but no mere infantrymen can halt my course towards Mali," replied Sunjata. (*Sunjata* IV.49)

Sunjata gradually closes in on Sumanguru, and their first engagement is at Negueboria. In spite of his deft moves, there is a touch of rashness in Sunjata. "As usual," we are told, "the son of Sogolon wanted to join battle straight away." The decisive battle of Krina eventually takes place, and Sumanguru is outclassed by Sunjata and put to flight. Sunjata and his ally Fakoli (the estranged nephew of Sumanguru) give chase, and the hero spares no risks in his pursuit of his man. He learns that Sumanguru is heading for the mountain district of Koulikoro. "I know a short cut to Koulikoro," Fakoli tells him, "but it is a difficult track and our horses will be tired." Sunjata's response is an unhesitating, "Come on." And together they "tackled a difficult path scooped out by the rain in a gully" (66).

Ozidi is, however, the classic irrepressible in the catalogue of African heroes so far encountered. Those who, like J. P. Clark, have seen his later fights (after he disposes of the assassins) as "excesses" may have overstated the case, because the myth of his personality permits that he should also eliminate these later adversaries. But these later contests are introduced in a manner that emphasizes the hero's restless thirst for action. We are frequently told that he and his attending musicians have gone out to "play":

one such play is his affair with the wife of Odogu the Ugly, which brings on the gruesome fight with Odogu (231ff.).[29]

Love of danger and of the din of battle and a contempt for the centainty of death are features that Homer similarly dwells upon in his portrait of the brave. To be sure, it sometimes happens that at the grim moment of engagement—after the final choice has been made, and the issue is left at the hands of the impartial war god—the hero experiences a brief sensation of fear, even considerable tremor of intent.[30] Still, turning his back on danger or death, with the terrible prospects of a life of shame that such a retreat would bring, is a step seldom contemplated by a true Homeric hero. Perhaps Achilles is the classic example of such a temperament. His withdrawal is a great sorrow to Achilles because "he longed always for the clamour and fighting" (Iliad 1.492). The rest of the tale is largely dominated by his painful awareness of his "evil destiny." He has had to make a choice between going home to enjoy a peaceful old age and winning eternal glory by dying on the Trojan battlefield. The former choice would of course be unthinkable for a hero of Achilles' stature, particularly as it eliminates the prospects of the grim battle with Hektor.[31] And for Homer, the effectiveness of his song depends considerably on his hero choosing the path of death. The opportunity comes with the death of Patroklos, which jolts Achilles decisively out of his withdrawal. Perhaps there is as much excitement as vengeance in his persistent haste in Iliad 19 to get back to the fighting; far more than Ajax earlier on (7.189ff.), he is all agog with the prospect of fighting with Hektor.

Love of danger and action is also a tradition in the heroic songs of medieval Europe. When Oliver tells Roland how vast the Saracen army is, Roland feels only exuberant joy for the coming encounter: "I thirst the more," says Roland, "for the fray" (1088). As he advances fully armed, we are told, "Nobly he bears him, with open face he laughs" (1159). A like spirit of daring and defiance propels Beowulf in his quests for glory. He would seem to be pushing his chances by grappling with the fresh menace of Grendel's mother, after he has disposed of the danger that drew him to Heorot initially. Yet he embraces the new struggle with equal readiness:

staked all on strength
On the might of his hand, as a man must do
Who thinks to win in the welter of battle
Enduring glory; he fears no death.
The Geat-prince joyed in the straining struggle . . . .

(1533-37)

But perhaps the classic example in medieval heroic poetry of the hero's fearless gamble is Byrtnoth's permission to the Vikings to step onto the mainland (*Maldon* 89ff.). The issue goes beyond a simple arrogance or even a willingness to give the invaders a fair fight. In fact, nobody places a premium on advantage quite as much as the hero; Byrtnoth is aware that the enemy may well benefit from the advantage that he is throwing away. But this is a risk that he, in his overzestful will (*ofermod*) to action, is happy to embrace. The danger of the invasion is not quite real, the grim appeal of battle play has not quite been realized, as long as the enemy is still a good arm's length away. The chance to lock with him in the fearful din, come what may, is, as Hektor aptly puts it, "the sweet invitation of battle" (*Iliad* 17.228).

The culmination of all these heroic qualities is action; and there is evidently no rule as to how long or how short the action should be. A long, drawn-out action, or a string of adventures concentrated over a limited period of time, may point to a performance in which the bard had considerable rapport with his audience. The show of courage, the terrors of fighting and dying, the breathless play of arms—all these have a tremendous appeal for the heroic bard and for the audience that encourages such details; the broader the compass of the action, the more satisfying will be the performance or narration. On the other hand, the show of strength could be a very brief one, particularly in stories in which the play of magical powers is emphasized. Some critics have seized upon this element in making an unnecessary distinction between what they consider true heroism and the shamanistic.[32] In fact, the bard is paying his hero the highest compliment possible by making him the wielder of incontestable powers. In *Kambili*, despite all the elaborate preparation for the contest with the lion-man, Cekura, the hero simply dispatches him with one shot of the rifle after weakening him magically. In *Mwindo*, the hero merely beats the dragon once with his *conga*, and the terrible beast drops and dies, although, in the hero's earlier career, there are several well-developed details of struggles with his father. The details of action and death may be piled high so that the terror achieves a cumulative effect (as frequently in *Ozidi* and the *Iliad*), or the terror may be conveyed by one sudden flash of wonder. These are varieties of the affective exploited by the bard, depending on the response of his audience or the content of his story. But to say that terror is better conveyed by naked strength than by magic or other supernatural devices is to misunderstand fundamental folk psychology.

IV

We cannot, in fact, fully appreciate the heroic personality without examining its supernatural dimensions. We are unlikely to find many traditions of the oral epic in which the hero achieves his amazing feats by sheer force of naked human strength. And considering that, in some of these epic tales, the denizens of the supernatural world are treated as dramatic characters—gods and spirits participating in the action of the tale—rather than simply as metaphors, it becomes hard to accept any definition of "true heroism" that underrates the influence of the supernatural on the personality and circumstances of the hero.

There are basically two angles from which we can examine this supernatural element. First, there are those moments in the career of the hero when he recognzies the supremacy of the divine powers and either actively solicits their aid or at least humbly acknowledges his indebtedness to it in his contest against insuperable obstacles. The fight between Sunjata and Kita Mansa provides a good example. The latter is a powerful sorcerer-king under the protection of the mountain *jinn* of Kita Kourou; on the basis of this power he resists the advance of Sunjata. But the hero addresses himself directly to these protective *jinn*. On the advice of his soothsayers, he "invoked the jinn of Kita Kourou and sacrificed to them a hundred white oxen, a hundred white rams and a hundred white cocks. All the cocks died on their backs; the jinn had replied favourably" (*Sunjata* IV.70f.). In this case, Sunjata has simply submitted himself, in pious appeal through sacrifice, to the good graces of the mountain *jinn*; without this measure, he would have found his naked human strength incapable of contending with the superior mystical or magical powers of the Mansa. For most of the story, Sunjata is cast in the mold of a defender of the Islamic faith against the evil might of infidels:[33] a reflection, no doubt, of the heavily Oriental influence in Mandingo culture,[34] but the essential point is that the hero owes his excellence largely to forces superior to the world of man.

The idea of divine aid to the hero can also be seen in *Mwindo*. After unsuccessfully aiding Mwindo's enemies, the lightning god, Nkuba, begins to take sides with him and stands by him in some of his more difficult struggles. In one of these Mwindo contends alone against the entire population of the village of Tubondo, who, having given protection to his errant father, Shemwindo, are now fighting on his behalf against the hero. To counteract such a force, Mwindo chants an appeal for aid from the lightning god:

My friend, Nkuba, may you be victorious.
I shall fight here in Tubondo,
Even if Tubondo has seven entrances.
Here in Tubondo seven lightning flashes!
I shall fight here in Tubondo.
I want seven lightning flashes right now!

(19)

May my victories be yours, Mwindo tells Nkuba, but first grant me seven lightning flashes. And seven lightning flashes he gets. The god unleashes these on the village and reduces the entire population—livestock and all—to dust, "and the dust rose up" (92). The same process is repeated, thematically, a little later when Mwindo confronts the Aardvark figure, Ntumba, who has given refuge to the hero's fleeing father (105).

All these instances recall the numerous cases in Homer when the heroes achieve their feats purely with the aid, solicited or unsolicited, of divinities. Thus Agamemnon, who firmly believes that if a hero is "very strong indeed, that is a god's gift" (*Iliad* 1.178), prays earnestly to Zeus to get his men out of a tight spot—

Let our men at least get clear and escape, and let not
the Achaians be thus beaten down at the hands of the Trojans

(8.243-44)

and gets his wish. We also have the interesting case in *Iliad* 6 in which Hektor organizes a propitiation of Athene by the Trojan women, obviously to see if the goddess can withdraw her impenetrable support of Diomedes (very much as Sunjata offers a sacrifice to the spirits protecting Kita Mansa); Hektor is simply making

107

a pious submission to the superior powers who are on the side of his enemy.[35]

Sometimes, however, the aid of divinity may not be so obvious; the hero himself is represented as the wielder of supreme magical powers. He has a tremendous confidence in his own innate might; the supernatural element is employed simply "to ritualize"—in Malinowski's memorable phrase[36]—his optimism. Indeed, the idea of the hero's ritualized belief in his own powers often represents a contrary attitude to the piety with which he seeks the aid of divinity. We have an interesting picture of this conflict in the *Kambili* epic, where the mismatch of Islam and cult magic, faintly evident in *Sunjata* IV, is quite glaring, especially in some of the gnomic lines with which the tale is dotted. At one time it is said, "Allah is not powerless before anything" (86); at another time the bard showers his praise on the superior power of magic and the occult:

Look to the talisman's Angel of Death for that not
  easy for all.
The praise for Tears of the Game.
No man becomes a hunter if he has no good talismans.
You don't become a hunter if you have no knowledge
  of the occult.

(2424-27)

The tale reflects the history of the struggle between the Islamic crusade and the traditional outlook in the western Sudan.[37] In a number of places in the song, Islamic figures and attitudes are mocked as a way of showing up their inadequacies in comparison with the powers of the cult, for example:

Ah! All the holymen are by the mosque,
But all of them are not holymen!...
All the holymen are by the mosque,
But they all don't know how to read.

(2009-12)

The "holyman" or Muslim divine who takes part in the Kambili riddle is treated as a treacherous schemer and a fraud, and subsequently dismissed from the scene in disgrace, to the advantage of Bari the cult sorcerer.

An even more subtle example of the conflict between Islam and cult magic in *Kambili* can be seen in an equation of the power of the "brave"—which in the context of the story means a strong man supported by sorcery—and that of "Allah." In the course of the long gnomic exordium that precedes the narrative, the bard says:

Almighty Allah may refuse to do something.
Allah is not powerless before anything

(85-86)

Much later on, Bari the sorcerer, assuring the childless warrior Kanji that he will certainly have an heir, says:

A man may refuse to do something.
But the braves are not powerless before
  anything.

(1042-43)

We may at once be tempted to see in this a simple formula, and to conclude—following especially Milman Parry's views on prosodic convenience—that there is no particular significance to the sentiment expressed in the latter passage; the bard has simply used a handy order of words to keep his song going. But the overall picture that emerges from the tale is of the heroic personality conceived as supreme in a world where all mystical or spiritual power is simply the tool of that supremacy; so that, in spite of the obtrusive tributes to "Allah" and "destiny" construed in vaguely Muslim terms and serving a vaguely gnomic purpose, the essential mystical force of the story emphasizes the hero's superior might, unsubordinated to any vague transcendences.[38]

The conflict between the appeal to divinity and the ritualized self-confidence is especially well dramatized in *Mwindo* where much of the hero's fighting is in fact against divinities. In the earlier part of his struggles, the lightning god, Nkuba, aids Mwindo's enemies against him, but the hero levels them all. Later he takes on the divinities Muisa and Sheburungu; the former he severely brutalizes and the latter he defeats in a game of wits, the *wiki*. In all these conflicts, Mwindo is supported by the magical force of his *conga*-scepter. In some other contests, as we have seen above, he is able to enlist the aid of Nkuba, the enemy turned ally; yet his final confrontation is with Nkuba, though this time Mwindo (perhaps because he does not use the *conga*) loses. On the whole, he is a hero who demonstrates extreme confidence in his own personality, supported by magical resources; even at the most critical moments he does not hesitate to oppose divine figures.

There is even less reliance on divinity in the Lianja epic. In the course of his struggles against various terrible characters, the hero transforms himself into a variety of objects and penetrates a number of others (for example, an apple) so as to elude his enemies and the more effectively do them damage (57-63). There are references to heaven—or perhaps the sky—in the career of Lianja; for instance, when he sends up his spear "to the sky" (presumably to be blessed, 50f.) and when he is translated "into the sky" at the end of the story (72). But, considering the overall scheme of his behavior, one is tempted to see in these translations an interpolation of Christian thought. The picture that emerges is of a hero who commands limitless inner potential. There are no rituals involved and no appeals made, simply an instant deployment of powers latently available to a personality than whom there is none greater. The personal potential is, indeed, the ultimate resource. "For characters," as Clark has ably put it "though aided by oracles and gods and other supernatural forces, remain complete agents of themselves. Either they must have personal resourcefulness to discover the secret chink in their opponent's armour or else succumb to greater cunning and courage" (*Ozidi* xxxiv).

These then are the varieties of the supernatural element in the heroic personality as revealed in the traditional African epics. There is either an appeal to the superior aid of divinity, or a situation in which the ego of the hero is supreme, and he simply exploits or coerces all supernatural resources for his benefit. In either case, the hero's world is somewhat more than human, and he needs more than ordinary human powers to cope with it.

It is perhaps true that the divine figures in the *Iliad* are too much masters of the Trojan situation, and the heroes simply have no way of constraining them as Mwindo is seen to do. But there seems to be a certain ambivalence in the character of Achilles. Sometimes he acknowledges an indebtedness to divine will (e. g., *Iliad* 16.233ff.), but at other times he displays impatience with this subordination to divinity and tends toward irreverence. At the start of Achilles' quarrel with Agamemnon, Athene descends from the heavens to plead with Achilles. "I have come to stay your anger," she tells him, "*if only you will obey me*" (1.207)—a clause that reveals much about Achilles' attitude toward the gods. Zeus himself later echoes Athene's misgivings when he instructs Thetis to persuade her son to accept a compromise on the body of Hektor:

Tell him that the gods frown upon him, that beyond all other
immortals I myself am angered that in his heart's madness
he holds Hektor beside the curved ships and did not give him
back. Perhaps in fear of me he will give back Hektor.[39]

(24.113-16)

Zeus's fear is not unfounded. Achilles backs down only because the immortals have made him an offer that is both handsome and honorific. Yet he will have it understood that the arrangement is

111

due to his good graces. To a Priam anxious for the body of his son, Achilles retorts in a language that demonstrates considerable impatience with the divine role in the whole business:

I know you, Priam, in my heart, and it does not escape me
that some god led you to the running ships of the Achaians.
For no mortal would dare come to our encampment, not even
one strong in youth. He could not get by the pickets, he could not
lightly unbar the bolt that secures our gateway. Therefore
you must not further make my spirits move in my sorrows,
for fear, old sir, I might not let you alone in my shelter,
suppliant as you are; and be guilty before the god's orders.

(24.563-70)

Clearly, Achilles does not suffer his pieties gladly. The prospect of violating "the god's orders" holds no special terrors for him, and if he defers to divinity, he does so only insofar as his honor and his self-interest permit. The divinities themselves are in much danger from the unsparing onslaught of his ego, especially in the heat of battle, when savage temper gets the better of sober judgment. Thus he has no hesitation in plunging into physical combat with the river-god Skamandros (21.2333ff.) and even means Apollo harm (22.20). Perhaps the most dramatic illustration of Achilles' defiance of divine will is at the moment when he kills Hektor. He is aware that his own death is near, but he is at least satisfied that by avenging Patroklos, he has at last done his duty as champion of his friends and lived up to his honor as the best of the Achaeans. So, standing over the fallen Hektor, he pronounces in all defiance:

Die: and I will take my own death at whatever time
Zeus and the rest of the immortals choose to accomplish it.

(32.365-66)

Rebel or not, Achilles owes his excellence to the supernatural element in his personality—whether we see this as divine will or his own ritualized will—and in a sense the classic appeal of the Homeric songs lies in the skill with which the poet has reduced the supernatural nuances to anthropomorphic terms.

In the African heroic myth the effectiveness of heroic might is achieved by magical devices more complex than the resources that Achilles exploits. The most significant of these devices is that by which the hero reaches into the very source of his enemy's personality and being and completely overwhelms him. This may be done in a number of ways. One way is to get hold of certain articles with which the victim may have had contact and subject them to a spell. We have an example of this magic of "contiguity"[40] in the conflict between the hero and Cekura in *Kambili*. Kambili's wife, Kumba, is instructed by the sorcerer Bari to go to Cekura, her former husband, and bring certain articles from his body. Says Bari:

Bring me a headhair,
Yes, bring me a hair of the lion's head,
And bring some hair from under his arm,
And bring some hair from his crotch,
And bring the sandal off his foot,
And bring a pair of his old pants,
And lay them on the omen board.
When we find a means to the man-eating lion,
Should we do that, the man-eating lion will die.

(2242–50)

This strategy does render Cekura ineffective—so ineffective that a single shot from Kambili's rifle is enough to finish off so powerful a sorcerer. In *Silamaka* 33, the hero's power is neutralized when an uncircumcised albino youth, charmed by sorcerers, is mounted on an albino horse under the tamarind tree by which Silamaka is accustomed to sit just before battle.

113

A more complex magical device involves the use of certain taboo items. It is believed in various African societies that, just as there is a guiding or protecting force in a man's life, there are also elements that can operate effectively against him. The protective life force is very often objectified by a "totem" or "double" that defines, in concrete zoomorphic terms, the essential character of the person's genial being. The animal symbol may represent the animal with which the person's family or cognate group has traditionally been associated, either because the ancestor(s) of that family or group once had a favorable encounter with that animal or because the animal represents the sterling qualities associated with them. Sunjata's mother is associated with the buffalo, and his father with the lion; the hero's totemic double is said to be composed of these two figures. Kambili's mother is called the Owl, and the principle is apparently the same.[41]

The totem will help the man; but there are other elements germane to a man's vitality which, when employed against him, will harm him. We will simply call the magic associated with these elements the magic of the counterforce, rather as a blanket concept comprising the various principles under which the counterforce operates. In the first place, there are certain objects that may be taboo to a man's life force. He should not have any visual or tactile contact whatsoever with those objects; if he does, his powers (especially if he hopes to achieve effectiveness in some endeavor such as ritual for a priest, war for a fighter) will be neutralized. Second, certain objects may have been used in concocting magical power for a man. It would be taboo for anyone else to know what these objects are; if they are known, similar objects can be used by some kind of homoeopathy to ruin the man.

One of these varieties of the counterforce seems to have been used against Sumanguru by Sunjata. The latter's sister, in that brilliant Samson and Delilah episode, is able to extract from

Sumanguru the secret of his magical power. She goes off to the king, pretending to be in love with him, but lays down the terms of their relationship:

She said to him,
"You shall not know me as a wife
Unless you tell me what will kill you."
He replied, "A spear will not kill me,
An arrow will not kill me,
A gun will not kill me,
Korte will not kill me,
Witchcraft will not kill me:
There is only one thing," he said, "which will kill me:
A one year old cock which crows,
Provided it is a white fowl."
He said, "you will catch it and kill it,
And you must remove its spur,
And you must put pure gold dust and pure silver
    dust inside it,
And you must put it in a gun.
If you shoot me with that,
I shall die."

(Sunjata II.1651-67)

The cockspur is used in a poisoned weapon—the above version says gun, but all the others say arrow—which ultimately destroys Sumanguru's power.[42] This magic of the counterforce appears in other African epics. To neutralize the power of Silamaka, the tip of an arrow is dipped in the ground bones of a black steer (*Silamaka* 33); the arrow is later used in shooting the hero. And Ozidi is able to destroy some of his enemies only after they have been confronted with certain objects that are taboo to their sight: Azezabife, for instance, is totally transfixed when he is made to look upon the mixed baggage of "a chicken, a newborn babe, a pot not yet through the kiln, a new plate also unglazed" (78); Ozidi seizes the opportunity to rain fatal blows upon him.

The fatal weapons used against Sumanguru and Silamaka introduce us to the last significant element of heroic supremacy: the weapon of invincibility. The logic behind this is that the means employed by the hero in his fights—material as well as metaphysical—should ensure the effectiveness of his maneuvers and finality of his victory. Sometimes charms may not be mentioned specifically as an ingredient in the texture of such weapons, but it will be clear from the circumstances of their fashioning or acquisition that they are designed for a special use or a significant occasion and are thus unconventional. Such then is Sunjata's gun/arrow, poisoned with the spur of a cock, which he used in fatally wounding Sumanguru. Indeed, the magical picture occurs, quite early in Sunjata's life, in the instruments and weapons that he wields. In his seventh year, when he finally overcomes his incapacity to walk, he has his mother tell his father's smiths to make him "the heaviest possible iron rod" (*Sunjata* IV.19). This is soon made by the master smith, Farakourou, and toted across to the boy-hero, who picks it up easily with one hand and bends it into a bow. Later, Farakourou makes Sunjata a special hunting bow; to this bow Sunjata's griot Balla Fasseke composes a hymn, and it is not long before the hero "received the title of Simbon, or master hunter, which is only conferred on great hunters who have proved themselves" (23). Kambili also has "the people of the smiths" fashion him "young boy's arrows" and "a young boy's bow" (1796ff.); with these he kills all sorts of beasts—leopards, buffaloes, bushbucks— at a shot. Ozidi's supreme sword is fashioned for him by a blacksmith whom the sorceress Oreame has summoned out of the bowels of the earth with a stroke of her magical fan (42f.).

The position of the smith in the African metaphysic should be explained, so as to make sufficiently clear the special nature of the weapons that they are fabled to have forged for these heroes. For instance, the Mandingo society of our epics is structured on the basis of castes, which are closely knit endogamous groups, each guarding its hereditary taboos and emblems jealously and faithfully observing the sanctions on which its kinship ties have been established. Of these castes, the hunter-smith group appears to be the most powerful and the richest in deadly, effective taboos. So prominent is the smith caste in this society that its origins are traced to the very beginning of things: "The world's first child was a smith" (*Kambili* 539). It is thus expected that when a smith makes a weapon for special use, particularly by the hero of the tale, that weapon has been treated with every imaginable taboo within the scope of the smith's powers and can therefore hardly fail in its aim. The smith is a master magician in this society; his art is of an intensely mystical nature. Of the smith Farakourou who makes Sunjata his fabled bow we are told: "The master of the forges, Farakourou, was the son of old Nounfairi, and he was a soothsayer like his father" (*Sunjata* IV.20).

The presence of the smith therefore makes all the difference to the career of the hero in such a society. The smith makes the weapon that ensures the hero's invincibility. It is recognized that the hero, if he is to execute his feats with effectiveness and finality, should be equipped with far from ordinary weapons, and these are often fashioned in an atmosphere of mysticism or acquired in far from natural circumstances. Thus in *Mwindo*, the hero is "forged" by the mystical Bat-figures, the Baniyana, in preparation for his final battle with his father:

The Baniyana said that they were going to forge him. They dressed him in shoes made entirely of iron and pants of iron. They told him: "Since you are going to fight your father, may the spears that they will unceasingly hurl at you go striking on this iron [covering] that is on your body." (82)

117

The idea of iron looks conventional enough, but there is clearly something otherworldly and eerie in the circumstances in which Mwindo is here being equipped. However, by far the most magical weapon that the hero uses throughout the epic is his *conga*-scepter, with which he confounds and overcomes men, animals, and divinities. The effectiveness of the magical weapon is generally final and sure.

Other African heroes also avail themselves of such weaponry. Before he is ultimately countered by other magical resources, Sila-maka has a charmed belt, made from the skin of the wildest serpent of a sacred grove, with which he frightens the whole world around him (*Silamaka* 16)—rather in the manner of the aegis worn by Athene in the *Iliad*. "The spear Tuluku Muluku, one place where it enters, nine places where blood comes forth"—such is the spear hailing from Mecca, wielded by the brave Fakoli in the fight against Sumanguru (*Sunjata* II.1431ff.). Lianja's spear boasts equal benediction: he hurls it up to heaven and three days after it returns, all blest and ready for the troubled journey to the promised land (50f.); he also carries a charmed knife (53). Abo Mama's magic club can travel unwielded and pummel the hero's enemies a long distance away (*Akoma Mba* 510ff.).

The magical weapon no doubt reminds us of Achilles' Pelian spear of ash wood: it was originally a gift to the hero's father from the medicinally skilled centaur, Cheiron, who has made it as formidable as it is phenomenal in weight. Magical, too, is the exquisite armor made for Achilles by the smith-god Hephaistos, whose smithy is attended by eerie automatons (*Iliad* 18.418ff.).[43] The poisoned sword is evidently an established European tradition. The hero Mehmed of the Serbian epic wields a sword "of fiery Persian steel tempered in fierce poison, which cuts angry armour" (*Smaila-gic Meho* 90). Beowulf also has such a sword: in spite of the obtrusive Christian portrait of him, the story does betray now and then its indebtedness to folk psychology. The sword, Hrunting, that the hero wields against Grendel's mother is "etched with poison" (1459); it fails only because a Christian Beowulf should eschew heathen magic. But the next sword, which succeeds in doing the job, has been made in the forge of Giants and—like Achilles' Pelian ashen spear, Sunjata's first bow, and the weapons Gilgamesh and Enkidu carry for the fight against the forest ogre Humbaba—is of monstrous weight (1560f.).

Whether the hero puts himself at the mercy of divinity and acknowledges his subordination to its will, or demonstrates extreme self-sufficiency and simply coerces otherworldly elements in ensuring his supremacy, the distinction between what may be called the "religious" and the "magical" instinct has always been a difficult one to establish. The essential mark of the heroic personality in many an African folk epic is its reliance on supernatural resources. The folk hero is generally objectified in folk myth by an otherworldly apparatus that ensures his successes. To say, as Bowra does, that magic is "unheroic and distasteful"[44] is to miss the point. Magic makes the hero all the more insuperable, his victory over his enemies all the more assured, deadly, final. It is, as Kirk has observed, "a special case of ingenuity, and exploits . . . a feeling of satisfaction at the neatness and finality with which an awkward situation is resolved or an enemy confounded."[45]

V

What, finally, is the value of heroism? What good to society is a figure who harbors such extraordinary potential? What does his career tell us as men?

The urge to question the paedeutic value of art has remained a healthy obsession among societies and generations of men who place the permanence of culture above the joy of the moment.

The bard of *The Mwindo Epic* sees fit to provide a didactic epilogue to his tale, as if he were bothered that the unfamiliar world of the tale would have no meaning for his fellows if he did not reduce the fanciful imagery of it to more familiar language. In *Kambili*, *Sunjata*, and in the songs of Homer, the numerous gnomic tags may have been intended as sobering didactic messages to an audience who would otherwise be thoroughly lost in the fancy of the outlook of the songs. Even Silamaka is made to reflect, from a Koranic conscience peculiar to his culture, on the consequences of his career of killing (*Silamaka* 32). And if it is true, as Djeli Mamoudou tells us, that Sunjata "left his mark on Mali for all time and his taboos still guide men in their conduct" (*Sunjata* IV.83), then we are indeed meant to derive enduring truths from these tales; those truths may fill us with noble expectations of our own human potential and cheer us as we grapple with the odds and risks of mortal life.

Perhaps the foremost value that the heroic image aims to emphasize is excellence or the quest for it; and by excellence is meant everything that makes a man more than just an inconsequential little being, one of the unaccountable rank and file—such as honor, fame, the permanence of his name and spirit long after he has ceased to be reckoned among the living. There is a considerable emphasis on grandeur and on glory, whether in terms of parochial interests or simply as a condition of life befitting the noble spirit.

Sunjata seems to have grasped quite early the importance of a glorious name in his fortunes. When his half brother, Dankaran Touman, who accedes to the throne of Mali at the death of their father, takes away Sunjata's griot, the hero is deeply hurt. We may not go so far as our bard in making the fortunes of Balla Fasseke the cause of Sunjata's war with Sumanguru, but the hero is certainly in his element once again the moment his griot returns to him: "Sundiata was very happy to recover his sister and his griot.

He now had the singer who would perpetuate his memory by his words. There would not be any heroes if deeds were condemned to man's forgetfulness" . . . (*Sunjata* IV.58). Sunjata keeps continually in focus his quest for distinction, and Alexander the Great— the doyen of Oriental epistemology—remains the measure of this distinction. Early in his youth, we are told, Sunjata is "enraptured by the story of Alexander the Great, the mighty king of gold and silver, whose sun shone over quite half the world." Later on, in the course of his family's exile, he has an opportunity to learn "many things about Alexander the Great" from a caravan of well-informed merchants. When finally he decides to undertake the momentous return expedition that will bring him into collision with Sumanguru, his "divines . . . related to Sundiata the history of Alexander the Great and several other heroes, but of all of them Sundiata preferred Alexander, the king of gold and silver, who crossed the world from west to east. He wanted to outdo his prototype both in the extent of his territory and the wealth of his treasury."[46] At every point of the hero's career, the urge for glory and distinction is kept clearly in focus; there is surely something attractive in a stubborn quest for the best, even in the face of exile and war.

Honor and distinction are not the central quest in *The Mwindo Epic*. The action of the tale is taken up largely with the hero's fight against his father, and in such an internecine struggle the scope for ambition is unlikely to be as large as in a contest with an external enemy. Still, it is noteworthy that early in his heroic consciousness Mwindo is fired with the desire for distinction. He chooses to be delivered through the middle finger because any other method would either level him with the rest of humanity or indeed bring him below it!

The sense of distinction and "name" is as strong in Kambili as it is in Sunjata.[47] In *Kambili*, the seminal concern is accomplishment of a great deed that will ensure everlasting renown worth celebrating in song. To achieve a feat, a man must have the gift of courage without which renown is an impossibility:

A coward doesn't become a hunter,
And become a man of renown.

(26-27)

The hero wins his renown by the might of his hand; it is not cheaply acquired as a legacy automatically bestowed on his line: "A name is paid for; a name is not to be forced" (95). The career of Kambili, expecially in his youth, may sound incredible in the telling; but nevertheless it is a heightened portrait of the beauty of rising above the common lot.

We find a similar quest for honor and glory in the world of Homer's heroes. Glaukos tells Diomedes that his principal aim is to outshine all others. Menelaos equates life itself with honor when he deplores the Achaeans' hesitation to stand up to Hektor
(*Iliad* 7.97-100).

On the Trojan side, the Thracian Iphidamas reflects the exuberant joy to be found in distinguishing oneself. A newlywed wife is a great pleasure, but nothing comparable with the chance of proving yourself more than just another married man:

Married
he went away from the bride chamber, looking for glory
from the Achaians.[48]

(11.226-27)

But distinction is nothing if it dies with the man; glory must survive the limitations of mortal life. Sunjata is joyous at recovering his griot Balla Fasseke because now he knows there is a singer who will make his name live in the perpetual memory of men. In *Kam-*

122

bili, the major consolation offered for the risks of the heroic life is, "Death may end a man; death doesn't end his name" (2543). Achilles is sure that he will die in Troy, but the pain of that knowledge is considerably offset by the certainty of an immortal fame. As he undertakes the journey to fight the forest ogre Humbaba, Gilgamesh is strengthened by the thought that "if I fall, I leave behind me a name that endures" (*Gilgamesh* 71).

Honor, distinction, the dignity of life, a sense of transcendence of the limitations of common mortality—these then are major concerns of the heroic spirit, ideals that the heroic personality aims to actualize. Often, too, there emerges a concern for justice, accommodation, and conduct befitting an ordered society. In many cases, the heroic tale portrays the hero as living in a society with a certain amount of organization, actively engaged in a cause involving the fundamental well-being of his community. It is therefore no surprise to find him demonstrating a certain concern for justice and decorum.

The career of Sunjata is marked, in youth and in adulthood, by an exceptional degree of consideration, accommodation, justice. Sassouma Berete, his mother's jealous co-wife, sends nine witches to plot the destruction of the child-hero. The idea is that they should steal from the vegetable patch of Sunjata's mother and destroy the boy if he assaults them. But the plot fails. Sunjata, moved at seeing such old women in want, treats them to his bounty. The witches are overcome by this exceptional concern; they hail him "child of Justice" and promise henceforth to watch over him (*Sunjata* IV.24–26). When his half brother Dankaran Touman takes away his griot, he lets him have his way and retires into exile, promising only to return someday and reclaim his heritage (27f.).[49] But the high moment of the hero's display of justice and consideration is after his conquest of his enemies. He spares the entire population of Kita after the fall of their king (71) and carves up the new empire of Mali in a manner that combines policy with fair play (77f.).

A sense of justice is evident in Mwindo. His struggle against his father is fundamentally a revolt against the injustice of preferring female children to male—a policy his father has tried to employ in safeguarding his position. In spite of the general ferocity of Mwindo's progress in pursuit of his father and after, he now and again shows his human heart and his desire for order and justice. When Kahindo, the daughter of the underworld spirit Muisa, shows him the way to her father in Mwindo's search for his own, the hero reciprocates her goodwill by washing her yaws and restoring her to good health (*Mwindo* 96). He listens graciously to his aunt Iyangura's pleas that he restore his destroyed enemies and pardon his own father. And the final episode of the story shows him establishing the principles that will bring harmony and prosperity to his community.

Other heroes also show a certain consideration and concern for justice. Ozidi's major program seems to be not only to avenge the murderers of his father but to eliminate all the terrible forces that plague the land. Nothing much remains after his victories, but at least the fact seems established that evil can be effectively countered.

There is a significant message in that episode in which in the absence of his sorceress-grandmother, Oreame, and thus of his formidable magical resources, the hero refuses to kill the defenseless sister of Tebesonoma and her child (*Ozidi* 252f.). Deep down, the hero does care; it is simply the wickedness of the world around him that fills him with so much fury and calls up the destructive potential in him. Against that wickedness of the surrounding world, the extortion and tyranny of Da Monzon's monarchy, Silamaka is an inveterate rebel.

124

Achilles remains perhaps the ancient European world's most notable rebel. His apostasy in the *Iliad* is motivated by roughly the same sense of affronted justice as we have seen in *Mwindo* and *Silamaka*. It is true that Achilles has provoked Agamemnon into a rash decision by offering unguarded words of encouragement to Kalchas; but it was bad judgment, as Nestor points out later (*Iliad* 9.108), for Agamemnon to have taken Achilles' prize away from him. The confrontation between these two underlines the difficulty of drawing rigid distinctions between honor and justice in the heroic society. But Achilles makes a convincing case as to why he should be the last to have his prize stripped from him:

Never, when the Achaians sack some well-founded citadel
of the Trojans, do I have a prize that is equal to your prize.
Always the greater part of the painful fighting is the work of
my hands; but when the time comes to distribute the booty
yours is far the greater reward, and I with some small thing
yet dear to me go back to my ships when I am weary with fighting

(1.163–68)

Moreover, Achilles is as capable of decorum and magnanimity as he is of an unbending ferocity. Andromache tells her husband, Hektor, of the Achaean raid on her town, during which Achilles killed her father Eetion,

but did not strip his armour, for his heart
respected the dead man,
but burned the body in all its elaborate war-gear
and piled a grave mound over it . . .

(6.416–18)

I have said that the hero is, in many cases, engaged in a cause that involves the well-being of his community. Despite the care he takes to place himself above the rank and file of society, he is very much a communal man, and, in the final analysis, the very qualities that make him so unlike other men operate to the advantage, and in accordance with the real interests, of his fellows. The heroic myth generally has a way of objectifying this strain in the heroic personality that reflects the cosmic interests of his community. In *Mwindo* (60), there is that horrid seven-day storm which devastates Tubondo and causes famine, beginning from the day that the hero is unjustly thrown away by his tyrant father: the Tubondo universe is revolting against that painful error. Otherwise, the cosmic interests of the society are figuratively portrayed on an object or weapon that the hero wields consistently. We have the bell of Itonde (or Ilele), Lianja's father, on which is represented everything from the beasts of the earth to the thunder and lightning of the heavens (*Lianja* 22); the bell is later frequently wielded by Lianja. In a similar vein we have the shield of Achilles, on which is represented the entire cosmic scene.

Because he is central to their cosmic order, the hero is thus frequently cast as a deliverer of his people. That cosmic bell of Itonde-Lianja is not simply engraved with all the objects known to the Nkundo world; it is explicity stated that whoever wants anything simply has to make a wish on the bell, and it will be granted. After he has avenged his father, Lianja leads his people on a long and painful trip to life in a promised land by a powerful river: perhaps there is a trace here of the history of migration in that part of Africa, but the myth in any case shows us a hero trying to ensure the vitality and survival of his people. Lianja constantly revives (at the request of his sister Nsongo, an ideal of feminine charm and tenderness) the enemies whom he destroys, and everyone is made to join the march of deliverance to the promised land. When they eventually arrive, Lianja settles them on fertile territory near the powerful river and even takes it upon himself to build them a village, houses, and a plantation (70-72). When all is done, he ascends to heaven.

The image of Sunjata as the champion and deliverer of his

people, one destined by the supernatural powers to save them and guarantee the right order of things, is established early in the story. There is something of this theme in the very turmoil of the elements at the hero's birth, which indicates that he is central to the transcendent interests and fortunes of his society. The point is emphasized by Gnankouman Doua, griot to Sunjata's father, when he sings that "the child is born whom the world awaited . . . and to announce him the Almighty has made the thunder peal, the whole sky has lit up and the earth has trembled" (*Sunjata* IV.14). But the promise of Sunjata the deliverer is not fully realized until Sumanguru puts an entire section of the Mali nation under his oppressive rule; this menace demands a saviour. This is the ultimate crisis for which Sunjata has been carefully prepared in the almost flawless hagiography of the bard. Many a hero owes his existence primarily to a communal crisis—"The hero is welcome only on troubled days," as Seydou Camara says frequently in *Kambili*—and this is certainly true of Sunjata. When the real moment of crisis comes to Mali, a group of envoys from its capital, Niani trace the hero to his place of exile and put the nation's problems at his feet. "We have consulted the jinn," the envoys tell him, "and they have replied that only the son of Sogolon can deliver Mali. Mali is saved because we have found you . . . . The brave await you, come and restore rightful authority to Mali. Weeping mothers pray only in your name, the assembled kings await you, for your name alone inspires confidence in them . . . " (45). When Sunjata defeats Sumanguru and returns to his native land, "peace and happiness entered Niani" (81). The heroic personality of Sunjata achieves its full meaning with the salvation of his community.

Professor Niane has cautioned that the story as told by these griots generally reflects a parochial concern for truth.[50] This parochial concern is even more evident in *Kambili*, which makes no efforts whatsoever to disguise its underlying cult mentality. The picture of life in Mande society is almost completely shorn of its real historical associations; even the historical figure of Samory Toure, the late-nineteenth-century emperor of the Segu Tukulor empire in the western Sudan, recedes into myth. All we see of Mande society in *Kambili* are the taboos of cult membership, the dangers of trespassing against the group ideal:

All groups can be broken;
However, a killing group cannot be broken.
Should you leave it, you will befoul yourself.
Man, if you were to do that,
A bit would be trimmed off your height.

(1614-18)

The story has less didactic interest than we find in the Sunjata epic, though its general gnomic flavor gives it a certain intensity (indeed ferocity) lacking in the latter. *Kambili* does emphasize the importance of one's loyalty to his kind, however. Even before his birth, the image of the hero is conceived in terms reflecting a community's concern for the security of life and economy. One expert soothsayer invited to predict the circumstances of the birth of Kambili says to Samory, the arbiter of the divination:

He will save your regiments,
He will rescue all our good sons,
And rescue the champion farmers,
And rescue all the wood gatherers.

(413–16)

Another soothsayer is no less emphatic about the hero's future role as the champion and hope of his community:

They will bear an invincible child.
The little one, hope of the group.
And bear a protector of orphans,
And bear a friend to the smiths.

(828–31)

As with Sunjata, the final proof of Kambili's heroic promise comes when he resolves the communal crisis. Kambili destroys the lion-man Cekura with a single blast of his rifle; in gratitude the hunters (the cult group that the epic celebrates) raise him up above their shoulders and salute his prowess:

You have taken us from under the execution sword, Kambili.
You have rescued the hunters,
And saved the farmers,
And saved the whole army.
May Allah not keep you behind.
May Allah not take the breath from you, Kambili.

(2633-38)

In *The Mwindo Epic*, the underlying hope seems to be that the ferocious firmness that the hero demonstrates in his struggle against his father's unjust rule will be turned to good account in the interests of the community. Many of the hero's actions can indeed be seen to reflect a degree of communal concern. For his kindness in rescuing the entire population and movable property of Tubondo, he is hailed the "eternal savior of people" (118). After he kills the dragon of the woods, he sees fit to apportion a whole mountain as property to the crowd he has saved from the monster's organs: "These are my people," he graciously declares (134). This communal outlook in Mwindo is well in accord with a heroic personality conceived as influential to the fortunes of his community, as demonstrated by that meteorological turmoil which occurs on the day when his father throws him away soon after his birth (60).

Other cultural heroes show a similar social sensibility. A Sumerian version of the Gilgamesh legend preserves an episode ("Gilgamesh and Agga of Kish") showing the hero (prior to his assumption of kingship) standing stoutly, in spite of meager sympathy, in defense of the land of Erech (Uruk) against the invading Agga.[51]

Beowulf is equally admirable in this respect. We cannot, I think, see his career at Heorot as a selfish quest for glory and his defense of his community fifty years later as a sign of social concern. Although the younger Beowulf does display some of the superior ego of most invincible warriors, all that happens fifty years later is that the champion of Heorot turns his energies to communal account. That the career at Heorot is only a foreshadowing of the sensibility of Beowulf's later days is suggested by Hrothgar's greatful prayer for Beowulf, in which the king contrasts the Geatish hero with the Danish Heremod:

Long shall you stand as a stay to your people,
A help to heroes, as Heremod was not
To the Honor-Scyldings, to Ecgwela's sons!
Not joy to kindred, but carnage and death,
He wrought as he ruled o'er the race of the Danes.

(1707-11)

Patriotism is another facet of the *communis sensus*, and Homer gives us an ample portrait of it in the person of Hektor. Some scholars have found this attitude rather out of place in the relatively individualistic outlook of the Homeric society,[52] largely because of an undue emphasis on the image of Achilles. But I do not find Homer's interest in him any the less. I have observed that one of the fundamental impulses of the heroic personality—intense self-love—is as evident in Hektor as it is in Achilles; and there is really little in Homer that makes the patriotism of the Trojans any less courageous than the buccaneering temper of the Achaeans. Hektor may be a less imposing figure than Achilles because he lacks divine parentage. But for a bard singing his tale before an audience of ordinary mortals the portrait of Hektor has its affective value; it is both moving and reassuring to know that an ordinary mortal is capable of putting up a good struggle amid impossible odds, especially in defense of hearth and home. And nothing in the entire *Iliad* approaches the rugged beauty of Hektor's defiant response to the sanctimonious caution of Polydamas: "One bird sign," declares Hektor, "is best: to fight in defence of our country" (*Iliad* 12.243).

It seems clear, therefore, that the hero represents the highest ideals to which a society can aspire in its search for excellence and security. Yet we cannot ignore other tendencies, inherent in his personality, which may not accord with the best interests of society. Whether or not this ambivilence is a deliberate search for balance on the part of the traditional artist is not easy to say, for his creative technique is fundamentally unlike that of the careful writer. But the epics do show us that a man who strives to stand out of the crowd may overstep the bounds which that crowd observes in its considered interests. Where, therefore, we find the cooperative will existing side by side with single-minded arrogance, we may rightly suggest that what we have is an undiscriminating representation of the contrarieties of human life; the hero is quite simply a comprehensive symbol of the ideals of human society and the dangers attendant upon such exaggerated expectations. Society does welcome honor and distinction and has the highest admiration for a man who surmounts all odds to see that his people survive. But it is also aware that the person who accomplishes such feats is not like the rest of his fellows and should be feared.

We find this complexity in the character of Mwindo. With the aid of Nkuba, Mwindo mercilessly destroys his enemies and the entire population of his native village, Tubondo; he seems justified in doing so, because they are standing in the way of his pursuit of his criminal father. But the same destructive, overbearing temper

131

shows itself again after he settles down as king of Tubondo. When the dragon destroys his subjects, he sets out to the forest and exterminates the ogre. Some of the villagers are so frightened by the feat that they are moved to observe that "he who has killed this one cannot fail to kill one of his relatives" (133). On hearing such careless talk, Mwindo kills the men right on the spot! This is apparently an act of excess, but it does not prevent the hero from demonstrating communal goodwill the next minute: he bestows land on the little men who have, thanks to him, been rescued from the insides of the dead dragon, thus graciously giving them a means of livelihood.

The bard, to be sure, does have a moral concern, and as a member of a society which desires perfect stability he is worried that the society is perpetually at the mercy of the random tempers of the brave. "The hero of yesterday," as Campbell rightly observes, "becomes the tyrant of tomorrow."[53] It is this concern for immanent justice which gives rise to the heavily moralistic denouement of the Mwindo story. We are first told that Nkuba "had made a blood pact with Dragon" (134). Killing the dragon seems therefore an act of overreaching, particularly since Nkuba has been so often instrumental to Mwindo's previous triumphs. The hero is accordingly translated into the sky and seriously cautioned. Yet, whatever significance there may be in Nkuba's blood pact Mwindo has clearly served the community by destroying the monster. Nkuba's relationship with the dragon may have a basis in Nyanga ritual, but Mwindo's heroic act has a logic of its own. Such then is the ambiguity of his heroic personality: he is both killer and savior, rebellious and cooperative, reflecting the varied potential in society.

There is perhaps a similar ambivalence in the career of Achilles. He is, to all intents and purposes, a representative of that heroic outlook succinctly summarized in Glaukos' notable line, "to be

always among the bravest, and hold my head above all others"
(*Iliad* 6.208); he received the same injunction from his father, Peleus (11.783). For this reason he wishes to reserve the highest hon-
ors to himself (as witness his injunction to Patroklos to stop short
of the Trojan walls); and his pride is injured at the slightest affront
to his ego, which is why he reacts to Agamemnon's insult by en-
dangering an entire army. But Achilles has also been raised by
Peleus under another moral code, as we learn from old Phoinix:
"Consideration is the better way" (9.256). He gives a fitting burial
to Eetion, Andromache's father, whom he had killed (6.416ff.); and
though, as the Greeks fall, he is pleased to have his revenge, he
takes anxious interest in their wounded and consents to let Patroklos give the Greeks a much needed relief. Though he is unbending to Agamemnon, at other times he is capable of admirable
consideration, as Zeus himself admits:

he is no witless man nor unwatchful, nor is he wicked,
but will in all kindness spare one who comes to him as a suppliant.

(24.157-58)

It has often been said that the tragedy of Achilles is the conflict
between his pride and his patriotism.[54] Yet where some see conflict, others see an all-inclusive pattern and an interplay serving the
varied affective interests of the bard at every turn of the tale.

We might best end this chapter by recalling the Yoruba god
Ogun, reputed to be the inspiration behind the *ijala* or heroic
hunters' chants among this Nigerian ethnic group. Ogun, the god
of smithery and of the hunt, is the source of much blessing to the
economy of the clan. But as the god of metal craft he is also the
god of warfare and reckless bloodshed, and his ungovernable lust
for blood is illustrated by numerous legends.[55] The Yoruba see
nothing incongruous in this dual personality, which is apparently a
mythic compromise between supreme good and supreme evil.

133

This power to blast and to bless, to sow weal with one hand and woe with the other, is myth's concrete image of the potentialities of the human character; the hero is simply the ordinary man writ large. Ogun's dual potential is perhaps best mirrored in the following portrait by the modern Nigerian poet, Wole Soyinka:

Ogun is the lascivious god who takes
Seven gourdlets to war. One for gunpowder,
One for charms, two for palm wine and three
Air-sealed in polished bronze make
Storeage for his sperms.[56]

It seems only right that, after the wanton carnage, the seeds of regeneration should be sown.

Four

ON FORM AND STRUCTURE

In examining the art of composition in the oral epic, we must bear constantly in mind the moment of performance—with music, histrionic resources, emotional relationship between singer and audience—which makes this tradition of art different from the literate variety. Each performance is the product of one specific moment or context and, in a creative tradition of the oral epic, is never exactly repeated. Though there are some fixed structural laws which the narrative will obey by the very nature of its oral medium, the results of any performance depend mainly on the particular audience, mood, and atmosphere.

Clearly, there can be no fixed pattern to the context in which a song is performed, and some of the peculiar features of a performance are due to a variety of circumstances. In an earlier chapter, we observed how the bard of *Kambili* has been forced to interlace his song with remarks to his accompanists on the inadequacy of the musical background. It is clear that to save his song from collapse he has either had recourse to his strophic or gnomic lines sooner than he needed to (e. g., 2106ff., 2252ff.) or has had to prolong the coral response from his accompanists beyond his apparent needs (2033f., 2053f., etc), or some such emergency measure.

There may well be other factors regulating the performance of the bard. For instance, the recording tape may run out, and he simply has to suspend his act until he can continue. The obligation to keep on singing until the tape runs out can be equally oppressive: Okabou, the bard of our version of *Ozidi*, draws much laughter from the audience when, at someone's observation that the tape is being changed, he responds, "If it's been changed say so, for in truth I feel like stooling right now" (362). Otherwise, there may be a tradition of performing the tale over a specific number of days. The *Ozidi* story is traditionally done in seven days (or nights); it is interesting to observe how at the start of every performance the bard feels his way for the last point of departure (though the recording may have been played for him so that he can get his facts straight).[1]

A good deal may also depend on the bard's audience. *Ozidi* as we have it is quite long, perhaps because the bard felt himself under pressure to stand up to his job in the presence of spectators who frequently challenged his usage and details (see p. 200), or because he felt obliged to overdo himself for a professor who was going to spread the fame of his craft; or possibly the general atmosphere (of criticism as well as frequent approbation) inspired him with the right fervor.

The patron has much to do with the results of a performance. The bard of *The Mwindo Epic* may have been blessed with a gracious one: the editor describes this particular version as "by far the longest, most comprehensive, most coherent, most detailed, and most poetic of all versions of the Mwindo story which I heard in Nyanga country" (*Mwindo* 19). An ungracious patron, on the contrary, would draw a short performance or one in which the bard was forced to interject a few unflattering lines; Nketia has mentioned this practice as a notable feature of performances among the Akan of Ghana.[2] Homer gives us interesting possibilities of the effect of an unfavorable audience response on the singer's performance. In the *Odyssey*, Phemios sings of the grievous homecoming of the Achaeans from Troy, and the memory of her missing husband moves Penelope to tears; the bard is asked to change his subject and sing more cheerful tunes, and his performance is thereby broken (1.325ff.). Also, at the Phaiakian court of Alkinoos, Demodokos makes Odysseus cry with his song about the Trojan experience, and the king asks the singer to halt his singing (8.535ff.); the punctuation of Demodokos' performances by athletic contests and other activities must also have some structural effects on a performance of that kind.

II

Despite these deviations, recent scholarship has firmly established basic structural patterns at the root of the composition of the oral epic.

The first such pattern is known as the "formula." From his observation of Homeric verse, Parry has defined it as "a group of words which is regularly employed under the same metrical conditions to express a given essential idea."[3] Parry is careful to exclude from his considerations the practice, in literate verse composition, of having phrases or lines repeated simply for their choral effect (as in Shakespeare's *Macbeth*) or lifted from other writers purely for their allusive or scholarly flavor (as in Euripides' *Philocteses* or Pope's translation of the *Odyssey*).[4] Parry's conception of the formula is that it must serve first and foremost a metrical purpose by its position in the verse: meaning is secondary to this prosodic function. Thus, Parry thinks Homer calls his hero "swift-footed Achilles" because that epithet is the only one that can be accommodated in the line; any of the several other epithets that could be used would ruin the perfect prosodic balance that "swift-footed" brings to the line.[5]

The study of the oral epic in modern Yugoslavia has failed to yield a comparable technical rigidity. Indeed, nowhere else has that rigidity been discovered in the numerous studies to which Parry's contribution has given rise, and this fact has raised the pertinent question as to how the Homeric epics as we have them today could have come into existence in the first place. Still, Parry is undeniably right in establishing the formula as a basic unit of oral composition; from a stock of phrases and lines that tradition and long use have stored in the bard's memory, he constructs fresh ideas and scenes and thus supports the overall fabric of his story.

African "verse" tales have so far not shown any of the Homeric rigidity, but the formula is certainly a feature of oral composition among African bards of the heroic narrative song. We can cite a variety of examples. Perhaps the simplest type of formula is the "noun-adjective combination,"[6] the combination of noun (e. g., name) and epithet or identification (e. g., patronymic or qualitative). In *Kambili*, the hero is frequently called "Kambili Sananfila," his mother "Dugo the Owl," and Samory Toure is "Toure ni Manjun" numerous times. In Banna Kanute's version of the Sunjata story (*Sunjata* II), Sumanguru is almost invariably called "Susu Sumanguru Baamagana," while in Dembo's version (*Sunjata* III) Sunjata's formidable ally Fakoli is constantly greeted with the double appelation "Faa Koli Kumba and Faa Koli Daaba." In *Akoma Mba*, the subject's fierce adversary is often called "Abo Mama, man Yemedziit" (of the Yemedziit clan). All these are noun-epithet combinations such as we find frequently in Homer and other epic traditons.[7]

The descriptive formula in *Akoma Mba* is particularly colorful. A beautiful lady is portrayed as one "whose charm dries up the saliva in your mouth" (461,602); the Ekang race is described as "those who believe nothing that they hear with their ears/until they have seen it with their eyes" (53f., 1214f.). Various other such formulas bear out the intense dramatic appeal of this performance, which was recorded in the lively atmosphere of a cultural festival.

The formulaic phrase is not restricted to the noun-epithet combination. In *Kambili* we have several examples of a verbal matrix being used for the construction of gnomes or praise-proverbs often occuring consecutively for several lines. These gnomic lines occur mostly at the opening, when the bard is trying to build up the pace of his performance as well as to articulate the transcendent ideas within which he sets the story of Kambili. The following is an example:

Look to the doorsill for the sight of all things.
Salute the co-wife's knife for leaving nothing behind.
Look to the salt for the success of the sauce.
Salute the sitting-stool for seizing all the smells.

(11-14)

This succession of lines has been built on a simple formulaic pattern. It consists of a verb or verbal phrase ("Look to" or "Salute") and a conjunction ("for"); on this pattern have been built numerous strophic or interludial passages with which the tale is dotted. Such lines may not take the story forward, but they prove the bard's versatile genius. True, the device can be overdone to such an extent as to leave the effect of an "empty fullness";[8] but if we consider that the bard is not simply telling the story but performing it, we can understand why he will devote some of his virtuosity to inflating his material now and then, particularly if he accompanies the verbalization with a fitting emphasis on the music—an effect that, unfortunately, will not be obvious on the printed page.

The formula as a verbal matrix also occurs frequently in Dembo Kanute's version of *Sunjata*. For instance, in a number of places where the bard laments the passing away of great heroic figures of the land, his sentiments are conveyed on a convenient pattern framed by the words "Don't you know that . . . is dead," as in the following lines:

(a)
Ali mang a long Darama Jallo la Fili banta.

(Don't you know that Darama Jallo's Fili is gone.)

(III.11)

(b)
Ali mang a long Tuuli Mbaalo la Cherno banta.

(Don't you know that Tulli Mbaalo's Cherno is dead.)[9]

(54)

Alternatively, the lament formula is framed as in the following examples:

(a)
N hakilo jaaka bula
Kelema ning Delema.

(My mind turns to
Keleman and Delema.)   (29-30)

(b)
N hakilo Jaaka bula
Bande banna, Jao banna la fana ku-ng o.

(My mind goes to
A wealthy Bande and to a wealthy Jao too.)   (40-41)

The two patterns are brought together in the following passage:

N hakilo jaaka bula
Ngana kika kika le fana ku.
Ali mang a long Marena muso la Seku Alifa Jaaju banta.

140

(My mind goes to
Many, many great men besides.
Don't you know that the Marena woman's Seku Alifa
        Jaaju is dead.)

(64-66)

There are also some functional phrases, built roughly on the pattern of Homer's "winged words," that help construct the main body of the narrative. By one such device, the bard of *Kambili* is able to establish a pattern for characters calling and responding to one another and thus initiating a dialogue between them. The simple formula for this is, "He said, ' . . . !' 'Yes?' the reply." On this pattern the beginnings of dialogues between characters in various scenes in the story have been constructed. The first such call and response occurs between the warrior Kanji (later the father of Kambili) and his lord, the emperor Samory Toure, when Kanji complains to Samory that he has failed to gain a child through any of his nine wives. Toure is about to assure Kanji that he will invite the soothsayers to probe the issue, and the dialogue begins, "He said, 'Kanji!' 'Yes?' the reply" (173). On another occasion, the formula is used to introduce a dialogue between Toure and one of the soothsayers, who regrets he is unable to solve the Kambili riddle: "He said, 'Toure in Kanjun!' 'Yes!' the reply" (474). On yet another occasion, the aggrieved Cekura is summoning his fellow lion-men to a bloody revenge upon the people of Jimini for robbing him of his wife, Kumba, whom the nobles have given to Kambili: "He said, 'Lionmen!' 'Yes?' the reply" (1907).[10]

These are examples of the call-and-response formula contained in one line. However, I hasten to observe that the prososy of *Kambili* has a quite different basis from that of the Homeric epos. The metric line of the hunter's bards, among the Mande of the western Sudan as among the Akan of Ghana and the Yoruba of Nigeria, is built on the basis of "breath groups:" the bard fits as many words as he can within a single breath, so long as this is done within individual segments of the rhythmic accompaniment from the background music. It is a kind of bardic *tour de parole*, which Charles Bird has described:

> The essential metrical requirement is that the singer keep in rhythm with his instrumental accompaniment. He may therefore form lines of one syllable or fifty syllables, depending very much on his virtuosity in rapid speech, and his subtlety in weaving the rhythms of his language around those of his instrument. The singer can play with background rhythm by forming couplets or even longer verses.[11]

The background rhythm of the *Kambili* song is of the 4/4 type; so, depending on how much bravado the bard can summon at any point of his act, he can manage to pack into one line what on other occasions he would have in two, and vice versa. This system gives the bard absolute freedom to do what he wants with his song, so that the call-and-response formula is occasionally broken up into two lines:

He said, "Sananfila Kanji!"
"Yes!" he replied.

(152-53)

The call-and-response formula is also frequently used in *Akoma Mba*, with no less dramatic sense of urgency than in *Kambili*, as for example:

(a)
A Endendem Obama o!
—Oo, ma va!
Zaa tilt ma nten avol!

(You, Endendem Obama!
—Yes, here I am!
Quick, come on and take down a note!) (34-36)

(b)
A Abo Mama o!
—Oo! ma va
Zaa san nten avol!

(You, Abo Mama!
—Yes, here I am!
Quick, come on and sign the resolution!)[12]   (155-57)

One frequently used formulaic matrix in the heroic tale—which depends for much of its effectiveness on a certain element of expectancy or alarm—is what may best be described as the formulaic alert. It does to greater dramatic effect what is frequently done in written literature by the exclamation mark, alerting the listener's attention to a detail. In *Akoma Mba*, the bard starts off the entire story with the words *Ma kam na* (Something makes me wonder), and the king Akoma Mba uses the same line when he is making the momentous decision to call his chiefs to a council of state aimed at portioning up the land (20). The words *Dyon te manga yen a na* (Look what I see [374, 453, etc.]) are also used for alerting us to a momentous scene. In *Kambili*, the prescriptions of the cheating Muslim in the divining contest are announced with the words, "Didn't you hear the learned holyman's words?" (1135), repeated in essentially the same words twenty lines later. Such a rhetorical question will be familiar to students of the south Slavic epic: as a character is about to send off a letter to another, we are frequently asked, "To whom did he send it?"[13]

The real place of the formulaic line, however, is in what Milman Parry has called the "theme"; Albert Lord has defined it as "a recurrent element of narration or description in traditional oral poetry."[14] The theme is somewhat larger than the formulaic line—

143

in Parry's words, "The distinction between the verse and the simple theme is only one of degree"—in the sense that it expresses, in more than a line, a sentiment or idea the oral poet finds capable of being deployed in several like situations. For instance, the idea of arming for battle, or entertaining a guest, or falling in a fight is a stereotype that can be used as often as such a situation occurs; in such cases the poet can repeat a whole passage without a radical change in verbal order or content. But perhaps because of the size of the passage, it is often not easy for the bard to observe in a theme the rigidity that characterizes the formula (at least in Homer); on this point Lord has observed: "It is not restricted, as is the formula, by metrical considerations; hence, it should not be limited to exact word-for-word repetition."[15] The essential thing in the theme is the idea that it embodies—the order of words can change a little here and there.

There are numerous examples of the theme in *Kambili*. The most notable involves the trial of skill that Samory Toure sets up for various soothsayers on the issue of who, among Kanji's wives, will be the mother of the hero-child, Kambili. The theme has become the appropriate unit of narration here because the contestants are going to be subjected to the same question, will fail the test on the same significant point of the hero's mother's name, and will be given the same order of execution. The words and the order of lines are not exactly the same in all cases, but the similarity would qualify them as themes in the Parry-Lord sense.

The soothsayers invited to participate in the contest include (a) the "blackbag man" (305), (b) the "cowrie thrower" (401), and (c) the "old sandal man" (443). The basic sequence of the trial is as follows. First Samory Toure invites the man to solve the child riddle, and the pattern of request is clearly a thematic one:

(a)
He spoke to the blackbag man.
"Man, come help me in this child affair."
He came with his black bag.
He came shaking his black bag. . . .   (305-8)

(b)
He called to the cowrie thrower.
"Come help me with this child affair,
You have no equal in reading omens."
Well, the cowrie thrower came.
He came with his winnowing basket,
And came with his ten and two. . . .   (401-6)

(c)
He called out to the old sandal man.
"Come help me in this child affair,
You who speak the bitter truth.
Hurry the old sandal man along, Allah!"
The old sandal man came.
He brought a piece of balenbon bark,
And the rib of a ram,
With a cowrie on the top of his head. . . .   (443-50)

After the invitation has been given, the man appears with the tools
of his trade and falls to the task of divining. He delivers a series of
lines proclaiming what a great hero is about to be born, but Samory tells him to stick to the main issue—which one of Kanji's
nine wives will be the mother. Says Samory:

(a)
'Man," he replied, "there's nothing wrong with that,
But nine women cannot be pregnant with one child,
So get yourself together and look for the mother's name
quickly. . . .   (355-57)

(b)
"Ah!" he answered, "Cowrie thrower!
I didn't ask you for a big pile of words,
Hurry up quickly and tell me the mother's name.
Nine women cannot be pregnant with one child. . . .   (417-20)

(c)
He said, "Old sandal man!" "Yes?"
"Nine women cannot be pregnant with one child.
Quick like a flash,
      Tell me the mother's name. . . . "   (467-70)

But none of the soothsayers is able to tell the name of the mother.
The symbols that the tools describe on the floor can only signify
features and qualities but cannot spell names. So the soothsayer
pleads with Samory:

(a)
"The bag is only for signs.
It does not know people's names"   (378-79)

(b)
". . . I have no means of knowing the mother's name.
The cowries are only for signs, Toure."   (428-29)

(c)
"I have no way of knowing the mother's name.
Their task is but to give signs,
Therefore the old sandals do not speak."   (476-78)

The soothsayer having failed the test, Samory orders that he be
put to death with the emperor's extraordinary sword, named
Konke. The execution is thematically described in terms of action
and result:

(a)
Ah! The bagman's head was cut off at his neck.
His two shoulders became inseparable friends.
And thus he died, quite dead.

(397-99)

(b)
The cowrie thrower's head was cut off at his neck.
His shoulders became inseparable friends.
He became a corpse, quite dead!

(435-37)

(c)
The old sandal man's head was cut off at his neck.
Big trouble has begun in Jimini!
The little man fell flopping about like a tramp in the cold.

(505-7)

The theme of execution is not confined to the soothsayers who
fail to solve the Kambili riddle. Later, when Toure orders the execution of the little old lady who tries to blackmail the mother of
Kambili, the killing is reported in essentially the same thematized
form in which the soothsayers' deaths have been described:

The old woman's head fell,
Cut off at her throat,
Her two shoulders became inseparable friends.

(1720-22)

Akoma Mba makes an equally fertile use of themes. There is
often a climactic touch to them, because they underline the heat
of action or at least an expectation of it. One such theme can be
designated "the hero dreams of killing." We have an example of it
in that scene where, on the night before he sets out to fight Otungu Mba, the hero Abo Mama falls asleep and dreams of slaughter:

147

Then he began to snore,
"Rrr . . . zig! Rrr . . . zig! I will leave, I will leave at dawn!"
He strikes and kills a man! hn! zig—who has he killed? Hn! zig!

(379-81)

The same murderous thoughts occur in the dream of the equally embattled Akoma Mba, Otungu's uncle, as he lies dozing in his palace, and the scene is reported in essentially the same words (557ff.). A second interesting theme, employed numerous times in this tale, can be termed "the frantic dash." Whenever a character has to run for it, whether on an errand or to save his skin, we are told that he

. . . dashed like the branch of a broken tree,
Like the furious racing of a young antelope,
Like a bird that takes off without saying goodbye to the branch.[16]

In the heat of anger and confrontation, one character is likely to threaten the other in the following thematized diction:

If you say another word,
I will bury you like a stub of cassava,
And you will go and join our ancestor Mebe'e in hell![17]

In all these passages there is a tremendous sense of urgency which is both an index of the pressure and challenge under which the bard is having to weave a tale that must keep moving, and a token of the lyrical feeling that the general fervor of the moment has engendered in him.

Banna Kanute's version of the Sunjata story (*Sunjata* II) gives us a few equally interesting examples, having to do mostly with the courtly atmosphere of Sumanguru. There is a tradition in the monarchical societies of West Africa (especially in areas influenced by Islam) of feting the arrival of a notable visitor to a ruler. If the genealogy of the visitor is sufficiently researched or well known, courtesy demands that he be greeted by the ruler's praise singers with details relating to that genealogy. But the praise singers must also recite the ruler-host's praises: it has to be brought home to the visitor that, whoever he may be, he should count himself fortunate to be introduced to the august presence of no less a host than the ruler. The singer's praises are thus a regular feature in any courtly scene of hospitality. Very much as on those numerous occasions in the *Odyssey* when hospitality demands that food be offered to a guest,[18] Sumanguru's praise singers hail him with the following appellation whenever a visitor arrives:

Cut and Sirimang,
It is forging and the left hand,
Senegalese coucal and swallow,
Cut iron with iron,
What gives iron its excellence,
Big *kuku* tree and big silk-cotton tree,
Fari and Kaunju.[19]

The formula and the theme, as we have seen, are useful for the forward growth of the story. But other repeated lines and passages only contribute toward a fullness of effect in the performance. Removing these lines will not hurt the story in any significant way, but the oft-repeated lines are a distinguishing mark not only of the oral poet's love of accretion but of the lyrical medium of his narrative. He is telling a story in song, and the oft-remembered line, so long as it is in context, has an immediate attraction for his genius.

Such repetition often occurs when a message or order is being delivered or rehearsed. In *Kambili* there are numerous examples, the best being when the lion-man Cekura is about to be overcome by the magic of "contiguity." The medicine man instructs Kumba:

Bring me a headhair,
Yes, bring a hair of the lion's head,
And bring some hair from under his arm,
And bring some hair from his crotch,
And bring the sandal off his foot,
And bring a pair of his old pants,
And lay them on the omen board.
When we find a means to the man-eating lion,
Should we do that, the man-eating lion will die.

(2242-50)

Kumba prepares for the mission and, on taking leave of her new husband, Kambili, she lets him know what she is off to do:

I'm going after the hair of his head, Kambili.
I'm going after the underarm hair, Kambili.
I'm going after the sandal, Kambili.
I'm going after the old pants, Kambili.
That done, the man-eating lion will die, Kambili.

(2270-74)

It is interesting that Kumba leaves out the detail of the crotch. Although the formular system imposes on the bard certain paths from which he does not much deviate, a good bard will try to maintain presence of mind and observe due proprieties as often as he can. It therefore becomes Kumba, who appears anxious to assure her new husband of her loyalty, not to bring it home to him that her mission will take her as far as his enemy's manhood.[20] But she has no hesitation in reinstating the detail when she finally gets to Cekura and bends the message to suit her purpose:

If you give me an old pair of pants,
They'll be used as a means to get Kambili.
Bring me some hair off your head,
We'll find a means to get Kambili today.

Bring me some hair from under you arm,
And give me some hair from your crotch,
And take off your old sandals . . . .
When all that's done, he'll become a corpse.

(2349-56)

The design works, and of Cekura's total surrender we are told:

Cekura gave some of the hair off his head,
And gave the hair from under his arm,
And gave some hair from off his crotch,
And gave the old pair of pants,
And gave the sandals off his feet . . .
"After that, there is only me."

(2367-72)

The above passages belong to a style of repetition that will be familiar to students of the Homeric epics or *Gilgamesh*. For instance, Patroklos repeats to Achilles, in almost exactly the same words, Nestor's plea that Patroklos be allowed to fight off the Trojans with the arms of Achilles;[21] Zeus's compromise on Hektor's body is conveyed to Priam by Iris in the same words in which she received the message;[22] and Telemachos berates the irresponsible princess at Ithaka at least twice in exactly the same language.[23] The *Gilgamesh* epic is probably not the record of a performance, but it is clearly indebted to the devices of the oral narrative song and copies them faithfully. Thus we have numerous passages in the story echoing one another; for example, the scene in which Siduri remarks, and Gilgamesh explains, the look of tedium and despair on the face of the wandering hero (*Gilgamesh* 101) is repeated when Gilgamesh meets the boatman Urshanabi (103), and again when he finally gets to Utnapishtim (105).

A message could be expanded as well as curtailed. Sometimes the messenger is inclined to presume further knowledge or infor-

151

mation than he has been charged to transmit; or the bard himself feels sufficiently moved to put more words into the mouth of the messenger; or perhaps the bard cannot remember the exact details of the message, and so he drags in a few more in the process. Thus, in *Akomba Mba*, when Ondoa sends someone to find out from a medicine man whether or not he will have a child, the messenger prefaces the message proper with a fuller description of the circumstances and the plight of Ondoa, taken from an earlier scene.[24] Such expansions are not unknown in Homer. We have, for instance, that passage in *Iliad* 8 where Iris gives Hera and Athene a message from Zeus (416-24): two of the lines (421-22), aimed offensively at Athene, are not in Zeus's original message (402-8).

Of the various other kinds of repetitions, perhaps the most interesting are those repeated songs and exchanges between two characters in a choral or operatic situation. An example is that delightful scene in *Kambili* involving Bari the shaman and the unhappy woman who later becomes the hero's mother, "Dugo of the Palace": in this scene, Bari assures her that her fortunes are about to take a turn for the better (872-926).

Technically, there is not much difference between these repeated passages and what we know as "themes." But there is a functional difference; for whereas repetition is a token of a lyrical feeling, the theme goes beyond an ordinary love of detail and singsong. In the case of *Kambili*, the themes of trial and execution are essential for the forward movement of the plot. Besides, the sequence of tragedies (of three soothsayers in a row) helps to build up the climax of tempers for the final battle of skills between the Muslim "holyman" and Bari, the hunters' divine. *Kambili* is a hunters' epic, and it is inevitable that our bard should show the hunters' man as succeeding where countless others have failed. In the *Odyssey*, the theme of entertainment at Ithaka, Lakedaimon, Scheria, and Aiaia describes formal procedures which custom invariably demands between host and guest.

Perhaps this is as good a place as any to say a few words on the question of the origin of repeated lines. There has been a long tradition of scholarship aimed at tracing the roots of every form of art to ritual or magic, and the formula has not escaped this exercise. In his discussion of the nature and growth of the formula, Lord says:

Its symbols, its sounds, its patterns were born for magic productivity, not for aesthetic satisfaction. If later they provide such satisfaction, it was only to generations which had forgotten their real meaning. The poet was sorcerer and seer before he became "artist." His structures were not abstract art, or art for its own sake. The roots of oral traditional narrative are not artistic but religious in the broadest sense.[25]

I have found these arguments rather unconvincing, particularly when Lord attributes formulaic epithets to the ritual of invoking religious figures by their names and their epiphanies.[26] When creative man felt the need to formulate or to compose a line, whether in play or as a ritual function, and felt like carrying on the exercise with speed and over a period of time, he must have faced the difficulty of formulating fresh ideas at such speed in unbroken sequence. The repeated line was clearly a mark of his anxiety at this point. But the time came when he felt that some of the lines and phrases that he had formulated were effective, aesthetically or otherwise. He therefore took joy in recalling them at several points of his chant; they were then either used for the purpose of formulating fresh lines that had a kindred message or were reechoed constantly for their sing-song appeal. Whatever the context in which it originally occurred (whether recreational or religious), repetition was first and foremost a token of the joy of recollection; it developed into a pattern mainly as a response to the pressure of a speedy or steady act of composition.[27]

III

We have so far confined our formal analysis of the functional repetitions in the epic to those of our texts that have been transcribed in numbered "verse" lines—*Kambili*, the version of *Sunjata* collected by Innes, and *Akoma Mba*. This perhaps suggests that we could not look for these formal elements in our "prose" texts and seems to support the long-held notion that formular composition belongs only in a quantitative context.[28] But any careful observer of the oral art in Africa would hesitate to make such a simple distinction between prose and verse. As we have noted earlier, prose placed in the rather complex environment of music and drama—such as *Mwindo* and *Ozidi* were narrated in—is not ordinary prose; it is prose supported by a musical feeling, and the story thus told, whatever the relative movements of its various segments, is a song. One would not, of course, go so far as to call *Mwindo* and *Ozidi* "verse" tales; the connotations that word has acquired from its long application to literate art are sufficiently discouraging. It will be sufficient simply to observe that a good singer who endeavors to give a warm and successful performance will find his genius considerably hindered by a quantitative regularity.

In many African societies, as the evidence so far suggests, the prosodic structure of the song (especially in a public performance) is treated as loosely as possible, so as to give the performing bard sufficient freedom to attend to music, dance, drama, and so on, and even allow impromptu repartee and other participation from the audience.[29] Whether the bard is performing to an unchanging musical tempo, or (as in *Sunjata* III) to a variety of accompaniments, he does not ever feel himself so bound by the constraints of the music that his words have to follow a rigidly regulated pattern. Foreign scholars, unfamiliar with the peculiar nature of such a traditional art form, may find it a little hard to understand it or to fit it into their neat schemes. But the answer is not to find a conventional slot for a new or unfamiliar art form. One may not help the situation by adopting an agnostic attitude, but it is hard to accept the definition that verse is any order of words or syllables delivered against a regulated rhythmic background.[30] In the study of the oral epic in Africa, one soon learns to shy away from these easy distinctions between prose and verse; as Lestrade has observed with regard to traditional Bantu literature:

The border-line between them is extremely difficult to ascertain and define, while the verse-technique, in so far as verse can be separated from prose, is extremely free and unmechanical. Broadly speaking, it may be said that the difference between prose and verse in Bantu literature is one of spirit rather than of form, and that such formal distinction there is one of degree of use rather than of quality of formal elements.[31]

If we accept that the looseness is not a disadvantage, it will be no surprise to find several formulaic and thematic elements in our ostensibly "prose" tales. Let us take *Mwindo* as an example. One of the most frequent formulas in that tale is of the order of Homer's "rosy-fingered Dawn," introducing a fresh stage of the story with the break of day: *"Bakie ebutu wamaca, mumukoma-koma."* (When the sky [or night] had become daylight, in the morning.)[32] Another frequent formula introduces choral chants which occur every now and then in between narrative portions; the formula is roughly of the order of Homer's "winged words": *"Mwindo . . . warekera enderi kubunu, wasimba."* (Mwindo . . . threw sweet words into his mouth, he sang.)[33] Yet another formula describes characters dressing up impeccably: *"wikia na buri kanyero kanko mwimbira"* (made himself like the anus of a snail in his dressing up).[34]

Several other examples occur in the chants. Of themes, there are two particularly interesting examples. One occurs twice in the story, when the lightning god Nkuba helps Mwindo destroy his adversaries. On the first occasion the hero is fighting his own village, Tubondo, which had offered sanctuary to his unjust father; on the second occasion Mwindo is battling Ntumba the Aardvark, who is also protecting the father. The thematic pattern of the aid from the lightning god can be seen from the following two passages:

(a) From the sky at Nkuba's, things came; there appeared seven lightning flashes; they descended on Tubondo in the village. Tubondo turned into dust, and the dust rose up. . . . (92)

(b) Nkuba sent down seven lightnings; they descended into Ntumba's cave; they cleaved it into a million pieces; the cave turned into mere dust; the dust flew up. (105)[35]

Another theme involves the contest between the god Muisa and Mwindo, in which the god tries hard to destroy the hero with a magic belt (*Karemba*). Muisa succeeds in doing considerable harm, but Mwindo recovers and employs his own magic *conga*-scepter in brutalizing Muisa. The idiom of the struggle in the following three passages will show their underlying thematic basis:

(a) [*Karemba*] fell upon [Mwindo] where he was; it made Mwindo scream; it crushed him; it planted his mouth against the ground—froth came out; he lacked the way of getting his breath out; urine and excrements agreed [to get out]; they lacked the one who could remove them. (99)

(b) When [the *conga*] arrived at Muisa's meeting place, it smashed him; it planted his mouth to the ground; the tongue dug into the earth; urine and excrements lacked mpunga-leaves, and the one who would take them away was also missing; breath found no way of coming out. (100)

(c) Muisa sent his *karemba*-belt; it went and smashed Mwindo on the tree; it planted his mouth into the trunk of the tree; his breath could not get out; urine and excrements trickled down from him. (102)

These are no simple repetitions. They mark three progressive stages in Mwindo's difficult search for his errant father; there is a forward movement to the story in each case. The bard has simply had recourse to a stock of useful descriptive touches and a pattern of action and result for which he needs no radical substitutes. As Albert Lord has observed, unlike the formula, the theme is not bound by word-for-word uniformity; I think it is clear from the above examples that the *Mwindo* bard has employed the same devices that we have identified in Homer and Seydou Camara.

Ozidi makes an even more fertile use of themes, perhaps reflecting the fervid, creative environment in which the tale was performed. One of the interesting themes in the story, which employs not so much the same ingredients as the same progression of cognate details, occurs when Oreame subjects the boy-hero Ozidi to various tests of courage—she turns first into an anthill, and then a leopard to see how the boy reacts (14-17). In each case the boy runs home ahead of Oreame; she arrives and scolds him roundly; then proceeds to bathe him in some medicinal herbs so as to strengthen his will power.

Another theme of considerable appeal occurs in connection with the fetish chamber of Bouakarakarabiri, the wizard of the bush who gives Ozidi his magical powers (28-30). Three animals go into the concoction that the wizard mixes for the purpose—a monkey, a kingfisher, and a lizard. Each first seeks a perch on the edge of the mortar in which they will be pounded; then cries in its characteristic sound; then alights on the mortar and is pounded to death by Ozidi, who has a pestle ready for the job. In the above two situations, the frame remains the same, and the diction has a certain amount of regularity too. Since the elements have to be put to the same use—as in that trial of the soothsayers in *Kambili*—there is hardly need for a radical alteration in the form in which they are presented.

The magical device from Bouakarakarabiri in turn spawns a further theme, which we may call the theme of the "destructive temper" in Ozidi. When Ozidi confronts an adversary, and they finally come to grips, the killing urge in the hero is often triggered by his witch-grandmother's calling his name or his attending musicians' beating the signature for battle. Then all those sounds from the animals which were mixed in Ozidi's magical device reecho in his bowels; he is at once driven into a fury, his sword tumbles out of his bowels (the seat of rage) through his mouth, and he begins to slash away at the enemy.[36] More often than not, Oreame summons this urge in Ozidi by simply calling his name when the time comes for him to act. In fact, so commanding is her instrumentality, and so pervasive the theme of anger in the circumstances, that even when, in one case (in connection with the helpless sister of Tebesonoma and her child), Ozidi is unwilling to kill, Oreame simply calls him to open his eyes (to the reality of his mission), and those demons in his bowels begin to resound (253).

Having killed the victim, Ozidi cuts off his head and dumps it in the shrine house; there follows a deafening clamor from the various heads of powerful victims whom the hero had earlier killed.[37] In the final stage of this interesting thematic sequence, the hero, now drunken with murderous triumph, begins to cut down the entire shrubbery in his premises, right up to the feet of his idiot uncle, Temugedege; the man is thoroughly frightened and prays that the citizens of the town will see fit to kill off the frenzied boy and put an end to his menace.[38]

There are two conclusions that we may draw from these discoveries. The first is that the texts of *Ozidi* and *Mwindo*, insofar as they were delivered to the background of music, may have been subject to the internal modulating influence of that music and therefore behave in a sense like "verse." But it must be counted verse of a most irregular or "unmechanical" kind, to use Lestrade's word. We have seen "verse" lines in *Kambili* and in the Innes editions of *Sunjata*, but we have also seen how the bards have remained totally unbound by "numbers." All this leads one to the conviction that for Africa, as far as the public performance of the heroic narrative is concerned, we must abandon those formal distinctions between prose and verse that literate judgment has taught us—if only for the fact that the performing bard does many other things which make up the poetry of his act, and cannot therefore afford to be held within narrow prosodic confines.

The alternative conclusion, to which we are logically led by this absence of a rigid formal distinction between prose and verse, is that there is nothing particularly prosodic about the formular device. No doubt we have all, at one time or another, seen a little child pressured to explain how he got involved in a fight. He knows that if he does not keep up a steady flow of narration, he will be judged guilty. But his vocabulary is limited, and he cannot manage an easy twist of details so as to present a winning case. His laboring imagination has nothing to fall back on but the most available conjunctives, such as "And I said," "And he said," or "Then I said," "Then he said." He clings to these phrases and may tend to overuse them, happy to have something that saves his argument from collapsing. Very much the same thing happens in adult oral composition. In this case there is a much greater variety of phrases, but that is because the bard has done the song many times before and can remember many more phrases that served him well. The regularity of phrases is determined not so much by the formal context of delivery as by the pressure of steady composition; in the case of our little boy, his formula is orchestrated by nothing but his anxiety. And if we also recall that formulas are often used even in prose narratives unaccompanied by any musical instruments,[39] we will no doubt agree that the formular device is simply a case of memory pressed into a pattern of convenience and is by no means peculiar to a prosodic context, much less to a ritual purpose. One must therefore take the following judgment by Lord with some caution: "Formulas and groups of formulas, both large and small, serve only one purpose. They provide a means for telling a story in song and verse."[40] The saving grace in this statement is the implication that a song may not necessarily be in verse.

IV

Indeed, the major breakthrough in recent scholarship on the epic has been the recognition of the essential structural looseness of narrative composition, its tendency toward a certain flexibility and modification. Perhaps because of Parry's earlier preoccupation in his researches on this subject, the formula was construed by many scholars to represent a kind of static, repetitive unit—undue emphasis was laid on repeated phrases and lines, which were even counted statistically—until it looked as if we were never going to get any further than these monotonous stereotypes. But, in more recent years, scholarship has succeeded in shifting attention away from the fixed and on to the variable aspect of the formular unit.

The foundations for this shift may well have been laid a few decades ago by Sir Maurice Bowra, who had a somewhat looser conception of the formula than Parry did.[41] Thereafter, in various books and articles, scholars like Hainsworth, Hoekstra, Russo, and Nagler[42] have endeavored to uphold the formula more for the potential it gives it for creative variations than for its role largely as a mnemonic tether in oral narrative composition. Nagler's book, *Spontaneity and Tradition*, is perhaps the most up-to-date statement on this principle of the creative uses of memory. It modifies the peculiarly Parryan tendency toward a rigid word count. Nagler has not entirely abandoned this attitude; like every scholar of the oral epic, he seems ever to feel the stern shadow of Milman Parry lurking in the peripheries of his path. But he does give this field of scholarship a certain breath of fresh air by applying some of the useful idioms and approaches of linguistics and anthropology.

Roughly stated, his book argues that the bard, in his narration, is guided not so much by the memory of specific words and details as by a subsumed frame—whih Nagler variously calls "Gestalt" and "motif." The motif is simply a frame of reference. For instance, the idea of stepping out into a hall with or without a group of attendants, or of killing an enemy in battle, can be used in any number of situations. If many such situations occur within the compass of one song or within a tradition of songs with which the bard is familiar, then there is already a neat package and progression within which he can fit in any number of details as each particular situation demands. The guiding criterion is simply that of a rough cognation; it is by no means imperative that all the details recognized for one situation be present in another. This leaves the bard enormous room for any amount of manipulation he may be forced or inclined to make as he faces the audience. "In the nature of spontaneous-traditional composition," says Nagler, "no one passage can be expected to show explicit realizations of all possible elements, nor need there be any one element common to every passage; to see the forest, one must simply make one's way through the trees by mental brachiation from one likely association to the next."[43]

This theory offers a long-overdue consolation to those phrases and passages which, because the odd familiar word or detail has been altered or omitted, have been isolated from the happy company of Parry's "formulas" and "themes." Those who have been inclined to see the formula in more rigid terms have often been perplexed or disappointed when a phrase or a line starts off in a familiar pattern but does not end as they expected. They conclude that the poet's memory is unreliable. In extreme cases, if the scholar is an editor working with a transcribed text, he tries to alter the new elements to what he thinks they should be on the basis of earlier passages of that kind: the Alexandrian copyists of the Homeric texts are known to have done this sort of thing often.[44] In this way, we are inclined to see the poet more as a slave to a fossilized pattern than as a skillful manipulator of sounds and ideas that continually suggest themselves to his mind in the rather challenging circumstances of his act. What Nagler has done is to see the formula primarily as a set-up giving scope for any number of words, phrases, or ideas that have either a kindred meaning or impact or a certain phonological kinship. That, basically, is his concept of the Gestalt or motif.

It is possible, I think, to distinguish between various levels of allomorphy which the concept of motif allows for. The first level involves those situations in which there is a relatively high percentage of repetition of familar details; a scene does start off in a familiar way, but it ends differently from a previous one because the bard has to take account of the new environment in which the motif is being deployed. Let us take the following two passages from *Sunjata* II as an example. Sumanguru has consulted these two marabouts about a child who, he hears, will in due course destroy him and his kingdom. The first marabout gives Sumanguru his findings:

(a)

    I went into retreat
For forty days;
I saw the seven layers of the sky,
Right to where they finish;
I saw the seven layers of the earth,
Right to where they finish;
I saw a black thing in a pond:
By the grace of God,
The creature which comes and gives me information in the night
Came and stood beside me and said,
"Allahu aharu rajaku fa mang kaana kaafa,
Ming muusi, janafang kumfai kuna."
God declares that by his grace,
Whomsoever he has created king,
He has made in his own likeness,
And nothing will be able to injure that person.
Those things which you must enjoy,
Enjoy them now, before this child is born,
For after he is born,
You will be powerless against him.
If you do not believe that,
You should release two white cocks within your compound,
And name one of them after yourself,
And one after this child.
Since you do not know his name,
You must mark it in some way;
You must fashion pure gold
And put it on your namesake's leg,
And you must fashion pure silver
And put it on the leg of the child's one.

(285-314)

The idea, of course, is that the two cocks should fight, which they

163

later do; the cock marked for Sunjata kills the one marked for Sumanguru.

The second marabout has been set a similar task. Of his report to Sumanguru we are told:

(b)
He too went into retreat;
After forty days he came out.
He came and said to Susu Sumanguru Baamagana,
"I have seen the seven layers of the sky,
Right to where they end:
I have seen the seven layers of the earth,
Right to where they end;
The creature which often stands beside me
Came and stood beside me,
A spirit in human form,
And it said to me, 'Hata nuta
Muslama utiya rusululai,
Wollahi alamu.'
It said that a created thing will not know God.
God declared that he had ordained this* and it could not be altered.
But if you do not believe it,
You must give two white rams as charity.
You must name one of them after yourself,
And the name of the person whom you fear,
That person whom God will make manifest,
His name must you give to the other ram.
You must watch those two white rams,
Because what happens with them
Will, if you touch this child,
Happen also with the two of you."

(449-74)

Later the two white rams fight, and the Sunjata ram kills the other.

*Sunjata's kingship.

The level of similarity between these two passages diminishes as we move further from their thematized beginnings. After the details about the retreat and the view of the Ptolemaic universe, the marabouts differ progressively on the natures of their epiphanies and revelations. And yet the details of both consultations are very closely related; the allomorphy is not very high. The pattern is essentially the same: a familiar figure appears in a vision and prophesies in some form of Arabic; the marabout interprets the message and prescribes what Sumanguru could do if he doubted his word. And the details echo one another rather strongly: the one set of Arabic words are just as much nonsense as the other; the message is about God's supreme will which cannot be contested, and the animals to be used as a test are both white. We are still working here within a compact frame that is not really different from Lord's concept of the "theme."

Something of this compact frame is reflected in two scenes that may be taken to represent a "motif of error and correction" in *Lianja*. In the first scene, Bolumbu's mother twice disobeys Bolumbu's request not to order her mysterious child, Yendembe, to do anything. While Bolumbu is away, the old woman twice compels the child to pluck her some bananas; the child dies each time but is revived by its mother with a drop of medicine in the nose. Later, of course, the error is irremediable (14ff.). In the second scene, Ilele twice disobeys his wife Mbombe's order (delivered in a dream) not to tell his name to anyone on their way to Ilele's home town; each time he disobeys, he is killed by the stranger but revived by Mbombe with a drop in the nose (32ff.). In these scenes, the echoes are strong, and the allomorphs have a rather close kinship.

A second type of motif—in which the level of allomorphy is somewhat higher than in the above examples—gives us a considerable insight into the associative nature of the oral narrative art.

In this category, a detail from one scene only needs to be mentioned in another, and it immediately drags into this second scene other details with which it was associated in the first scene. Let us take another look at passage (a) (from *Sunjata* II) above, noting the details about the cocks: they are white, and they are to be treated, one with gold and the other with silver. Now let us compare that scene in which Sumanguru reveals to Sunjata's sister the only thing that can destroy him:

"There is only one thing," he said, "which will kill me:
A one year old cock which crows,
Provided it is a white fowl,
He said, "You will catch it and kill it,
And you must remove its spur,
And you must put pure gold dust and pure silver dust inside it,
And you must put it in a gun.
If you shoot me with that,
I shall die."

(1659-67)

It would appear to be the tradition that Sumanguru was effectively neutralized or killed by Sunjata by means of a weapon poisoned with the spur of a white cock—all the available versions state that fact. If this is the case, then one is strongly tempted to suggest that it is the prospect of that fact that has influenced Banna Kanute to introduce a white cock in the earlier scene where Sumanguru's destruction is foretold by a marabout; the marabout scene may simply be a foreshadowing. The simple motif that links the two scenes is the death of Sumanguru, which is strongly connected with a white cock (for whatever reason, mystical or mythical). It makes no difference in what context the motif of his death occurs—whether the prophesy of a marabout or confrontation on the battlefield. It simply follows that the details about gold and silver will fall into place in the combination. Alternatively, all we need is a reference to the death of Sumanguru, and we find the details of white cock, gold, and silver following suit; the death is the basic "preverbal Gestalt" (to use Nagler's phrase) that transcends all contexts in which it may be realized. We can therefore represent the frame of associations in either of the following ways:

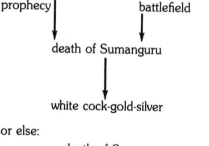

prophecy

battlefield

death of Sumanguru

white cock-gold-silver

or else:

death of Sumanguru

white cock-gold-silver

The level of allomorphy as revealed in this category of motif is evidently higher than in the case of the two marabouts quoted earlier. Here the motif of Sumanguru's death is roughly the same in both cases, but the contexts of its gestation are not at all similar. The dissimilarity of contexts is the major consideration in a similar example from *Kambili*. When Bari the shaman is about to consult his oracles on the chances of Kanji's having an heir, he prepares a divination charm in a pot, warning the wives of Kanji (who are present) to turn their backs at once, because

(*Passage 1*)

No woman can see a Komo's pot.
If your eye falls on the Komo's pot,
    Your body will swell.

> Head lice will land on you.
> Body lice will cover you.
> They will rustle in your hair,
> And get in your underarm hair,
> And go attack the hair of your crotch.
> Don't you look at my pot.

(1000-18)

The oracles having declared that Dugo will be the mother of the hero, Bari then has to find a way of getting Kanji and the woman together without arousing the envy of the other wives. So he sets up a trick: he declares that he is "going to put my talents into action" to enable Kanji to have a child. He warns the wives that for a certain number of weeks none of them should look into Kanji's sleeping hut.

(*Passage* 2)

> Should you put your head in there,
> The Komo pot will get you,
> And swell up your body.
> You will get stuck in the door of the hut.
> Head lice will cover you.
> Body lice will cover you.
> They will rustle in all your hair.
> They will make your underarm hair rustle.
> And go twist and turn the hairs of your crotch.
> Don't dare go near that pot.

(1356-65)

After a month, during which Kanji and Dugo have been making love unbeknownst to the other women, the favorite wife becomes impatient; she rushes out of her quarters, snatches Bari's medicine pot, and smashes it on the ground, declaring it a worthless device. The shaman reacts with a curse: the favorite wife must procure a white sacrificial kola nut, or disaster will surely strike her.

(*Passage* 3)

If you don't bring out a white kola
And sacrifice it to my birth pot ...
Ah! Favored wife, you will swell up,
You will stick in the door of the hut
And there you will become a corpse.
Body lice will cover you.
Head lice will cover you.
They will rustle all your hair,
And rustle the hair under your arms,
And twist and turn the hair of your crotch,
If you refuse the kola.

(1422-32)

Much later on in the story, Bari is to be involved in yet another preparation of a charm or spell. The climax comes with the fight between Kambili and the formidable lion-man, Cekura. In order to destroy Cekura's magical powers, Bari sends Kumba, the wife of Kambili who was previously Cekura's wife, to procure certain articles from the lion-man's body; these articles will then be subjected to a spell. Says Bari to Kumba:

(*Passage* 4)

Bring me a headhair,
Yes, bring me a hair of the lion's head,
And bring some hair from under his arm,
And bring some hair from his crotch,
And bring the sandal off his foot,
And bring a pair of his old pants,
And lay them on the omen board.
When we find a means to the man-eating lion,
Should we do that, the man-eating lion will die.

(2242-50)

In passages 1, 2, and 3, it is clear that Bari is delivering a curse.

169

The basic details of the curse are the swelling of the body and the attack of lice on clusters of hair on the victim's body, and in each case there is a touch of indignation (whether real or feigned) in the shaman. Those three passages would therefore qualify strongly as themes in the Parry-Lord sense, since the bard has used the same ingredients in three independent and progressive contexts. But we do not get quite the same effect in passage 4. To be sure, the relationships between this passage and the first three are significant. There is the idea of a spell, involving a woman. There is no indignation as such, but the injunction is the product of a long and frenzied oracular consultation (2210-41); so there is the same basis of an emotive charge. But in passage 4 the curse/spell is not even ready; and in place of lice attacking the hair of the victim, we have an instruction to Kumba to go and procure not only hair but a number of other things connected with Cekura's body.

Passages 1, 2, and 3 therefore qualify as themes, but passage 4 does not, in spite of Lord's qualifying statement that "the theme is in reality protean";[45] the context of passage 4 is just not the same, and the theory of theme rests on similarity of context. Between passage 4 and the others there is only a notional "corresponsion."[46] Lice regularly attack clusters of hair, so it makes a lot of sense for the details of head, underarm, and crotch to be enumerated. In passage 4—though one is careful not to take Bari's mystical business lightly—there seems no particular reason why the hair should come from all those parts. The only accountable reason for the details of the head, underarm, and crotch occurring in passage 4 is that, once the bard has thought about *hair* in relation to a spell, he immediately thinks head, underarm, and crotch. His "art language" is basically an associative one that cuts across situations. We may construct the following representative pattern for the above passages:

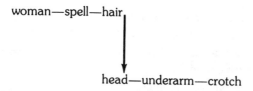

woman—spell—hair

head—underarm—crotch

We may be quite sure that if the bard were to have in his story a scene in which Kambili was driven to singe an opponent's hair, the hero would be made to invade those three parts of the body; for hair immediately suggests those parts. The device is well within the associative resources of his art; every echo, of idea as well as sound, is well worth exploiting, if only because it will help the bard sustain the steady flow of his song.

We have moved from examining a pattern of motifs with similar contexts but a number of variant elements to one with different contexts but a potential for an association of cognate elements. We now come to a final category of motifs that can be considered "preverbal" in the broadest sense of the term. Motifs of this kind perhaps go beyond the limited style or repertoire of the individual artist and belong in a body of myths known either to a community of artists who continually re-create it or to a more universal pattern for which there are no ascertainable origins. The Stith Thompson index gives us the ultimate information so far on this category; all the artist has is a broad, general concept that transcends everything from the man and the situation to the very details that illustrate the motif.

Many scholars are not very happy about this proliferation of terminologies—formula, theme, motif, etc.[47]—but I think there is a basic distincition that is worth making. The distinction between theme and motif may be a fine one; but there is clearly a qualitative difference between the narration of a standard action in which we can recognize a tendency to employ the same or very much the same details, and a situation in which the details do not matter nearly so much as the broad—indeed, vague—general background from which they derive.

Eliot Youman makes an interesting point in his examination of themes in the Homeric *Iliad*;[48] his understanding of the word "theme" was innovative and approaches the more Naglerian concept of the "Gestalt" or "motif." The level of allomorphy is exceedingly high in the variety of examples he gives, as we can see from an examination of a few of those passages. One theme he designates, "not destined to enjoy a long marriage," as exemplified by a number of scenes. The first of these has to do with Protesilaus, who has led a contingent of warriors to Troy:

τότε δ᾽ ἤδη ἔχεν κάτα γαῖα μέλαινα.
τοῦ δὲ καὶ ἀμφιδρυφὴς ἄλοχος Φυλάκηι ἐλέλειπτο
καὶ δόμος ἡμιτελής.

but now the black earth had closed him under,
whose wife, cheeks torn for grief, was left behind in Phylake
and a marriage half completed.

(*Iliad* 2.699-701)

The second passage is from Andromache's lament to Hektor as he prepares to go back to the fighting:

Δαιμόνιε, φθίσει σε τὸ σὸν μένος, οὐδ᾽ ἐλεαίρεις
παῖδά τε νηπίαχον καὶ ἔμ᾽ ἄμμορον, ἣ τάχα χήρη
σεῦ ἔσομαι.

Dearest, your own strength will be your death, and you have no pity
on your little son, nor on me, ill-starred, who soon must be your widow.

(6.407-8)

The third describes Iphidamas, who has left wife and home in search of martial glory:

γήμας δ' ἐκ θαλάμοιο μετὰ κλέος ἵκετ' Ἀχαιῶν

Married, he went away from the bride chamber, looking for glory from the Achaians.

(11.227)

The rest of this passage describes how Iphidamas is killed in combat by Agamemnon. The rest of Youman's discussion of this motif mentions (among other things) how Achilles, foreseeing an early death in war, refuses when Agamemnon offers the hand of his daughter in marriage as part of the settlement of their quarrel.

These can only be called "themes" by a forced analogy, for they are far from belonging to the same level of cognation as, for example, those "typical scenes" of entertainment in the *Odyssey*. The echoes are too faint (the diction in one scene scarcely suggests that in another) and the variants a little too remote from one another for us to see the passages otherwise than as deriving from a vague common background or motif. The wood—to use Nagler's imagery—may look somewhat familiar, but one would need to wade through a large number of trees to be able to recognize it. Yet, for the very skill with which the poet is able to fashion new material and fit it into a given mold, he should be accounted more poetic than if he were to belabor the same scenes and diction endlessly. There are echoes, but they remain just that; every scene has an almost entirely independent life though it belongs in a larger community of ideas.

The entire compass of the heroic tale is built on motifs of this kind. In the last chapter, we talked about the tendency of the tale to make selective use of sentiments and ideas; we cited examples from *Mwindo* and the *Iliad* to show how the bard is able to build a whole collage of moments from a mere handful of concepts reinforced with an accumulation of details. This is very much the principle that operates in this final category of motifs. We can illustrate the point with *Ozidi*. A seminal motif there can be described as "success after initial setbacks." If we can grasp the implications of this motif, we will have taken account of the entire plot of the story; for on that pattern is built just about every episode of confrontation, and the story is largely an assemblage of confrontations. The motif provides the scheme by which the Ozidi family first suffers the assasssination of the senior Ozidi, and rises again to triumph with the birth of the boy-hero and his steady elimination of one opponent after another, from the assassins right down to the Smallpox King and his attendants. It also explains why the little Ozidi first fails the trials of courage that his witch-grandmother, Oreame, sets up for him in the bush but overcomes his weaknesses thereafter (14-22); why the confused Awka blacksmith fails twice in his attempt to fashion a sword for Ozidi but succeeds the third time (42-47); and why, in the various fights that Ozidi undertakes, he is first overcome by his opponent, but rises—after Oreame has in turn failed and then succeeded in finding the right magical counter to the discomfiture—and defeats the other with little trouble.

Even the array of opponents is guided by a principle that we may call "the hero's enemy appears insuperable." There is always something unusual about each successive opponent—one has a giant scrotum, another has seven heads, yet another walks on his head—that makes the audience think, "How is he going to deal with this strange creature? This time he's finished!" In fact, there is a certain gradation—sensed by the audience—in the gravity of the menaces that the hero faces. Azezabife boasts to Ozidi that he is not the one to stand arrested in one spot, like the last victim, Agbogidi, for Ozidi to slash up as he likes (70); the Scrotum King boasts that, though Ozidi has killed or put everyone else to rout, there is no way the boy can get past his giant scrotum (210); and several other victims reveal exaggerated notions of their superiority, right down to the Smallpox King himself, who hopes to put an end to this evil boy who has laid a whole nation waste (375f).[49]

I am not attempting here to construct any kind of unitarian logic about the structure of *Ozidi* or any other heroic tales of the kind. It is well known that the order observed for one performance (or series of performances) may not be observed for another. In *Ozidi*, the encounter with the Smallpox King remains the last in the series because a long tradition of narration has sanctioned that position; but the order of the details within the main body of the tale can be altered depending on how they come to the mind of the bard or appeal to certain moods. The sort of "climax" that Youman recognizes in the pattern of "themes" in the *Iliad*[50] should therefore be taken with a grain of salt. Even if we accept a build-up of details for one narration, we may be faced with a different build-up in the next narration of the same tale. Though the bard is inclined to make an increasing impact on his audience, every episode has a force all its own, and the whole structure can be altered at will, though the tendency toward a mounting effect remains the same. The heroic tale, as we have constantly observed, is little more than a narrative collage of affective moments and moods.

We shall end this discussion of typical scenes by examining some of the broader implications of our discoveries. First, how useful is this device of matching one scene with another? I believe Lord first pointed out that narrative inconsistencies in heroic tales are often traceable to the bard's tendency to transfer to one situation a narrative idea or theme originally employed in another situation; he illustrates his point with a reference to the Yugoslav guslar Demail Zogic, who interpolates the theme of the poor hero who borrows his arms into a scene of recognition.[51] It seems obvious that unless the device is cleverly handled, the bard is likely to spoil the credibility of his work. It may not matter to the audience, which often is too carried away by the total impact of the moment to detect the occasional "nod" of the artist. But the fact does matter for our understanding of the creative processes of the oral narrative art.

We must be careful, however, not to dismiss as a slip the occasional detail in a passage that may appear to be extraneous to its context or to belong more properly in another body of information. One example from *Kambili* springs readily to mind; it appears in that scene where the bard warns Samory Toure about the grievous consequences of punishing Nerikoro, the soothsayer attached to the cult of smiths, who fails to solve the riddle of the hero-child. Says the bard:

Nerikoro, the Komo man has come!
  Fakoli was a smith, Samory!
  If an insult is made to a smith, pleasure will sour.

(536-38)

Fakoli is not a character in *Kambili*, but in the Sunjata legend. Yet we cannot rightly call his introduction here an interpolation or a narrative inconsistency. He is mentioned here simply as a warning to Samory. "Remember Fakoli," the bard seems to say, "how an insult to him brought Samanguru to grief"—very much as Christ uses Lot's wife, or Mohammed the examples of fallen cities, as a warning to men against certain evil tendencies.

We would, however, regard as a narrative inconsistency that detail in *Sunjata* II in which the bard makes gunpowder out of cockspur mixed with gold and silver dust (1663ff.). In defiance of "tradition," perhaps in an effort to impress his listeners with the modernity of his repertoire, the bard has decided to use a gun instead of an arrow as a weapon, unaware that he is violating all probability. A mixture of those ingredients could be glued to the tip of an arrow, but it is difficult to see how such a mixture could fire from a gun. And, if the combination of cockspur, gold, and silver dust is indeed suggested by that earlier scene where they occur in connection with the prescriptions of a marabout (305ff.)—as the bard himself seems to imply soon after (317ff.)—then it becomes quite clear that he has simply transferred a stock of elements from one context into another without making the necessary adjustments.

But there is a far more serious inconsistency which the use of typical scenes and motifs tends to promote. We argued in chapter 1, in our discussion of the relation between myth and ritual, that the confrontation between Ozidi and the Smallpox King can hardly be seen in the light of retribution and purification, in spite of societal interpretations of the attack of such diseases in those terms. What the bard has done is to subject Smallpox to the same pattern of confrontation that the hero has survived with earlier opponents: Smallpox wants to test his powers against Ozidi confident that he will put an end to the menace of the hero; he succeeds in putting Ozidi out at first; Oreame probes around and finds an antidote to Smallpox's powers; the hero recovers from the initial setback, pounces on Smallpox, and destroys him. It may well be that the bard had in mind the communal rite of retribution and cleansing; but his *Kunstsprache* demands the deployment of certain patterns that make it difficult for him to be flawlessly loyal to that rite.

Something of this inconsistency with communal rite may be seen in the *Iliad* when Achilles slaughters twelve Trojan captives, among other creatures, in retaliation for the killing of his friend Patroklos:

[He] drove four horses with long necks
swiftly along the pyre with loud lamentations. And there were
nine dogs of the table that had belonged to the lord Patroklos.

Of these he cut the throats of two, and set them on the pyre;
and so also killed twelve noble sons of the greathearted Trojans
with the stroke of bronze, and evil were the thoughts in his heart against
them,
and let loose the iron fury of the fire to feed on them.

(23.171-77)

Nilsson has argued that in this passage Homer "does not understand the custom, he does not know that such things were intended to serve the dead man in another world."[52] But I think the explanation for the anomaly should be sought elsewhere. Not only does the powerful diction reveal the conscious affective intent of the bard; the passage has an equally significant structural place. Youman has more correctly identified Achilles' purpose as belonging in a larger motif of that epic which he calls "the mathematical idea of revenge."[53] Revenge and recompense are so overwhelming a motif in the *Iliad* that they seem to shape the entire plot: the punishment of Troy for the abduction of Helen; Achilles' sworn intent to pay back Agamemnon and the Greeks for dishonoring him; the constancy with which Zeus balances the killing on both sides of the fighting line; the restitution Agamemnon and Priam offer to Achilles; and so on. In particular, when a hero loses a companion in battle, he makes sure to kill a certain number of people on the other side, considering this an appropriate exchange for his lost companion. It is therefore no surprise that the same pattern should prevail—and to a larger degree, as is fitting—in the case of Achilles' treatment of the Trojan captives, though it would seem a gross contradiction of the sobriety of the moment for Achilles to be slaughtering people, not on the battlefield, but amid the hallowed rites of burial. The situation is dictated by a structural device that coerces new element into a given pattern. Nagler may seem to be overstating the case when he says that "from a generative viewpoint . . . all narrative episodes are 'type scenes' ."[54] From our considerations above, it is hard to see how one can disagree with him.

A second implication of the motif theory, which Nagler has identified and which I believe I established from a somewhat different angle, is the pointlessness of making any distinctions between prose and verse. Nagler still finds his phonemic and lexical echoes within verse units or *cola*, but that is because he is working mostly with a Homer that has been severely cosmetized by ages of editing. Still, in place of metrical cola, Nagler speaks of "psychological cola or rhythmical groups of some sort bearing a hitherto undetermined relation to formulas, and based upon factors that are not always statistically quantifiable . . . . Whatever may be the larger implications of these observations for metrical theory," he continues, "it is clear that objective metrical criteria, as now known, will not provide an indispensable *differentia* for every member" of those groups of phrases in Homer echoing one another.[55] I have used the formal patterns of *Mwindo* and *Ozidi* to demonstrate that, in view of the prosodic looseness that characterizes most African oral art, a system of analysis overemphasizing statistical count, and thereby setting up distinctions between prose and verse, may not take us very far. But since music accompanies performances (whether in prose or in verse) and makes all the difference to the balance of the performance, we should concentrate on how the music works in relation to the words,[56] not on how often a particular phrase is replaced by another containing the same number of syllables and occurring in the same part of the "verse." Musicologists could help us here.

V

A major formal issue concerns the internal movement of the heroic narrative—its mode of expansion and contraction. Here again, if we can but see the tale in the live, oral context, we will be able to understand why internally it works a little differently from the written story.[57] I am not sure that in an oral epic it makes that much sense to talk about the "unity" of the material, a tendency in a good deal of Homeric scholarship, inspired largely by Aristotelian notions of wholeness.

Admittedly, there is a beginning, a middle, and an end very much along the lines that Aristotle has identified. No one took greater care than the oral artist to announce the progressive stages of his work; the beginning and the end are at least very clear. In many cases, the bard will announce the broad subject of the story and offer some sort of prefatory comments and observations. What Innes says about the eighty-one-line prelude of *Sunjata* III is particularly illuminating:

The main purpose of this prelude is probably to give the listeners time to make the mental switch from the everyday world in which they find themselves to the heroic world of the Sunjata era. The griot cannot plunge straight into his narrative without giving his audience time to make the mental adjustment needed for the proper enjoyment of his narrative. The prelude helps to create the appropriate mental set toward the forthcoming narration.[58]

In *Kambili*, we have an exeptionally long proemium that not only announces the remote and immediate subjects of the story—*Ah! Master, Kanji and his good journey!* (1) and "The Jimini conflict was not easy" (114)—but also presents in numerous gnomes the overall outlook of the world of the story. In *Sunjata* IV, Djeli Mamoudou, after establishing his claims to truth and authority, announces that the subject of his tale is Sunjata and the history of Mali (1-2). Homer in the *Iliad* announces the remote and immediate themes of his tale (the will of Zeus, the anger of Achilles), and the format seems to have been maintained in the performances of a later generation, the Homeridae.[59] The Yugoslav guslars also often have elaborate preambles to their songs.[60]

Sometimes, too, the end of the song can be quite clearly expressed. *Sunjata* IV ends markedly with praises of the immortal nation built by the hero and with various saws and admonitions. *Sunjata* I.872-1305 (nearly a third of the entire story) is a didactic coda documenting the history of Mali kings and culture from the time of Sunjata. *Mwindo* ends with a moralistic epilogue, and *Kambili* with a long praise song in honor of Kumba, the loyal wife. In Yugoslavia the bard often ends by observing that he has sung his song as he has heard it.

But perhaps what counts most significantly in the oral song is the behavior of the details in that "middle" portion of the song; this is where it shows a marked difference from a written story. The writer moves consciously toward a *telos*, avoiding "redundancies" like repetitions; in this way he presents us with a final product whose parts neatly guide us toward its resolution.[61] But the oral artist continually postpones the *telos* of his tale, using devices that to him are not redundancies but are a welcome part of the full package in a successful performance. It is true that he remains ever aware of where he is going and tries to prevent his tale from breaking down. But he does not hesitate to expand the material at every chance he gets. In a discussion of the internal behavior of the oral epic, therefore, instead of Aristotelian unity we should speak of fullness; the effect is achieved not by an unwavering pursuit of the end of the tale but by an expansion and ventilation of the body.

There are several modes of ventilation in the oral narrative song. One of these is the use of gnomic lines and passages, proverbs, and other reflections. The *Kambili* epic in particular is characterized by an extensive use of these gnomic reflections and aphorisms. More often they exist as independent, paratactic comments in their own right, merely demonstrating the bard's virtuosity at articulating various saws at a high speed. But sometimes they

181

expand on an idea suggested by or emanating from a scene in the story, rather in the style of choral strophes in Aeschylean drama. There are two good examples of this in *Kambili*. The first relates to the trial of skills between the Muslim "holyman" and the hunters' sorcerer Bari, during the Kambili riddle. The former is about to set up a ruse aimed at confounding Bari and ensuring Bari's failure to solve the riddle; so he sends Bari off to kill game and fetch it, the idea being to get him out of the way while the snare is laid.

Bari the Omen Reader went off into the bush, Allah.
The learned holyman will prepare a plot in Bari's
    absence.
Ah! Treachery is not good!
Treachery always ends up on its author.
When the well gets old,
Its frame no longer sees the light of day.
It has fallen down into the well.

(1147-53)

In time, says the bard, the holyman's treachery will catch up with him, just as in time the frame of the well caves in upon it. Or take the scene in which Kumba is commissioned to bring some of the hair and clothes of the lion-man Cekura. Before she leaves, she announces her mission to her new husband, Kambili, and the bard reflects on the power of women:

If you are not afraid of females, Master,
If you are not afraid of females,
You're not afraid of anything.
The woman's hand knows how to strike a man's
    desires in any case.

(2275-78)

The reflection is significant because, in her enumeration of the things that she has been asked to get from Cekura (2270-74),

Kumba has left out the detail about the hair from the lion-man's crotch: evidently, this has been done to avoid stirring the suspicions of her new husband, Kambili. As the bard suggests, a woman surely has the key to a man's sensitivities!

The bards of the Sunjata story also use these strophic passages. Niane's edition has some good examples. It is not exactly clear how the griot framed them in the original text, but they must have punctuated the old bard's story with just as much measured pith and cogency as we have them now. Sometimes they comment on a past event, and sometimes they reflect on a growing tendency with a pointedly fatalistic tone, as in the observation on the corrupting influence of power in the fortunes of Sumanguru:

The tree that the tempest will throw down does not see the storm building up on the horizon. Its proud head braves the winds even when it is near its end. Soumaoro had come to despise everyone. Oh! how power can pervert a man. If man had but a mithkal of divine power at his disposal the world would have been annihilated long ago. Soumaoro arrived at a point where he would stop at nothing. (*Sunjata* IV.41)

There are a good many aphorisms in Homer.[62] They are mostly tied up with a character's speech, but often they appear at the end of it, so that one is tempted to see them more as the poet's thoughts than the character's words.[63] In *Beowulf* there are many reflective passages, often delivered in a pretentiously Christian tone either independently by the poet or as part of a character's speech.[64] In these several ways the heroic narrative receives an internal airing. There is a consistently outward or centrifugal movement, which rescues the story from the narrow compass of the bare details of action.

Another mode of ventilation is the use of passages with a certain operatic or fuguelike flavor to them, passages in which the bard lends an added touch of the musical feeling to the general run of his narrative: we may call the phenomenon the song within a song. Such passages usually take the form of duets, or lyrical chants, or songs sung by a bard who is a character in the story. We have numerous examples of this airing device in *Kambili*. The Ode to Nunkulumba, ancestor of the smiths (545ff.), the operatic duet between Bari the sorcerer and Dugo the estranged wife (873ff.), the Ode to Jealousy (1650ff.), and the final paean to Kumba (2693ff.) are all devices to infuse fresh life into the bare account of the Jimini conflict. In *Sunjata* IV, the story is punctuated now and then by chants credited to Balla Fasseke, griot to the hero, such as the "Hymn to the Bow" (21), the instant praise song for Suman-guru (40), the "Niama" (75), and the "Hymn to Abundance" (79). *Mwindo* has countless chants in which the hero flouts his enemies, or celebrates himself, or summons his magical powers; the same is true of *Ozidi* and *Lianja*. Whatever the event may be, in such cases there is a certain lilt to the performance; the bard simply abandons himself to the lyrical resources of his tale.

We have similar effects in Homer. The friendly dialogue be-tween Diomedes and Glaukos in *Iliad* 6 may not readily be seen as a ventilative device, but it has surely been introduced to give not merely a touch of fellow feeling but also a lyrical respite from the cheerless sequence of deathly blows and savage words in combat. Perhaps the most brilliant fuguelike piece in all of Homer is that scene in which Idomeneus and Meriones celebrate their valors (*Iliad* 13.248-327);[65] it is clear that the poet is giving vent to a lyrical feeling and joyfully breaking out of the narrow confines of narrating battle action. Other examples of the song within a song are the performances of Demodokos in the *Odyssey*. In these ventilative moments Homer can choose to be either lighthearted, as in Demodokos' song about the luckless love of Ares and Aphro-dite, or heavy, as in the Trojan story that brings Odysseus to tears. The touch of sadness is more apparent in the lyrical lament, as in the mourning of Hektor (*Iliad* 24.725-75).[66] The lyrical scenes have been woven rather neatly into their contexts, though we cannot be too sure that we have them the way an oral Homer would have sung them.[67]

A further evidence of accretion or expansion in the oral epic is the presence of digressions, internal and external. The internal digression is a product of the subtle associative tendencies of the creative imagination, and the potential for it is particularly high in an open performance in which the bard is under the stress of steady delivery. One word or idea suggests a similar one until the imagination is entangled in a chain of closely connected ideas. There is an interesting case of the internal digression in *Mwindo*. Mwindo has been translated into the sky by the lightning god Nkuba, who cautions him against further heroic excesses. In a chant, the hero laments that it was his father that pushed him into the problems that he has caused. At this point, however, the bard is getting tired and pleads to be replaced by one of his accompanists:

My little father threw me into palavers.
Substitute, replace me now!
My father believed that I would faint away;
He threw me into palavers.

(140)

The significant line here is the third. The bard is actually exhausted and is afraid that he "would faint away" if he was not replaced. But the idea has a delicate connection with the hero's conflict with his father. When his father heard that a baby boy had been born to him, he devised several ways of destroying it, and the last measure he took was to have it stuffed into a drum and dropped in a pool of water in the swamp, in the hope that the baby would be stifled to death. But the boy eventually escapes from the drum and de-

185

clares war on his father, pursuing him in a series of adventures in which the hero demonstrates his defiance of and superiority over the natural and supernatural worlds. So it was his father's original attempt to stifle him—to make him "faint away"—that has brought the hero into a palaver with Nkuba; but the detail has been brought in by an associative imagination grappling with the bard's desperate need of a substitute!

A similar situation occurs in *Ozidi*. The hero has been rendered powerless by the magic spell of one of his opponents, Akpobrisi. Ozidi's grandmother, Oreame, beats about frantically but is unable to find a counter to the spell. The scene is well into the third night of the performance of the story; Okabou, the bard, is already feeling the strains of the job, and his tiredness finds fitting articulation in the plight of the cramped and powerless hero. The following passage, which captures the plight of the bard and the efforts of the audience to give him new energy, begins when Oreame disappears to search for further aid against the enemy:

This woman, that instant, flew out of sight.
       [Laughter]
Caller: O STORY!
Group: YES!
Okabou: Let those concerned now put in a little. I'm tired. Of course I'm tired.

Though Ozidi bestirred himself, his belly!
Yabuku: Agadaakpen yenyen!*
Okabou: Never pick at fire!†
Although he roused himself, his belly would not respond.
"Oh," he said, "help then . . ."

                     (133-34)

---

* Bard's praise title.
† His usual response to it.

The lines about tiredness, credited to the bard, could be the hero's, and that last cry for help is as much the bard's as it is the hero's: in an internal digression of this kind, the line is not always so easy to draw!

Internal digressions are also to be found in epics from other cultures. Homer, for instance, shows a peculiar strain in his similes. Sometimes one simile follows another in a chain of vaguely complementary images. A good example is the resistance to the Trojans by Telamonian Ajax, which Homer illustrates with a chain of two similes reflecting the attitudes of both attackers and defenders.[68] Sometimes, too, a single simile is internally complicated by one word or idea setting off a fresh image relating to it, as in the following description of the stout advance of Polypoites and Leonteus against the menacing Trojans:

They were in the likeness of two wild boars who in the mountains
await a rabble of men and dogs advancing upon them
and as they go tearing slantwise and rip the timber about them
to pieces at the stock, the grinding scream of their teeth sounds
high, until some man hits them with his throw and takes the life from them:
such was the grinding scream from the bright bronze covering their chests
struck hard on by spears, for they fought a very strong battle....

(*Iliad* 12.146-52)

In this simile, the "grinding scream" is a secondary phenomenon in the charge of the boars, subordinate to the tearing movement of the animals; but it is a powerful picture, so powerful that it dominates the second half of the simile, which normally should have recalled the original picture of the stubborn challenge of the boars.

The internal digression merely expands the scope of an idea within the story, giving it an added compass and flavor; though the imagination strays, the digression is still conceptually tied to its context. The external digression, on the other hand, is clearly extraneous, sometimes intended for a humorous effect. It can often be omitted at little cost to the story's integrity or to the clarity of the particular scene. But it is a sign that the bard is responding to the performance environment. The tale he is telling may have been told countless times, but for him the tradition is by no means frigid and indeed receives fresh relevance and appeal from the warm human context in which it is continually recreated. Hence he feels free to throw in, now and then, comments about himself or observations about members of his audience.

Kambili has a proportionately large number of these external digressions. In the long prefatory passage of gnomic lines that help the bard build up his tempo, he compliments himself, his apprentice Sacko, and the audience:

> *It's the sound of the harp-playing Seydou from Kabaya.*
> *Dugo's Kambili! the lion is evil!*
> *Look to Sacko for the thing not easy for all.*
> *Gaoussou Sacko, I salute you!*
> > *I say, my apprentices, I greet you.*
> > *Guests, I greet you.*
> *Respected guests, I greet you, Allah!*

(53-59)

Another such digressive tribute takes its cue from a praise line to a hunter. In it the bard pays homage to his hunter-patron in superbly elevated language:

> *You who have offered me a skull*
> *As a face-washing bowl,*
> *And offered me a skin*
> *As a covering cloth.*
> *You have given me a great tongue*
> *So that I may speak to the world.*
> *The brave offered me fresh blood*

As face-washing water,
And gave me a tail
As a hut-sweeping broom,
And offered me a thighbone
To use as a toothpick.
It is the hunter who has done this for me.

(240-52)

A similar homage is paid by Banna Kanute to Mr. Sidibe, who organized the performance:

The person on account of whom I am relating this story
Is himself a great one for stories.
His father is Keeba Sidibe,
He is descended from the people of Wasulung . . . .
Keeba Sidibe was the father of this young man
Who has brought myself and this white man* together.
Moreover he himself is sitting,
All ears for the Sunjata story which I am telling.

(*Sunjata* II.391–98)

The external digressions in *Mwindo* present an interesting problem. Like the bard's plea for a substitute (140), they are a bit difficult to isolate from their context because they take their cue from an adjacent word or idea relevant to the story. They can be removed without much harm to the story, but the dexterity with which the bard exploits his associative resources is remarkable. In the following chant, the embattled hero tries, with the aid of his magical powers, to draw away all the comforts belonging to his father, Shemwindo, in the village of Tubondo:

And the chickens that Shemwindo possesses,
May the chickens also join Mwindo.
The cheerleaders are in unison;

*Innes.

189

They thus having achieved unison long ago.
The cheerleaders are in unison;
They have achieved harmony in the middle of the village . . .
The dogs that are in Tubondo,
May the dogs join Mwindo.
The dogs barked, saying,
"Oh father! let us join Mwindo."
We are seated stretching out our voices
Like the diggers of pits.[69]

(85)

The fundamental idea is that of "joining," from the hero's wanting to pull everything away from Tubondo and assemble them all beside him. The idea gives rise to the bard's digressive observation that his musical group ("cheerleaders") has achieved unison and harmony at the scene of their performance. Later in that chant, the dogs respond to the magic call and "bark" their desire to join Mwindo; this in turn moves the bard to note the strain that the interminable singing is exerting on the voices of the group—digging a pit being in itself an endless affair, since the earth is bottomless.

Other external digressions indicate the physical resources of the performance—such as the *Kambili* bard's frequent warnings to his harpists to attend to their strings, or the injunction by the bard of *Akoma Mba* to one of his accompanists to "stop shaking those bells!" (629).

In all these digressions we are reminded that the oral epic belongs in a lively human environment. If we cannot change the "historic truth" of the story, we can at least give it a recognizable contemporary stamp and appeal by paying due tribute to the moment and context of its re-creation. Admittedly, the tendency to do this will vary among bards and communities. But it seems reasonable to suggest that the digressive tendency is characteristic of the narrative song in performance, particularly in a society where such songs depend for their permanence more on re-creation than on recitation.[70]

A final element to consider, which constitutes the real evidence for the accretiveness in the oral epic, is the simple piling-up of details. Milman Parry's view that "there is no example in oral narrative poetry of a detail being interesting by itself"[71] is, I think, only partially true. If we see the tale first as a performance and then as a narration—in which, to quote Lord again, "the tale's the thing"—we will no doubt be better equipped to assess the value of the text at any one point in the story. True, much of the diction does not help the story forward in the geometrical sense; the bard exploits it largely for its affective value in his search for audience empathy and as part of a lyrical act. Take the following chant in *Mwindo*, which describes the hero's magical resuscitation of life and property in the devastated village of Tubondo:

each one who died in pregnancy resuscitated with her
pregnancy;
each one who died in labor resuscitated being in labor;
each one who was preparing paste resuscitated stirring
paste;
each one who died defecating resuscitated defecating;
each one who died setting up traps resuscitated trapping;
each one who died copulating resuscitated copulating;
each one who died forging resuscitated forging;
each one who died cultivating resuscitated cultivating;
each one who died while making pots and jars resuscitated
shaping;
each one who died carving dishes resuscitated carving;
each one who died quarreling with a partner resuscitated
quarreling.

(119)

191

It might make sense to argue that, for the magic to be truly effective, it is necessary for the bard to mention every aspect of life in the village by name. But it is difficult to overlook the sheer comic intent in the detail of copulation, of value primarily for eliciting audience response in an open performance, and only secondarily for the technical needs of the story. A bard who knows his craft will lose no opportunity for establishing rapport by incorporating such a detail in his song.

An even greater sense of fullness is revealed in the following passage from *Kambili*, in which the warrior Kanji laments to Toure that the soothsayers have brought him all loss and no gain in his quest for a child:

The Jimini reason-seekers are evil, Imam!
The reason-seekers have gone through my cow herd.
They have gone through the sheep herd.
They have gone through my goat herd.
And gone through my chicken flock.
They have gone through my good gowns.
They have gone through my good hats.
They have gone through my good caps.
And gone through my good pants.[72]

(155-63)

The effectiveness of such a passage has a great deal to do with its context. As written poetry the passage would probably fail not only for endlessly belaboring its phrases but indeed for its preference for padding over cogency. The argument is not whether the soothsayers took away every one of the items enumerated by Kanji. They may well have done so; but all those details could have been taken care of in one phrase. The bard, in ignoring that device, shows that for him there is special value in stringing details one to another. The method is only relevant in an oral context, which encourages a fullness of effect through elaboration and accretion;

the idea, as Aristotle has said, scarely goes beyond an exhaustion of detail.[73] I believe that in Homer a similar fullness of effect is intended in the numerous battle episodes, the interminable trivia in isolated scenes like the Diomedes-Glaukos colloquy, perhaps even in the Catalogue (in spite of arguable political interests).

We must appreciate why the oral poet has this tendency to ventilate his song and seek a fullness of effect. It is not simply that the pressure of constant delivery forces him into the expediency of repeating himself over and over again. There is also the factor that, invariably, the song or its main subject is known to his audience at large. He is not expected or even inclined to introduce any details into the story which are totally alien to the known facts of it, for that would be an unacceptable violation of "historic truth." The only manipulation that he is therefore permitted is structural and stylistic; the proof of his excellence is in the nature of his presentation of that "historic truth" of which he is an imaginative trustee. Aware of this challenge and of his duty to give his patrons their money's worth, he explores the full and varied potential of the song, expanding the lean, skeletal resources of his legacy. In the final analysis, he is considerably less interested in the meager plot of the story which tradition has put in his hands than in the richness which it might attain through his poetic skill.

We must not, however, leave this issue of the bard's love of detail without asking ourselves a question or two. As we said much earlier, Professor Clark's transcription of *Ozidi* is particularly useful because he has given us a good picture of the atmosphere of performance—as in all those cases in which the bard quarrels with some members of his audience over the odd detail in his narration. A few of the spectators' comments are noteworthy for their insights into the intrinsic poetics of oral art. For instance, in *Ozidi* 343-52, the bard so builds up the details of the confrontation between Oreame and Ozidi on one side and Azema and Azema-roti on the other, that at one point a spectator is moved to interject, "Let nobody flag, you people" (346), and at another point, "Now for the fight!" (351). These comments may be understood to be helping the bard generate excitement. But well into the real fight between the two sides (which takes up quite a few pages), a spectator throws in, "Leave off when he hasn't killed" (367). All this leaves one wondering: When the performing bard piles detail upon detail in his narration, is he merely padding out of self-consciousness and a desire to impress with words, words, words, or has he a more artistic purpose? Is the oral narrative truly built on a spontaneous and paratactic basis, or does the artist consciously withhold and build up carefully toward the climax, in the manner of a modern thriller writer? When we find a spectator telling the bard to "get to the point," how do we—from the text we see before us—draw the line between the virtues of a "fullness of effect" and the possibility that the bard may not in fact be doing such a good job? These are questions well worth pondering.

VI

The spectator's injunction to the *Ozidi* bard to get on with the job indicates that, despite the virtues of fullness, a certain amount of control is needed. The bard himself feels this need sometimes, and that he does is demonstrated by a structural device of the oral epic which has been called "ring composition."[74] The formular and accretive devices ensure the progressive movement and growth of the tale; the ring, on the other hand, brings stabilization and control. The bard's fertile imagination has a tendency now and then to digress from the main track of his story. A word or an idea suggests various associations; a line or an idea recalls an event or a tune; and the imagination is drawn off on a tributary trail. The bard may also feel like giving a few explanatory details on a point that he has made—because he wishes to impress his audience with his fund of knowledge, or because he considers his meaning unclear, or his impact inadequate, without the explanation; he therefore has little hesitation in making a deviation. To be able to continue with the main subject of his performance, he often has to return to the *locus ex quo* by repeating the word, line, or idea that gave rise to the digression. It takes a considerable presence of mind for the bard to pull himself together by this device whereby he "interrelates the parts of his material which are centrifugal."[75]

A fairly simple ring, of the more or less explanatory kind, can be found in Banna Kanute's version of the Sunjata epic. The bard begins to narrate an episode, digresses a bit to drop an etiological note bearing on the episode, then makes a quick return to the main line of the narration. In the following passage, one of the marabouts whom Sumanguru has commissioned to consult their oracles on the coming menace of Sunjata reappears to prescribe that Sumanguru should set two rams against one another to test the truth of his prophesy:

He went into retreat;
After forty days he came out.
That is why,
Among us black people,
A white cock is prescribed as charity,
For every boy.
Afterwards, when you grow up and build your own compound,
A white ram is prescribed as charity for you.
As to the origin of this custom,
This is how it came about.
He too went into retreat;
After forty days he came out.

(*Sunjata* II.439–50)

On Form and Structure

First the episode is begun (A); then the explanation is introduced with "That is why, . . . " (B); the explanation proper follows (C); we return to the introductory idea with "As to the origin of . . . " (B), and finally to the beginning of the episode (A).

A more interesting ring appears in Dembo Kanute's version. It involves that episode in the story where—according to Dembo, for no other available version says so—the griot Dookha (Niane's Doua) is sent on a mission to Sumanguru for military aid; he sees a xylophone hanging on the wall of the king's house and plays a winning tune on it; Sumanguru is so impressed that not only does he put aside Dookha's mission but he forces the griot to stay by cutting his Achilles tendons and renaming him Bala Faasege, reputed ancestor of all present-day griots. This incident hastens the confrontation between Sunjata and Sumanguru. The entire ring commences with Fakoli's seeking volunteers for an expedition aimed at recalling Sunjata to Mali (Manding), which is at the moment under Sumanguru's despotic rule:

Faa Koli asked them "Who will volunteer to join me and go there?"
When he was saying that,
It so happened that when Sunjata had left Manding
At the height of Sumanguru's power,
He came and destroyed Manding nineteen times
And he rebuilt Manding nineteen times.
It is in reference to this that the griots say:
    It is war which destroyed Manding,
    It is war which rebuilt Manding.
Where did that song originate?
It originated with a griot.
Who was that griot?
He was called Nyankuma Dookha.

(Sunjata III.259–71)

The rest of it tells how Dookha fares with Sumanguru, and how the latter ends up cutting the griot's heel and giving him the new name of Bala Faasege (Fasseke) Kuyate. The ring closes with the following lines:

The griots are all descended from that Bala.
The people of Manding heard what had happened to him,
And they say of it that it was that which gave rise
        to the war between Manding and Susu.
He destroyed Manding nineteen times,
He rebuilt Manding nineteen times.
They say, "It was war which destroyed Manding,
It was war which rebuilt Manding."
He became master of Manding.
Faa Koli gathered all the elders of Manding together
And said to them, "Let us go and find Sunjata . . . .

(329-38)

In this whole episode, first there is Fakoli's summons (A); then mention of the destruction and rebuilding of Manding (B); and the popular ditty recalling that war on Manding (C); and finally a detail of origins connected with a griot (D). We return to the story proper via a detail of origins connected with a griot (D); then a detail about war involving Manding (C); next the destruction and rebuilding of Manding (B); the popular ditty (C); and finally Fakoli's summons (A). The mode of expansion and contraction, as well as of associations, is remarkable.

Kambili gives us further examples of the ring device. There is, for instance, that long operatic scene of exchanges between Bari the Shaman and Dugo, Kanji's despised wife, who is destined to bring forth the hero-child (865-935). The scene begins with Bari taking a "horsehead kola" nut to Dugo; the omens have revealed that she will bear the child, and the kola is meant to ensure the

197

success of the affair. When Bari gets to the goatpen in which Dugo has been isolated from the rest of the household, he finds her weeping over her lonely plight. There follows a long operatic dialogue between the two—introduced by the formulaic line: *He said, "Beloved Dugo!" "Yes," the reply*—in which Dugo wails and the shaman tries to console and reassure her. The already inflated piece is further extended by a fresh digression of gnomic lines (927ff.), these having in turn been suggested by the idea of unavoidable death (921ff.). Finally, the story continues with Bari giving Dugo the kola to eat. This superb ring opens with the lines

Bari took the horsehead kola
And went to find Dugo . . .
He said, "Beloved Dugo!" "Yes," the reply

(865-67)

and ends with the lines

And Bari of the Omens said, "Dugo!" "Yes," the reply."
Take this horsehead kola . . . .

(935-36)

It may be said that Dugo's lament is a fresh scene in the story; but it is strained beyond the bare needs of the plot and gives rise to a further spate of reflective lines that do not really advance the main thread of the story. Yet the bard makes a drastic return to the kola by way of the formulaic line of address. Homer may not have such operatic inflations; but I think the presence of mind demonstrated here by Seydou Camara is strikingly similar to that shown by Homer, as in the nineteenth book of the *Odyssey*.[76]

Most of the other ring passages in *Kambili* are shorter, however. Usually they involve a chant or a speech neatly enclosed by two quite identical lines or ideas, as in the following warning to Kanji's wives by Bari the sorcerer:

No woman can see a Komo's pot.
If your eye falls on the Komo's pot,
>Your body will swell.
>Head lice will land on you.
>Body lice will cover you.
>They will rustle in your hair,
>And go in your underarm hair,
>And go attack the hair of your crotch.
>Don't you look at my pot.

(1000-1008)

Or we may have a short digression in which the bard spins off a number of his gnomic lines but picks the story up again from the line or idea that led him off. A good example is the passage that introduces the Muslim "holyman" into the Kambili riddle:

Ah! The holyman has come....
The man of the Koran has come, Kambili!
Man, the hero is only welcome on troubled days.
It is not good to put aside tradition for one day's pain.
Death may put an end to a man, it does not end his name.
There is no other source of pity beyond Allah.
Hearing the wretched out is better than mine-is-at-home.
>Ah! the holy man has come!
>The holyman of the Koran has come!

(719-27)

In such a ring passage, it is particularly interesting to observe why the bard finds it easy to pick up the thread of his story from where he left it. The ideas expressed in the gnomic lines are intrinsically related to one another and are all united by an associative thread which helps the straying imagination back again into the open road—a kind of Thesean thread. In the above ring passage, "Kambili" in the second line suggests "hero" in the third; "trouble" in the third suggests "pair" in the fourth; "grain" in turn suggests

199

"Death" in the fifth; it is to "Allah" (sixth line) that the brave go when they die; "Hearing the wretched out" (seventh line) is an act of "pity" (sixth line); the "holyman" (eighth line) is the ostensible servant of Allah, who is the ultimate source of pity—we are finally back to the original line about the holyman!

The above ring is complex and adventurous; bravado and versatility are combined with a stern sense of direction, without which the story would probably have collapsed. Homer has some ring passages built on a fairly similar pattern. The digression is usually a simile, the latter portion of which endeavors to swing us back again to the initial word or idea. The following example describes Hippodamas' death at the hands of Achilles:

He blew his life away, bellowing, as when a bull
bellows as he is dragged off for Poseidon, Lord of Helike,
and the young men drag him. In such bulls the earth shaker glories.
Such was his bellowing as the proud spirit flitted from his bones.

(*Iliad* 20.403-6)

Homer achieves his Thesean thread in this passage by repeating the verbs "bellowing" and "dragging"; this helps him stay within the single picture of slaughtering and maintain the main line of his story.[77] It is a considerably safer approach than that of *Kambili*, whose bard reflects in his style the adventurous spirit of the heroic world he sketches.

But what happens when the digression is not of the bard's own making—how, for instance, does he survive the distractions imposed on him by his audience and carry on with his narration? The question is adequately answered by an interesting scene in *Ozidi*, in which the hero, still thirsting for action after disposing of Tebesonoma, informs his mother that he is anxious to go out and "play." She eventually agrees but warns him to be wary. The following passage shows us how the bard wrestles with a spectator's intrusion:

"If you must go far, don't take the turning to the right. That leads to
Odogu's. That's where Odogu is."

Spectator: Isn't that where he previously went to woo a woman?

Yes, the very same place!
"You went once to say hello to Odogu's wife,
You said. Nobody accosts Odogu's wife. So
don't ever go in there as you did before."

(275)

It is possible that Ozidi's mother never really meant to add the
detail about his earlier experience with Odogu's wife: it should be
obvious to Ozidi that his mother's warning is against a repeat of
the previous encounter. But the spectator, apparently anxious to
show off his grasp of the facts of the story, forces the addition on
the bard. The bard returns to the mother's warning, but not without taking account of the spectator's point in his main line of
narrative. The scheme of this scene may be represented as follows:

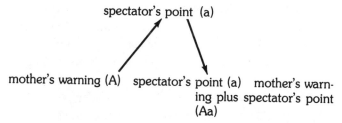

spectator's point (a)

mother's warning (A) spectator's point (a) mother's warning plus spectator's point
(Aa)

The environment of a live performance is often uncertain, even
tempestuous, and these various examples of the ring device show
us how ably the artist can manage to steer his craft of song
through it. He is anxious to make an impression on his audience
by showing what a full and extensive performance he can give, but
he realizes what a fool he will make of himself if he lets his act be
driven out of control. The ring device reflects this need for stabilization and sanity.

Five

ELEMENTS OF THE
ORAL NARRATIVE STYLE

In the last chapter, we discussed the basic principles of growth and control in the heroic narrative. We will now examine some of the peculiar stylistic touches that the tale is subject to in performance. We have touched upon some of these in our discussion of the accretive and digressive tendencies of the bard. Indeed, in a study of the oral epic it is rather difficult to draw a rigid line between structure and style, for often the mood of the bard determines the structure of the song, its coherence or total dislocation, its balance or its unevenness. The situation is not strikingly different in a written work, but in that medium there are greater opportunities for control and sobriety. What we shall try to observe here are some of the techniques that the oral epic relies on under the pressures and influence of its live context.

One of these is humor. Sometimes this is plain, lighthearted humor aimed at making fun of a discomfited character. For example, in *Kambili* 1300-1328 the bumbling "holyman" is coarsely laughed out of the child riddle, just as in *Iliad* 14-15 a wheedled Zeus is ridiculed for his love-struck folly. But on the whole the humor is down-to-earth, crude, carefully aimed at the raw passions of the crowd, and often delivered with sensuality or roguish mischief. We saw something of the sensual humor in *The Mwindo Epic*, in that magic resuscitation scene in which the hero pronounces that "each one who died copulating resuscitated copulating." It is conceivable that the audience would be tickled at such a detail, especially in view of the rather serio-comic mix of activities that the narrator mirrors in his tale. Or take the following description in *Kambili* of the villainous "favored wife," who is bent selfishly on being the one to bear the hero-child; the passage reveals a humor at once sensual and saucy:

She sprang up quickly, buttocks like a bush hut roof,
Her great belly looked like a Moorish drum.
The incorrigible's head was flat like a Mande drum,
Her mouth, like a Mande tobacco box.
She sprang up with her great belly rolls,
Galump, galump, galump . . . .

(1399-1404)

The language is even more unabashed in *Ozidi*. The idiot Temugedege feels mocked when his nephew, Ozidi, addresses him as father; the old man responds:

Oh, you people of Orua, have you come again to laugh at me? Since I grew up, I have fathered no child. That's how I am. I've found no cunt to fuck. That is how I have lived till this day . . . . (41)

Saucy humor is the keynote of the episode involving the Scrotum King, whose giant scrotum gets in the way and frustrates all efforts by the hero to kill him. The audience explodes with constant laughter (214-29) as the scrotum bounds from one spot to the other and is all over the hero! The sexuality is still more openly indulged in the episode involving the hero's all-too-brief affair with the wife of Odogu, in which we are shown some love scenes between the boy and the woman ("Now how shall we do it?" "Well, how should we do it?" [234]). The woman is frightened of the consequences of her husband's knowing of this secret affair, and she seems sometimes to have more his interests than those of Ozidi at heart; yet she begins to develop a weakness for her lover when the two enemies come to mortal grips and Odogu seems to have the upper hand:

Pity for Ozidi now filled her eyes.

    Spectator. He must have slept with her already.

You don't have to say it!

    [*Laughter*]

These exchanges between the bard and the spectator make clear that the bard's sensual picture was effective.

The sensual touch may be due in part to the character of the bard himself; many field studies of bards have revealed that they are frequently known to be fun-loving men. But sensuality in song would seem to be a standard means of attracting emotional responses from the audience. The following passage from a song by the Yugoslav guslar Salih Ugljanin suggests that the device is a universal one. The bard has been singing of the wedding of the brave Halil and the princess Nastasija:

May Halil kiss her whenever he awakes, and may he go to her as strong as he can, so that they may breed grey falcons and bring discomfort to the emperor and the kaiser. May he enter the race from afar and throw himself upon her from the mattress, throw himself upon her and ply her well!

                                                      (*SCHS* 178)[1]

The humor begins to be fearsome when the situation is one of conflict or of murder and bloodshed. This is particularly true when one character is shown to be locked in the magical spell of another, who may then proceed to make short work of his victim.

Something of this order occurs in *Akoma Mba* when the hero Mengono, who has gone off in a rescue search for Otungu Mba, arrives at the land where the latter is being held captive and is himself caught in a magic spell by Otungu's captors—so effectively that he cannot lift his feet from the ground! (2118ff.) The humor could be grimmer: one wonders how a rhapsode would have "interpreted" that scene in the *Iliad* where Patroklos is struck nerveless, naked, and dazed by the divine hand of Apollo, only to become the butt of savage blows from Euphorbos and Hektor (16.788ff.). In Africa, both performer and audience are frequently conscious of the play interest even of the most fearful scenes in the heroic tales; the tragicomic potential is given full vent. This is why, in *Ozidi*, the audience laughs when Ogueren is struck insensate by the magic touch of Oreame (124),[2] only to be cut to pieces by Ozidi (126); or when Oreame uses the same magic on Odogu's mother Agonodi, whose head snaps off and spills over on the ground (306).

Such macabre humor is effectively exploited by the *Kambili* bard in his descriptions of the fearful act of killing. The effectiveness of such statements derives from the sheer seriocomic mismatch between their tone or idiom and the nature of the event that occasions them, as when the act of decapitating a man is described with phrases like "trimmed a bit off his height," or "his two shoulders became inseparable friends." In his bloody rampage the aggrieved cuckold in the story, Cekura, is said to be "really playing in Jimini":

Whoever went out to defecate,
He was made into a toothpick.

(1918f.)

Or take the following description of the execution of the "old sandal man" who fails to solve the Kambili riddle:

The old sandal man's head was cut off at his neck.
Big trouble has begun in Jimini!
The little man fell flopping about like a tramp in
    the cold.

(505-7)

Here we are reminded of much morbid humor in Homer. For instance, the Trojans who go down before Agamemnon are said to be "lying/along the ground, to delight no longer their wives, but the vultures" (*Iliad* 11.162f.); Diomedes warns Paris that whoever gets a blow from him dies instantly and "rots away, and there are more birds than women swarming about him" (11.395); or take the following passage describing the death of Kebriones, Hektor's charioteer, at the hands of Patroklos:

    The sharp stone hit him in the forehead
and smashed both brows in on each other, nor could the bone hold
the rock, but his eyes fell out into the dust before him
there at his feet, so that he vaulted to earth like a diver
from the carefully wrought chariot, and the life left his bones. Now
you spoke in bitter mockery over him, rider Patroklos:
"See now, what a light man this is, how agile an acrobat.
If only he were somewhere on the sea, where the fish swarm,
he could fill the hunger of many men, by diving for oysters;
he could go overboard from a boat, even in rough weather
the way he somersaults so light to the ground from his chariot
now. So, to be sure, in Troy also they have their acrobats."

(16.739-50)

    The value of humor in the narrative art can hardly be overstated. However sober or dignified the context of the narration may be, the oral artist is sufficiently aware of his duty to make an impression and so, once in a while, spices up his account with a few affecting details. We may borrow some examples from two traditions of oral literature involving the narrative art. The first is the homiletic verse from the Islamized societies of Africa; the "Song of Bagauda" is a good case in point. It is possible that when such historical accounts moved from the courtly environment and become part of the repertoire of itinerant musicians (some of them beggars), they lost something of the high seriousness of their original material. But the changes cannot have been extensive, considering that each narrator would feel obliged to respect the Koranic flavor of these homiletic accounts. One is therefore touched to find, now and then, lines of mischievous humor like the following from the Bagauda account (the bard has been talking about the need for women to remain in the *purdah*);

It is the word of God; is there any who is slow to obey it
Save only perhaps the rustic malams of the village
  With their satchels that contain only cockroaches,
And their fez hats crowned with turbans?
  At the naming ceremony and the funeral assembly
Their zeal is all for a little grain and dough;
  On a ball of dough their attention is fixed.
The blind man comes to seek one to guide him,
  And finds a guide whose own eyes are falling.[3]

(A18.32-40)

Our second example comes from the oracular verse tradition of the Yoruba *Ifa*, which is as serious as anything relating to ritual divination can be. The client's consultation is usually answered by the priest with a body of narrative exempla (called *ese Ifa*), which tell the client of previous cases of the kind that he has brought up and how they were resolved. One such story concerns the creator god Orunmila. At the dawn of creation, when Orunmila still inhabited the earth, he named a day of festival, at which his children were duty-bound to pay respects to him. One of them turned rebellious and refused to pay homage; Orunmila became angry and left the earth at the cost of untold suffering to mankind:

The result was that pregnant women no longer delivered.
The barren one remained barren.
The sick remained infirm.
Small rivers wore garments of leaves.
Semen got dried up in men's testicles.
Women no longer saw their menstruation.
New yam tubers appeared but could not develop.[4]

(1.87-93)

There is a touch of dark humor in the details about congealment in the sexual organs. The client may not laugh, yet he cannot but be a little uneasy. The bard has made his point.

From dark humor or tragicomedy it is only a short step to full-scale horror, and in a song of terror the bard does not hesitate to make the most of that element without the least intent to amuse anyone. To this day, the bard of a public performance generally feels free to impose on his audience if he thinks he will make a point that way (the frequent "ululations" in our text of *Ozidi* clearly indicate how fully Okabou must have exerted himself). If, for instance, a scene calls for the killing of a child, the bard will go so far as to reach into the audience for a child, swing the matchet down on his prostrate body, and arrest the blade only an inch away from sure harm. As the crowd gasps in panic, the performer releases the child with a leonine grin on his face!

Ozidi makes full use of horror. Nothing could be grimmer than that scene where one of the flying pieces from a broken sword smashes the brains of Ofe's child (44); or where the boy-hero Ozidi chops up the wives of Ofe and Azezabife, and the dripping pieces fly off in disarray to report to their husbands that the son of their old victim is up and about (55ff.); or where the frenzied hero descends with his blade on Tebesonoma's sister and her child and, for all the woman's begging and crying, slices them up with one blow (259). In *Silamaka* we have a scene approaching the Jacobean in sheer chill. After he has killed his adversary Fularadio, Silamaka severs the dead man's head and throws it, with its long tresses studded with gold, into the feeding bag of his horse. On arriving home after the campaign, he cheerfully announces to his sister that he has a war gift for her and asks her to get it from the feeding bag; the little girl is quite overcome with fright when she discovers that the object she has pulled out of the bag is the head of a man (*Silamaka* 30). In the grim contests between Mwindo and his enemies, mouths are smashed to the ground, breath is stifled, and urine and excrements slobber over the brutalized victim (99, 100). In *Kambili*, some of those portraits of decapitation seem simply to have congealed into formulas in which the horror stands out with all the morbid grin of a skeleton. We are reminded of so many chilling scenes in the *Iliad*; the following is particularly representative of the sheer physical horror of many a Homeric fight:

Idomeneus stabbed Erymas in the mouth with the pitiless
bronze, so that the brazen spearhead smashed its way clean through
below the brain in an upward stroke, the white bones splintered,
and the teeth were shaken out with the stroke and both eyes filled up
with blood, and gaping he blew a spray of blood through the nostrils
and through his mouth, and death in a dark mist closed in about him.
                                                                    (16.345-50)

By stressing humor or horror the bard aims to keep our interest during his performance. Another device is the use of pointed, rhetorical lines that draw the audience's attention to a statement made by a character or to a fresh event. It may not always be clear whether or not the statement or event is significant in the scheme of the story; from what we have said about the accretive or paratactical tendencies of the narrative song, it would follow that quite often individual scenes or episodes are developed for their own independent appeal and may not significantly advance the plot of the story. Consequently, the rhetorical line may or may not be a way of introducing us to a significant turn or moment in the story; it may simply be the bard's way of reactivating his fancy or of rekindling the flagging interest of his audience.

Let us briefly examine one example of the rhetorical question from Dembo Kanute's version of *Sunjata*. This version concentrates on the career of Fakoli, Sunjata's chief ally against Sumanguru—glorifying his person, his antecedents, and his role in the legend—and is named after him. Early in the story, we are alerted to his personality by the following verses:

But now I want the *Janjungo* tune to be played
So that I can tell him* about Faa Koli;
Play *Janjungo* and change it.
Sora! This (tune) is calling Faa Koli.
Faa Koli—
He it was who cut off Kunkuto Lamini's big head from his big neck;
He rolled over like a sacrificial ox in Manding.
Faa Koli—
He it was who cut off the Wolof King's big head from his big neck;
He rolled over like a sacrifical ox in Manding.
Faa Koli—
He it was who cut off the king of Kajori's big head from his big neck;
They called him King Karajata Job.
But who was Faa Koli?
Faa Koli was one of Sunjata's great commanders.
What sort of a great man was Faa Koli?
This tune was played for Faa Koli;
This is *Janjungo*
The griots have changed *Janjungo*
And dedicated it to Jula Jekereba Bayo.
Faa Koli—
His maternal uncle was Sumanguru Kante.

(III.82-103)

*The host.

We can observe here an interesting "ring" passage enclosed by details about the Janjungo tune. Within that ring we are told first about Fakoli's exploits, and then we come to those rhetorical questions about Fakoli. But the answers do not tell us significantly more about the hero than his victories over those kings do. It is true that the rhetorical questions bring us closer to the facts about Fakoli that relate more directly to the main subject of the Sunjata story (i. e., the details about Sumanguru, etc.). But the questions are a little remote from these facts; they basically are a token of the periodic gain in excitement characteristic of the heroic narrative song in performance.

A somewhat similar situation occurs in *Kambili*. The following passage introduces the "blackbag" soothsayer into the child riddle:

Ah! The bagman has come!
And come shaking his bag.
What words did he say?
He spent a long time shaking.
He said, "My father Imam, my mother Imam . . . . "

(343-47)

There are two rhetorical points in this passage. The first line reveals considerable elan, particularly since the entry of the bagman is the first of a long sequence of such entries into the Kambili riddle. We can thus concede that that line does represent a climactic moment for the bard. But we cannot easily say the same for the third line. The distance between the rhetorical question and its answer, covered by the repetition of the detail about bag shaking, suggests that the bard may be having a little trouble coming round to the actual words of the bagman, or else that his mind is struggling to contrive a more mannered way of reporting the bagman's address to Samory Toure.

These rhetorical questions and statements may not yield any

new insights or advance the story; but even when they fall flat in the print—as does the following question from *Kambili*

There was one young boy among the boys of the village.
What was his name? His name was Samson.

(1092-93)

they show that the performer is anxious to sustain the level of excitement.

The tendency to jolt us every now and then must be attributed to what we shall call a *sense of moment* in the performing oral artist. The sense of moment is of course present in written literature: there comes a time in a novel, for instance, when we feel that a critical point has been reached or a significant turn taken. Far more regularly than written literature, however, an oral performance alerts us—by a recognizable technical or structural device— to significant moments in the story.

The alert may sometimes not be sounded by the bard himself. There are, for instance, those moments in a performance when the audience is considerably impressed by a turn of phrase, a wellrepresented detail, or even a histrionic movement by the bard, and a member of that audience throws out a phrase instantly in recognition of the bard's excellence. On numerous occasions the bard of *Ozidi* is greeted in this way. For instance, he is showered with his praise name "Agadakpa yenyen" when he portrays the tension and fear involved in Akpobrisi's threat to come to the hero's house and pack him away (135). More often in that tale, however, we encounter those phrases of call-and-response with which the audience shows its recognition or encouragement of the bard's good job: "Egberi Yo!" "E!" This device is, of course, often used to reenliven audience interest, especially if the narration is a long one. But quite often we find it at moments when the bard has let drop a weighty situation: for example, when Tebesonoma, as he is

212

taking Ozidi off to destruction, is benumbed by an instant magic spell from Oreame (246); at the celebration of Ozidi's slaughter of Odogu's wife (295); at the point where the frenzied hero rises from his trance and cuts down both Odogu's mother and his own grandmother, Oreame (307); and various other scenes. These are all momentous points, and the text of the tale usually bears marks of the audience's recognition of the importance or effectiveness of those points. Perhaps we have a similar phenomenon in the periodic "AOI" of *The Song of Roland.*

Otherwise, the bard himself alerts us to the climactic points of his story. We have observed that some rhetorical questions and alerts are not so effectively placed and do not prepare us for any really significant moments. Others, however, do the job effectively and are placed so that we get a good feel of the critical force of the scene. A good example can be seen in *Akoma Mba.* Some of the prominent men of the Ekang race, who had gone in search of Otungu Mba, had been imprisoned by the men of Mfim Ekie. The king of the Ekang, Akoma Mba, finally decides to rescue his subjects. The confrontation with the powerful enemy promises to be a heated one—"A war is at hand," as we are told (2301)—and so it is; for Akoma starts off by locking the entire population (foe and friend alike) in a solid rock which he ties up with a metal cord. The whole episode, from the approach of Akoma Mba until his men move in to try to open up the rock, is punctuated with phrases like "Then I see," "And I see" (2306ff.).

This climactic use of alerts resembles what we find in the Parry collection of Yugoslav epics. For instance, in Salih Ugljanin's "Song of Bagdad," after the hero Derdelez Alija has summoned the generals and they begin to arrive one by one, it is clear that an important point in the story has been reached, as we look forward to the siege of Bagdad. This significant moment of the gathering of the armies is indicated by a line that invites us to take fresh interest in Alija: "Now let me tell you of Derdelez Alija" (*SCHS* 74). When Fatima of Budim, the betrothed of Alija, dons her disguise in order to forestall the military preparations and take Bagdad by a trick, we are introduced to that episode by a fit alert from the bard: "Now let me tell you the strange tale of Fatima, of Fatima of the city of Budim!" (76). When Fatima has finally disguised herself and ridden up to Bagdad, we are once more introduced to a significant moment in the story—the deceit of the queen of Bagdad by Fatima of Budim—with the following arresting line: "Now see the queen of the city of Bagdad!" (82).

Nor is the climactic alert unknown in Homer. Take those occasions when the poet appeals to the Muses to help him narrate a momentous scene. For instance, the Catalogue of Ships (like the assembly of the generals in Ugljanin's *Song of Bagdad*) is a major episode in the story—the sheer size of the Greek fleet is a jolting spectacle—and Homer aptly exploits the affective potential of the moment, having prepared us for it by an appeal to the Muses (*Iliad* 2.484ff.). The appeal is also used to introduce major turns in the actual fighting, to highlight the display of valor by notable warriors—as in the *aristeiai* of Agamemnon and Hektor, and the series of slaughters by Greek heroes led by Ajax.[5] Homer also uses his similes frequently to introduce fresh pitches in the fighting. Indeed, the very first killing in the battlefield of the *Iliad* (done by Antilochos) is preceded by a simile that pointedly describes an avalanche of water (4.452ff.). Thereafter, as the fighting progresses, similes are frequently spun off one after the other in crowded sequence to mark a critical point in the conflict, as in the frenzied tussle over the body of Patroklos at the end of *Iliad* 17.

But there is a device, more complex structurally than the simple alert, which the performing bard employs frequently in underlining the major accents of his tale. The climactic chant—which in the last chapter we grouped under the song within the song—does this job quite well and can be used in a variety of situations. For instance, there are those moments when the very act of the hero bestirring himself (whether in conflict or in the prospect of it, or in council) is greeted with a series of his traditional praise titles or with a song glorifying him. Thus when Karta Thiema, ambitious to fight against the power of his overlord Da Monzon, raises his massive hairy arms to the view of his entire court, his griot unleashes a series of praise lines chanting the glory of the "red lion of Karta, king of kings" (*Karta Thiema* 180f.). Likewise, when Sunjata finally rises to his feet after several years of not walking, his griot greets him with a song announcing to the world that "the lion has walked" (*Sunjata* IV.21). These are all significant prospects of action, and their significance is recognized and realized in an instant chant.

The climactic chant is also employed at moments when heroic figures deliver a boast, whether independently or against one another. For instance, before he gets into a confrontation, Mwindo frequently breaks into a chant bragging that the adversary "is powerless against Mwindo." In *Kambili*, when Kambili is informed of the bloody acts of Cekura, he reacts by swearing that he is going to finish off Cekura with only one shot. The spirits of the bard are at once fired by this display of bravado, and the result is a series of intoned lines (2118-29) lamenting the cooling of the heroic temper among the men of his own day. But the more exciting chant in this category comes off as a fugue. An exchange of boasts between two heroes before or in the thick of battle is a matter of high spirits, and the entire scene is often done in a chant. Thus we have that beautiful series of exchanges between Sunjata and Sumanguru before the battle of Krina (*Sunjata* IV.60f.), and that equally beautiful scene in *Karta Thiema* where, before the confrontation with Da Monzon, Hambodedio and his griot rehearse the credits of the former in a series of counterboasts (199-200). The latter scene particularly reminds us of the exchanges between Idomeneus and his henchman Meriones in *Iliad* 13.249-327.

By far the most affecting, perhaps, of these climactic chants occurs when an alarming event takes place. A truly momentous point in the song has been reached, and the bard does not hesitate to exploit the impression which he believes his narration has made on his audience. In *Kambili*, a good example is at that point where Nerikoro, the leader of the Komo (the smiths' cult group), is baffled by the child riddle and, rather than be executed by Toure like the other sorcerers who have failed, turns into an eagle and flies away; the bard chants:

Ah! Toure ni Manjun!
The Komo hyena danced and danced.
And changed himself into an eagle,
And rose, wings flapping,
Saying his powers were not for earthly battles, Kambili.
    Ah! E! My time has come.
    Yes, the time for rising off the ground has come!
        Now's the time.
        Rising off the ground time has come!

(615-23)

There is a subtle metaphysical as well as poetic moment involved in this scene, and it has given the bard some highly affective resources for his act. The Komo Society, of which Nerikoro is leader, is the ultimate mystical authority in the cult life of this Mandingo group: "The world's first child was a smith," we are told earlier in the story (*Kambili* 539). It would therefore be inconceivable for the leader of such a powerful body to be subjected to the common lot that has befallen the other sorcerers. But justice demands that he cease to exist, so he takes a dignified way out by turning into an eagle and lighting on a mountain at Kona (where, we are told in the notes, he is fabled to be still living). The charged mystical force of that scene, and the impressive act of Nerikoro's taking wing, combine to fill the bard with a tremendous poetic afflatus which erupts into a choral chant of considerable length (620-47). The bard himself has taken wing!

Other epics have similar pitches accompanied by songs. In *Ozidi*, there is often a song when the hero kills an enemy—as at that point where he cuts up the wives of Ofe and Azezabife (54f.), or where he kills Badoba without any struggle worth mentioning (152), or when finally he destroys the Smallpox King and his retinue (386). Ilele and Mbombe, the parents of Lianja, are united after a heated and tumultuous wrestling contest that Ilele has to win: this climactic moment is punctuated with songs (31). And the final crisis of the Sunjata epic as performed by Banna Kanute, describing the flight of Sumanguru before Sunjata in the last encounter, contains snatches of song as well as praise lines (*Sunjata* II.1920-83). Perhaps the closest to this phenomenon in the older European tradition is that tendency of the bard of *Roland* to repeat whole laisses as a way of underscoring the climactic force of the scenes or speeches, as in Laisse 42.

It may be said that the chants that occur at some of these critical moments in the heroic tale are a way of softening the harsh impact of the scenes or statements;[6] indeed, what we observed in the last chapter about the "ventilative" character of the song within the song may indicate a certain tendency on the part of the bard to relax the intensity of the moment. What matters, however, is that the bard recognizes that a critical moment has been reached; the chant is a token of that recognition.

The implications of the sense of moment for the oral performance of a heroic song are far-reaching. If the bard recognizes so many significant crises within the compass of one song, then the song is indeed built on something of an episodic pattern. Bowra has cogently observed that the epic poet concentrates on one episode at a time;[7] the tale is conceived of in units. The episode about the fortunes of Nyankuma Dookha/Bala Faasege at the hands of Sumanguru (*Sunjata* III.266ff.), which is introduced with a chant and a rhetorical question, is one such convenient unit. The value of the episodic plot is that when the bard may not have the time or encouragement to sing the entire story, he can select those segments of it that time will allow or that can appeal to the special tastes of his audience. In fact, there may never be time enough on one occasion to sing all of a full-length heroic song; the periodic elevations in the tempo of the narrative thus represent the physical divisions of it into episodes and may help the bard make the choice, when the time comes, as to which part or parts of the song to sing and where to begin his singing.[8] The point is worth noting because it seriously questions the validity of applying Aristotelian notions of unity to an oral performance in a creative tradition. The bard may have the broad lines of the plot of the story in his mind; but, because he seldom sings the song in its entirety, each episode has its own integral logic and appeal which may or may not agree impeccably with those of another.

This may be one more reason why Homer "nods," and other epic bards get the details and logic of their songs mixed up now and then. Let us take an example from *Kambili*. When the young hero orders weapons to be made for him, he makes it clear what he wants:

Tell the people of the smiths,
To make some young boy's arrows,
And to strike a young boy's bow.
The rifle will never be for me.

(1796-99)

Yet, when Kambili finally kills Cekura toward the end of the story, he uses a rifle:

218

He made his one leg like a fork of the bush,
And made his elbow like a hanger of the bush,
And separated Danger from Imprudence,
And fired the packed-down powder at the right time.
> Ah! the shot went off like an iron drum, Master.
> Dust rose up behind the man-eating lion.
> The bullet travelled straight and true.

(2611-17)

If the bard had maintained a monolithic view of the personality of his hero and was *that* scrupulous about the consistency of his details, it is unlikely that he would allow himself to be so "self-contradictory" when describing the two most momentous events in the career of the hero: his first display of daredevilry and his final triumph. But he had probably never sung the story in an unbroken sequence before and could not flawlessly coordinate its parts. More importantly, each of these two episodes has its own affective appeal, and this consideration must have outweighed any urgency to see them as mutually complementary and inseparable parts of the same heroic portrait. When Kambili orders a young boy's bow and arrows to be made for him and disowns the rifle, it appears that the bard intends to accentuate the marvel involved in a little child's effortlessly dispatching leopards and buffaloes with only one shot of the puny dart. But for Kambili to be seen as a full-blown hunters' hero, he must own a rifle. Besides, in a contest with a tremendously powerful enemy like Cekura, the thunderous sound of a gun is only a fitting backdrop to the action and lends it considerable forcefulness. Either of these two episodes could be performed exclusively as an evening's fare, so that the bard or his regular audience will seldom pick holes in the "organic" frame of the tale.

This, in addition to considerations of the thematic device, may likewise explain why Pylaimenes is killed by Menelaos in *Iliad* 5

219

and comes alive in 13, or why in *Iliad* 3 Priam, ten years after the Greeks have been battering his city, is only beginning to learn the names of their leaders.[9] Each of these episodes or lays has its special accents and represents at least one *moment*; in celebrating it (especially in an exclusive performance) the bard can afford to pass over the other episodes so long as the immediate purpose is served. The overall tale is a collage of so many affective moments, and the organic links are only secondary to the respective accents of the performance. Milman Parry has observed that the heroic song "for the oral audience has an interest of its own apart from the plot."[10] I think we should look to these accents and moments for the fundamental device by which the bard endeavors to gain and to hold the interest of his audience.

II

We have discussed those stylistic elements and tendencies in the heroic narrative that affect the mood of both bard and audience. These are perhaps the most essential features of an act undertaken in an environment of considerable excitement, one in which the oral artist (unlike the writer) cannot afford to ignore the physical presence of his assessors. It will not, however, be out of place to examine briefly some of the verbal nuances of this medium of art. The bard of the heroic tale makes some of his best impressions by means of the spoken word, and it is only proper that we take a look at one or two devices which he sometimes weaves from the sounds and combination of words.

One such device is exclamation. Not every bard uses exclamation to any considerable extent, and those that use it do so in their own various ways. Some find it particularly useful in opening their songs and attracting the attention of the audience—like the *Kambili* bard, who in his very first line of the tale announces his subject with an exclamation, "Ah! Master, Kanji and his good journey!" Other bards use exclamation for emphasis. Dembo Kanute uses it in underscoring his sense of loss of a hero of a bygone day: "Ah, Kadi Darame's Cherno too is dead" (*Sunjata* III.42). The *Ozidi* bard frequently uses the phrase *gbabo* (believe me) or *be gbabe* (on my word!) for putting his details in sharp relief; and numerous kinds of exclamation are found in *Akoma Mba* (e. g., "A yeee!") (373).

But the exclamation serves especially to underscore a critical situation, reflecting what we have described as the bard's sense of moment. The *Kambili* bard is particularly quick to recognize the dramatic potential of any scene that he considers significant. Thus, when he is about to introduce that trial of skill in which various soothsayers are going to lose their necks over the child riddle in the land of Jimini, he begins:

Ah! The battle has begun!
Jimini will not be pleasant!

(299-300)

When finally Kambili and Cekura face each other in a gunfight, and the hero fires that fatal shot at the lion-man, we are jolted to recognize the terror of the moment with an exclamation:

Ah! The shot went off like an iron drum, Master.
Dust rose up behind the man-eating lion.
The bullet travelled straight and true.

(2615-17)

These exclamations would normally be expressed with the strongest possible voice to achieve their impact because the voice, if it is not powerful, is not much good for the master of words.

The sound of words is particularly fundamental to such phon-aesthetic devices as onomatopoeia and ideophone. The latter is one of the most notable features of daily speech in African societies and comes in quite handy in most oral art.[11] In the heroic narrative, with its accent on afflatus, the bard, anxious to put a movement or an action in the starkest possible relief, may use a flourish of sounds where so many words would have done the job of description. Some translators prefer to leave the original sound rather than let the foreign idiom distort its effectiveness, as in that line describing the clumsy trundle of one of the women in *Kambili*: "A little old lady came forward, *gwiligigwologo*" (1475). Other translators are not so loyal, either because they think the indigenous language sticks out rather clumsily in a sea of foreign words or because they feel confident that they can produce a version that retains much of the flavor of the original. John Pepper Clark, himself a notable poet, manages some impressive efforts in his translation of *Ozidi*—for example, take the scene when in the battle against Azema and Azemaroti, the hero's magic sword renews itself for further action:

E-e, Ozidi gbai me kekene agbodo be temi temi ke temi de. Kerepu, kerepu, kerepu, kerepu, kerepu, kerepu.

(That one sword of Ozidi now resharpened and forged itself afresh upon its target. The grating sound of filing and flying flint filled the air with each blow.)

(361)

The sexual appeal of Ozidi's wife is described almost as effectively in Clark's English as in the original Ijo:

Endoubo wo, wo, wo . . . kene yereke yereke.

(Her bosom was full and large, all yearning and yielding).

(372)

But the rendering of the cumbersome movement of the Scrotum King is not quite as successful:

222

Kene kpiridi, engbe kiri kpon pake tekie
tekie tekie tekie.

(Rolling, his balls trundled along.)

(211)

Nor is Gordon Innes any more successful in his translation of the movement of a crocodile on dry land:

Ye daa yele a ma bamba kendo
Nyati, nyati, nyati a funtita bungo kono.

(When they opened the door the live crocodile
Came waddling out of the house.)

(*Sunjata* II. 1762-63)

The picture conveyed by the sound of the original African language is often so inimitable that one cannot help wishing the translator had left the sound as he found it.

Akoma Mba is full of ideophones, which the editors have mainly left alone. The sound *Yaaaannnng* is frequently used in denoting the infinite stretch of a scene or an object in motion. The messenger sent by Akoma Mba to assemble the chiefs of Ekang land for a summit is said to have taken off swiftly like a bird flying *Kpa yaaaannnng* (63). One of the heroes who goes off in search of the exiled Otungu Mba comes to a river, which is said to stretch before him *a Yaaaaaannnnnng* (1581). Abo Mama sends his magic club to pummel Otungu Mba; Otungu tries to hide from the unrelenting blow of the weapon but continues to hear it bounding after him *kungum kum! . . . Kugum Kum! . . . kugum kum! (522).* The performance of this epic was evidently fervid, for the sound patterns of our text give us a truly "speaking picture" of the scenes and experiences of the tale: beauty, laughter, fury, even the snoring of a man deep in sleep, all come alive in the sheer sound of words. Perhaps the closest parallel in the ancient European epic is Ho-

223

mer's description of the patter of the feet of the many men who go to fetch the wood for Patroklos' funeral pyre: they are said to be going *polla d' ananta katanta paranta te dokhmia* (*Iliad* 23.116)

Linked closely with this play on sounds is the use of phonological echoes as in the twin devices of assonance and alliteration. This is particularly evident in the flourish of words with which the griots of the Innes collection of *Sunjata* seem to tell their tales. There is music in the sheer drop of words, and the griot makes the most of it, as when Dembo Kanute laments the passing of some celebrity of an earlier day: "Bande banna banta" (The wealthy Bande is dead) (III.43). In fact, so strong is this tendency to construct and deliver sounds that it appears the bard is frequently driven to formulate various words that have no traceable meaning but are simply there to give the impression of a rich phonological repertoire. Such is the impression one gets from those lines that Banna Kanute puts in the mouth of the marabout who, commissioned by Sumanguru to consult the oracles on the advent of Sunjata, emerges to announce that a spirit has spoken to him thus:

Allahu aharu rajaku fa mang kaana kaafa,
Ming muusi, janafang kumfai kuna.

(Sunjata II.295-96)

Innes calls these words "completely unintelligible," and it does seem that their major appeal is phonological: the bard is attracted by the assonatal and alliterative uses of the *a-u* and the *kaa* sounds of the first line, and the *m, ku, fa* sounds of the second.

This reliance on sounds tempts one to reexamine the fundamental mythic premises of the oral epic in such a tradition. The Mandinka do stress the power of words, and the bards recognize this power.[12] It is therefore no wonder that these bards tend to rely heavily on verbal impact in the entire fabric of names and situations that feature in the myths they re-create. Take the names or titles commonly associated with the hero Fakoli of the Sunjata story. He is given the praise names "Kiliya Musa" and "Nooya Musa" by Bamba Suso (*Sunjata* I.599f.) and Dembo Kanute (III.6), and is also greeted with the appellations "Faa Koli Kumba" and "Faa Koli Daaba" by these griots (especially Dembo). It is difficult to ignore the appeal of assonance in the first pair of titles; so dominant, it seems, has that appeal become in the mythic fabric of Fakoli's personality that it is not now easy for us to reconcile various versions of the tale on the exact signification of "Kiliya." Niane's edition makes "Keleya" the name of the hero's wife (*Sunjata* IV.42). Dembo Kanute, on the other hand, makes "Kiliya"[13] the scene of the quarrel that Fakoli had with his uncle Sumanguru, who took the hero's wife away from him; Dembo gives the town a location: " Wo Kiliya, wo le be Bugu ning Buguning tee" (Kiliya is between Bugu and Buguning) (III.223). This line further emphasizes the phonological purposes of the bard; and this makes it difficult for us to see "Kiliya" and "Nooya," or for that matter "Kumba" and "Daaba," as little more than convenient verbal echoes reflecting the mythmaker's preference for beauty over historic truth. Once this principle is grasped, we shall perhaps rest easier in our researches over those fanciful names that we find every now and then, as in the following lines from Dembo's *Sunjata*:

My mind turns to
Kelema and Delema.
Delema, great man and wizard.

(III.30-32)

Just about every "man" who occurs in the griot's tale, ranging from Sunjata to Sumanguru, is both "great" and a "wizard"; besides, the fact that Dembo has not bothered to describe Kelema apparently indicates that he is no different from Delema, or from any other hero whose name can be dragged into some chance phonological link with his.

There are numerous other such examples in African tales. In the Lianja story, the charming lady caught by Lonkundo in a trap gives the names of her father and herself as "Ensombyankaka" and "Ilankaka" (18). In Yoruba heroic myth, the phonological appeal can be achieved by a mere change of accentuation. We have a good example in the tragic tale of Kujoyi, from Babalola's *ijala* collection, especially in that scene where the bard talks about a hunting experience involving his "father" and Kujoyi:

Kujoyi reached Réfúréfú Forest in his search for elephants.
He found no elephants there, no elephants praisenamed Laaye.
My father reached Rèfùrèfù Grassland in his search for Elephants.
He found no elephants there, no elephants praisenamed Laaye.[14]

The editor does not offer any explanation either for Refurefu or for the accentual changes, no doubt because none are needed: Refurefu is of interest simply for its interplay of echo and variation.

This principle of phonological appeal and convenience may well apply to other cultures: it may, for instance, explain why in the first *Iliad* Homer makes Chryses the priest of Chryse and father of Chryseis. There is beauty and music in these echoes—more so, perhaps, if the words are close to one another.[15] The needs of the myth are well served if the narration is executed with the power and appeal of words, even if factual authenticity—especially for tales that have an historical basis—has to be compromised in the process.

III

To conclude this chapter, we shall briefly examine the fundamental realism, the sense of intimacy and of immediacy, in the heroic song. A cursory look at the material would leave the impression that it had a too otherworldly character to it—especially in view of the unbelievable might of its heroes—to have any interest for men such as we are. It might also be thought that the story reflected a vanishing outlook or way of life, and should be treated with all the distance that its obsolescence deserved. But a closer examination soon reveals the bard's efforts to make his subject concrete and familiar. Because his story deals with action, he strives to make his ideas come alive and to reduce the most abstract concepts into vivid, perceptible images and ordinary terms.

We can start with one simple example. The character of man in general or of a people is portrayed not in abstract philosophical terms but in terms of a particular action by which the type can be distinctly identified. Thus the bard of the Sunjata story characterizes the heroes of old Mali, assembled in the fight against Sumanguru, as "all those who say 'N'ko', all who speak the clear language" (*Sunjata* IV.55).[16] We are reminded of those passages in which Homer distinguished men by their eating bread, in contrast to beasts and monsters such as the Cyclops Polyphemos, who

was a monstrous wonder made to behold, not
like a man, an eater of bread, but more like a wooded
peak of the high mountains seen standing away from
   the others.[17]

                                    (*Odyssey* 9.190-92)

This sense of realism, the tendency to identify with the familiar environment, accounts for those instances in the heroic tale in which familiar customs feature in the unusual world of the heroes; indeed, some of those customs are traced to events in the tales. The heroes may be involved in the most superlative actions, but the fantasy of their world is a reflection, albeit remote, of the aspirations and dreams of the society of which the bard is very much a part. Thus, in *Kambili*, we have situations in which the superlative exists side by side with the mundane:

There was an old woman there of fine speech,
She pounded the herb with one blow of the pestle,
And took out the herbs,
And put them under Kambili's tongue.
That is the Wasulu people's mouth medicine.

(1584-88)

The Mandingo audience would surely be flattered to know that the extraordinary child is treated just like the regular child growing up among them—as a Homeric audience, listening to those descriptions of hospitality in the *Odyssey*, would be flattered to know that the superior beings of the bard's tale lived a rather familiar lifestyle.

In Banna Kanute's version of *Sunjata*, the bard tries to trace certain contemporary habits and taboos to events in the tale. Take the following about the Kante clan, said to trace from Sumanguru:

As you may know, the members of the Kante family do not eat white chicken,
And the reason for this is
That when Sunjata and Susu Sumanguru met,
It was a white chicken which killed the latter.

(II.371-74)

Another etiological digression links the custom of charity giving with the fortunes of Sumanguru by having the prophesy about Sunjata tested first with a white chicken and later with a white ram:

That is why,
Among us black people,
A white cock is prescribed as charity,
For every boy.

Afterwards, when you grow up and build your own compound,
A white ram is prescribed as charity for you.
As to the origin of that custom,
That is how it came about.

(II.441-48)

The history of the Mandingo world is so closely linked with the legend of Sunjata that the intelligent bard can easily mine the broad field of local customs for details that can help him bring the world of his tale closer to that of his audience. By carefully inserting the explanatory line, he invites his audience to empathize with his tale by recognizing its roots in the familiar society.

Another aspect of realism involves treating abstract or inanimate ideas with warmth and animation. The bard tells a tale of action; there is little room for the passive, lifeless, and immobile. The practice of giving names to weapons probably has its roots in traditional ritual or magic; but in the active world of the heroic song it is particularly fitting that even weapons are endowed with personality and the potential for action which names imply. In *Kambili* we have a rifle named "Kume," belonging to Bari the sorcerer. Samory Toure's sword of execution is named "Konke" and is said to behave very much like Samory (*Kambili* 381). The hero of *Silamaka* has a spear called "Moutonniere" (Fleecy). The magic spear used by Fakoli in the war against Sumanguru has been brought from Mecca and bears the name "Tuluku Muluku" (with the power of inflicting nine wounds at one thrust) (*Sunjata* II.1434). We are reminded of numerous such cases in the heroic myths of other cultures: the breastplate of Gilgamesh is named "Voice of the Heroes;" Arthur's sword is "Excalibur;" the herald Unferth loans Beowulf a sword named "Hrunting" for the fight against Grendel's mother; Beowulf's own sword, which he uses in his last fight against the dragon, is called "Naegling."

There is an even deeper interest in the animation or personification of natural scenes and phenomena. We have numerous examples of this device in *Mwindo*. As the hero and his aunt Iyangura advance toward Tubondo, where Mwindo will fight the decisive battle against his father, they are beaten by "Kiruka-nyambura . . . bearer of rain that never ceases" (83): the rain is fabled to be an old woman in the sky who drags rain along with her. Later in the story, the hero relates how he won the *wiki* game against the divinity Sheburungu, who has warned him that Heaven and Earth had previously lost the same contest; the example is particularly interesting because the chief editor, Biebuyck, notes that he had "not found these personifications [of Heaven and Earth] anywhere in Nyanga tales" (116n). But the most interesting example occurs in the scene involving the translation of the hero into the sky. There he confronts the personified figures of Lightning, Sun, Moon, Rain, and Star, who caution him against further heroic excesses; as punishment for his misdemeanor, Moon "singed [his] hair" and Sun "harassed him hotly," and he is warned in the most familiar and homely language (138). These personifications remind us of the raining Zeus in the *Iliad*; of Iris the rainbow goddess flitting across the sky on divine errand; of the fighting Skamandros, tossing with rage after Achilles.[18]

By giving names to inanimate objects and human agency to nonhuman phenomena, the bard makes the superhuman world of his heroes familiar. Using vivid images from the natural world can serve the same purpose. For instance, one of the characters in *Akoma Mba* has the name "Bivin Binkumba Biaka Amvus Biaku Amebum," meaning "the bark of a dried up tree falling both forwards and backwards." The name signifies his peculiar capacity to achieve both good and evil in anything he executes. Whatever its fabulary background, it adds vividness and intimacy as well as heroic scope to the story.[19]

Similes also capture for us in familiar terms the fantastical scope of the figures in heroic lore and the actions credited to them. The heroes Sunjata, Silamaka, and Karta Thiema are likened to lions in rampage. A lion may not exactly be commonplace, but it is the closest that the mythic imagination can get to capturing the terror of heroic action. Often the simile mirrors the familiar environment, as in those many instances in *Akoma Mba* when a character's hasty movement is compared to "the furious racing of a young antelope"; or when Ozidi scans helplessly from far below the towering figure of the Ogre Tebesonoma, "like one scanning an oil palm tree to see whether it has ripened" (238). Homer achieves similar results by evoking scenes of the pastoral life in his similes.

Occasionally historical experience is evoked. For instance, when Ozidi and the Scrotum King pause for a rest during their breathtaking encounters, they are portrayed in language that recalls the experience of World War I trench tactics:

It was like the white people's war, with one sitting this way and the other sitting that way, each waiting for the other. So they waited for each other . . . . (*Ozidi* 227)

The search for familiarity does, of course, have its problems. Because he is so anxious to enlist the empathy of his listeners by bringing the facts of his tale as close to their experience as possible, the bard is sometimes unaware of anachronisms and other anomalies in his song. In the last chapter we saw how Banna Kanute, in his version of *Sunjata*, has substituted a gun for an arrow as the weapon used in shooting a fatal charm at Sumanguru

(II.1937f.). No doubt he thought that his audience would be more impressed by his knowledge of modern weaponry and warfare than of antiquated stuff like arrows, and he has simply fitted the detail of a gun into the conventional scheme of his performance without making any adjustment to the context of the information. For a similar reason, Homer has put the detail of a trumpet in a simile (*Iliad* 18.219ff.) referring to an age when trumpets were unknown. Such improprieties of detail are part of the chance the bard takes in trying for intimacy; and it may well happen that the odd member of his audience will chastise him for violating accuracy (as happens frequently over diction in *Ozidi*). But this is a hazard the bard can live with—better for him to err in striking a familiar chord than to alienate his listeners outright by choosing a rigid loyalty to the unfamiliar outlook of his art-world.

Of all the devices that the bard employs to make his tale as intimate and as down-to-earth as possible, perhaps the most aesthetically effective is the tendency to weave his personality into that of his characters: to give us the benefit of his judgment, or to so mesh his voice with his material that it is difficult to tell where dialogue ends and narration resumes. The tendency towards this device may depend on native cultural attitudes; but where it is successfully employed, we can detect a depth of empathy without which a performance is little more than a recitation.

The search for empathy can be seen in the bard's holding, during his performance, an object with which the hero of his tale is traditionally associated. Many bards would claim that without this sort of contact they would not get any inspiration for their performance. Anthropologists have generally been inclined to view such a claim in terms of ritual, in the sense that the artist is consecrating his art to the cult figure of his tale; but it seems to me there is more an aesthetic than a ritual purpose in the act. By thus coming close to the personality of his subject, the bard is better equipped psychologically to re-create the hero's career convincingly. Hence Rureke holds the *conga*-scepter of Mwindo; the *Lianja* bard holds his hero's spear; and a narrator of the Ozidi story would normally hold Oreame's fan in one hand and the hero's sword in the other. The job of re-creation is made easier if the bard can identify with the hero in some palpable form, and if he can succeed thereby in weaving the mythic psychology of his subject into his own creative consciousness.

In the text of the tale, the authorial empathy may reveal itself when a gnomic line or an observation formulaically "intrudes" into a character's speech. In the Sunjata story, for instance, when the king Nare Maghan becomes estranged from his wife Sogolon because she has borne him an infirm son, the bard gnomically laments, "How impatient man is!" (*Sunjata* IV.16). Shortly after this, the king's griot Gnankouman Doua tries to console his sad lord;

"When the seed germinates, growth is not always easy; great trees grow slowly but they plunge their roots deep into the ground."

"But has the seed really germinated?" said the king.
"Of course," replied the blind seer. "Only the growth is not as quick as you would like it; how impatient man is." (17)

In *Kambili*, one of the bard's frequent gnomic lines is, "Death is not hard but for 'Who comes after me?' " (87); the same language is used by the despised wife Dugo (923) when she pleads with the sorcerer Bari to ensure that she be the one to bear the hero-child. Something similar to this may be found in *Iliad* I: that Hera loves Achilles and Agamemnon equally is first stated by the poet (196) and then echoed by Athene (209) as she urges Achilles to exercise patience in the quarrel. These may not be so striking an example of the authorial voice or "intrusion," as they do only illustrate the formulaic technique by which the oral poet exploits a serviceable idea or line for building other lines. But they do point to the poet's total proprietorship of the views expressed in the work as a whole, and they suggest the difficulty of drawing fine editorial distinctions between him and his characters. Earlier scholars of Homer were in the habit of rejecting such coincidences as interpolations, not realizing that they are of the very nature of oral narrative poetry.[20]

Sometimes, too, the poet gives us the benefit of his thinking about events or characters in his tale. The action of the characters may be conceived within a supernatural compass, but they basically mirror certain tendencies in human conduct and so give the bard an opportunity to reflect on anything from human caprice to human destiny. As he observes the mad anxiety with which Agbo-gidi prepares to enter into a fight with Ozidi and thus into certain death, the bard laments, "O life, does God create to kill?" (*Ozidi* 65). This fatalism achieves its most gloomy proportions with the bards of the Mandingo world of Kambili and Sunjata; the hand of Destiny is immutable, and everyone—whatever the quality of his life—is destined to die.

The poet's portraiture of characters also reveals his personal views. Heroes and villains are who they are not merely from what they say and do but indeed from the sense of commitment with which the bard draws their features or assesses their behaviors. It is clear in *Kambili*, for instance, that in the rivalry between the wives for the honor of being mother of the hero, the bard sides with Dugo against the mischievous favorite wife who has "buttocks like a bush hut roof":

The preferred wife's child won't succeed.
The whore wife's child won't succeed.
The big bottom-swaying wife's child won't succeed.
The thieving wife's child won't succeed.
The slut wife's child won't succeed.

(950-54)

All through the epic we can see a deliberate effort to glorify Kambili as the ideal image of valor and sorcery, the proud marks of the hunters' cult group to which the bard is attached.

Perhaps *Mwindo* represents the extreme of authorial intrusion. The deliberately didactic denouement reveals a depth of concern for communal mores. Though it is, as we have seen, slightly out of alignment with the internal logic of the myth itself, it reflects the bard's effort to weave his personality into his work.

That the bard cannot be altogether impartial is similarly shown by Homer. Our well-manicured texts are probably not a good guide to his true nature; but there is little to show that, where it occurs, "the introduction of the poet's personality," as Leaf observes, "is a mark of a late origin."[21] We may not be certain who Homer was. He may not be as enthusiastic a judge of conduct as the bard of *Mwindo*, but his portrait of Thersites leaves us in no doubt as to his view of the wag in the context of the noble gathering before Troy:

[He] knew within his head many words, but disorderly; vain, and without decency, to quarrel with the princes with any word he thought might be amusing to the Argives. This was the ugliest man who came beneath Ilion. He was bandy-legged and went lame of one foot, with shoulders stooped and drawn together over his chest, and above this his skull went up to a point with the wool grown sparsely upon it. (*Iliad* 2.213–19)

Like the "preferred wife" in *Kambili*, Homer's Thersites has an ugly body and an ugly mind. The picture is not just obvious—the poet by his diction says so explicitly in a tone of judgment—and the portrait is that way because Homer positively wants to enlist the reactions of his audience in support of his feelings about the particular tendency that Thersites represents.[22] In heroic poetry performed in public and nourished by an empathy between bard and audience, impersonality is not much of a virtue.

By far the most significant proof of the bard's intimacy with his story is his tendency to identify himself with its characters and to speak in their respective personae. When he does so, drama and narration are inextricably merged in the warmth of the performance, creating editorial problems for collectors. Take the scene in *Kambili* when Bari the sorcerer is reading the oracular symbols in the dust as he prepares to solve the child riddle. In the charged mystico-poetic moment, the bard intermittently calls to his chorus men ("Namu-sayers"), as though *he* were reading them the signs:

Ah! Namu-sayers!
The brave put his hand into the dust.
Kumadise has appeared!
Maromaro has appeared!
Karalan has appeared!
Jibidise has appeared!
Teremise has appeared!
Nsorosigi ni kate has appeared!
Ah! Namu-sayers!
Yeremine has appeared!
Teremise has come!
Namu-sayers!
This one has become jibidise!
This one has become karalan!
The omen has come out!
The omen has become yeremine.
It's the omen for the birth of the child . . . .

(775-91)

The drama of this scene is highly powerful; we are reminded of that moment when the bard achieves vicarious elevation from a Nerikoro who turns into an eagle and takes flight (*Kambili* 615ff.). Or take the scene in which the lady Kumba goes to Cekura to secure the articles needed to destroy his magical power. She first succeeds in fooling him into believing that she is fed up with her marriage to Kambili; Cekura, highly flattered, showers gifts on Kumba:

He went and bought some grains of rice,
And went and bought some white chickens,
And went and bought ten white kolas,
And came and gave them to my Kumba.

(2320-33)

The bard is here impressed by Kumba's ingenuity and gratified by her service to the hero of his song; he has therefore no hesitation in addressing Kumba as if she were his own wife—"my Kumba."

An even more complex example of the authorial empathy appears earlier in the story. The blackbag man is the first to tackle the child riddle. He consults his oracular symbols and pronounces the qualities of the destined child; but Samory Toure, the judge of the contest, is unimpressed:

"Man," he replied, "there's nothing wrong with that,
But nine women cannot be pregnant with one child,
So get yourself together and look for the mother's name quickly.
    Will it be my dark wife?
    Will it be my favourite wife?
    Or will it be my outcast wife?"

(355-57)

The last three indented lines are delivered in an intoned chant—according to the editors' textual arrangement (see *Kambili*, p. ix)—and the use of possessive pronouns seems bound up with the overall empathic feel of the scene. The name of the wife is the real crux of the riddle. The wife in question is not the wife of Samory (though he asks the questions) but of Kanji, and the possessive pronoun has simply been thrown in under a lyrical impulse by a bard who feels that he has a stake in the fortunes of the trial. As written literature, the piece would be unacceptable for its failure to make the right distinctions between its characters, but the audience in an oral performance is quite content with the affective value of that lyrical moment: they accept that the bard and his characters—especially his favorite characters—are one.[23] "By identifying himself with his characters," as Bowra says of such a bard, "he can indulge emotions and sentiment, and adds greatly to the richness and variety of his poetry."[24]

We cannot, of course, state that this is a universal phenomenon. Our present texts of Homer do not reveal any such confusions, though we do not know how much tinkering was done with Homer by earlier editors (e. g., the Alexandrians), and we may or may not accept that the Peisistratids had to standardize Homer from several variants. But in the affective vocatives used for Patroklos and Eumaios we have a close approximation to the authorial empathy in heroic song. Nor do we often find the poet meshing with his characters in Yugoslav heroic songs. But the singers do sometimes jump right into a speech without making it quite clear whose speech it is, as in the following conclusion to Sulejman Makic's "Battle of Temisvar":

Then the vizier from Stambol departed and with him his army of a hundred thousand men. They went to Zlatna Jabuka and there they found Dano of Sarajevo. He had captured the seven kingdoms and seized countless treasure. He delivered them into the hands of Cuprilic Vizier. "I honour you for capturing all seven kings. I honour you, O elder, for your empire!" (*SCHS* 284)

Lord's note to the last couple of lines, reflecting this happy confusion of persons, indicates that the words could be taken "as being addressed to Cuprilic either by Dzano or possibly by the singer himself."[25]

Evidently, the performance character of the oral epic is much stronger in Africa than elsewhere, with a greater emphasis on the musical and dramatic elements. A situation like that would thus encourage a deeper affective interest on the part of the bard than has been noticed in any of the European traditions. But it would seem that not enough attention has been given to the existence of these elements in the European and other epics (the above note by Lord was only a cursory observation); as a result, those texts have been subjected to the rather augustan standards of judgment established by generations of scholars nourished by the scribal culture. By paying a closer attention to some of these stylistic nuances—for example, the bard's sense of intimacy with the characters of his tale—we will be well on the way to establishing a proper poetic for the oral, traditional epic, especially as yielded by performance.

Six

CONCLUSION

It will not be easy to summarize everything that has been said so far, given the variety of contexts in which we have examined the oral epic in Africa. But if anything has been firmly emphasized in this study, it is the peculiar demands of the very context of performance. There seems no doubt that the duty to affect an audience (in an act involving singing, musical accompaniment, and some dramatic movement), and the challenge of avoiding a collapse of the fervid act, impose upon the epic certain distinctive features. In content, not only may the story occasionally distort the accepted facts of a body of belief or of true history but the details of one performance may not be in total agreement with those of another performance of the same story, since each performance reflects the specific context that gives rise to it. In form, the oral epic demonstrates, under the pressure of steady delivery, a peculiar combination of economy and extravagance, or what Nagler has called an "intriguing mixture of sameness and variety."[1] In style, the bard employs certain techniques aimed both at manipulating the passions of his audience so that they accept the peculiar terms of his myth and at ensuring that there is enough of the familiar touch and voice in the tale to make it acceptable in contemporary, human terms.

We have endeavored to examine the African traditions of the

oral epic side by side with the Homeric and other traditions, because the numerous parallels between them are too close to be overlooked. No attempt has, of course, been made to establish an irrefutable one-to-one correspondence between one Homeric epic (e. g., the *Iliad*) and one African (e. g., *Kambili*); that would be a pointless exercise. No sensible scholar of the epic will contend that any traditon of the oral epic is exactly like the Homeric, for the obvious reason of cultural differences; in the words of Geoffrey Kirk once again, "the different preoccupations of mankind . . . do not express themselves in the same way or the same proportions from culture to culture." The works of Milman Parry and Albert Lord, and of the various scholars who have taken to the field after them, have in large measure increased our understanding of the fundamental character of the Homeric bard and his work. But none of these men would pretend that what they fetched in their recordings was exactly like the Homeric epos; for example, the Serbo-Croatian songs of the Parry-Lord collection have scarcely anything like the amazing divine apparatus of Homer. Similarly, Bowra's *Heroic Poetry* gives us an interesting gathering of heroic traditions from the Western and Eastern worlds, but many of them reveal aspects of heroic behavior different from Homer and one another. The Homeric epos is a towering classic, by the general agreement of centuries of scholarly opinion; yet it does not embrace all the conceivable possibilities of the genre that it represents so well.

The burden of explanation therefore rests with those scholars who, for reasons best known to themselves, bandy about phrases like " 'epic' poetry in the normal sense of the word" and contend that on the whole the heroic narrative traditions in Africa yield little more than "certain *elements* of epic."[2] We have tried to establish, in the last three chapters at least, that, viewed against the background of the genre as a whole, African heroic narratives are epics in spite of differences of detail here and there. With regard to the frame of performance itself, the following comment by Hainsworth gives as clear a picture as anyone may need: "Both modern observation and inference from old poems indicate that the plain recitation of epic poetry is unusual. The verses are at least intoned and usually sung. Instrumental accompaniment by the singer or by an assistant is regular. A second singer may repeat each verse after the first. There is consequently wide scope for histrionics on the part of the performer."[3] As our analysis has revealed, Hainsworth could very well have been talking about Africa. If, therefore, this much common ground exists between Africa and other societies where the oral epic has been found, it seems we are immensely well-equipped by a wealth of perspectives to examine the basic ingredients of this genre of art. Though the vagaries of global politics have so painfully shaken our faith in universal ideals, there is still room for an honest observation of two ways of life that impress us by the degree to which they mirror each other.

This book therefore makes an ambitious but sincere double effort. On the one hand, it tackles the various problems raised by traditional African poetics both within a local cultural context and against the background of worthwhile insights from non-African scholarship; on the other hand, it reestablishes the faith of more recent Africanists like Ruth Finnegan in "the relevance of African oral literature for comparative literature in the wide sense."[4] It should, of course, be clear that I have not given as much space to outlining the broader comparative implications of my views on the African material as to illuminating that material; this is the first full-scale effort to examine a genre of art that Africa was generally thought not to have, and it seemed to me that the duty to make the facts known and to attempt an intensive analysis of them in context was preeminent. I have, nevertheless, given due attention to some of the wider theoretical conclusions which that analysis may suggest in our study of the art of the heroic narrative. Structurally, for instance, a bard under the pressure of the audience out there endeavors to encompass more that rigid metric form can allow, and so some of the fashionable conclusions which have been framed largely on prosodic considerations need a little re-examining. And stylistically, since it is clear that the bard endeavors to impress that audience with the peculiar appeal of his style, however long-established the tradition which he re-enacts, we must go back and look a little deeper into the affective purposes of certain tendencies in the acknowledged classics like Homer whom we have for so long seen in terms not of the pre-literate artistic background from which they derive, but of sophisticated literary culture. As a comparatist, I can only hope that my ideas will invite certain scholars to open their eyes to evidence from areas that they have hitherto thought of no cultural account.

I also hope that this study will open the door to further investigations of this aspect of African culture, especially by Africans themselves who have grown up hearing these tales, and in particular those who have taken the trouble to collect them from the field. A large number of these epics have been collected by various scholars (some with greater care and professional skill than others),[5] but there have been very few serious attempts made to analyze that wealth of material or to formulate fairly comprehensive judgments on the strength of this analysis. If we can only do this, we will be treading on much safer ground when we make the kind of sentimental journey that is reflected in the following statement by Leopold Sedar Senghor:

Black voices, being undomesticated by the school, reveal all the nuances of ideas steeped in feeling; drawing freely from the unlimited dictionary of nature, they borrow her sonorous expressions, from the lucid songs of doves to the dark bursts of thunder.[6]

The scholar can do better, for his carefully worked out conclusions can stand the test of intelligent challenge.

NOTES

1. AN INTRODUCTION TO TRADITIONAL AFRICAN ART

1. See, for instance, W. E. Abraham, *The Mind of Africa* p. 41. Cf. J. Knappert's view of the religious function of minstrelsy: "The Epic in Africa," p. 172; also Ulli Beier, *Contemporary Art in Africa*, p. 25.

2. J. P. Clark, *The Ozidi Saga*; D. Biebuyck and K. C. Mateene, *The Mwindo Epic from the Banyanga.*

3. Cf. D. J. Crowley, "The Uses of African Verbal Arts," p. 131: "The breaking of the most sacred sanctions and the shocking distortions of proper behaviour are the very mark of story telling . . . . " Something of this disalignment between art and real or accepted forms is implied by Sir Walter Scott when he says, "This last high and creative faculty, namely, that of impressing the mind of the hearers with scenes and sentiments having no existence save through their art, has procured for the bards of Greece the name of ποιητής" (In *Minstrelsy of the Scottish Border*, E. F. Henderson, ed., p. 4).

4. Abraham, *Mind of Africa*, wades between phrases like "rationalistic philosophical" and "essentialist" (p. 47), and Stanley Macebuh has an interesting idea in his "oceanic infinitude" ("African Aesthetics in Traditional African Art," p. 20). The trouble with "infinitude" is that it denotes a too romantic reluctance to construe the world in *finite* terms.

5. Lucretius, *De Rerum Natura* 5.1183ff. and Statius, *Thebaid* 3.661 derive religion from fear, as does Freud in his idea of the formidable father-image (*The Future of an Illusion*). The Bachama of Nigeria also have a legend that traces the origin of religion to the fear of death: see J. Carnochan, " 'Nzeanzo and Won': A Bachama Folktale," p. 237. For the view of magic as the parent of religion, see Pliny, *Natural History* 30.1, and J. G. Frazer, *The Golden Bough*, 11.75.

1. Traditional African Art

6. See, for instance, the Baga and Senufo masks in P. Meauze, *African Art*, pp. 13, 17.

7. E. B. Idowu, *African Traditional Religion*, p. 134.

8. Elsy Leuzinger, *The Art of the Negro Peoples*, p. 47.

9. *Ibid.*, p. 26—which, incidentally, contradicts her claim on p. 24 that medicine men produced some of "the most important works of sculpture."

10. Matthew Arnold, *Preface to Poems, 1853*; cf. Leuzinger's comment on Baluba art, *Art of the Negro Peoples*, p. 198.

11. Cf. Leuzinger, *Art of the Negro Peoples*, p. 34

12. S. A. Babalola, *Content and Form*, pp. 46, 50. The idea of divine patronage is little more than a veiled claim to bardic authority and excellence, which is made by bards everywhere from classical Greece to contemporary Africa. The interesting picture of the frenzied bard in Tynnichus the Chalcidean (Plato, *Ion* 534d) is just another of the philosopher's unflattering views of poetry.

13. Babalola, *Content and Form* p. 41.

14. Indeed, it seems plausible to argue that the great moment of traditional African art came when the artist was removed from the staying influence of ritual to the relatively secular environment of the king's court, as witness Ife and Benin. Though she laments the reorientation, Leuzinger bears witness to the virile growth of artistic activity in the atmosphere of competition for the royal patronage, *Art of the Negro Peoples*, p. 34.

15. See Bruce King, *Introduction to Nigerian Literature*, p. 23.

16. See Meauze, *African Art*, pp. 63, 69, 129.

17. *Ibid.*, p. 79.

18. See Leuzinger, *Art of the Negro Peoples*, p. 128, and M. Trowell, *Classical African Sculpture*, plate XVIIA.

19. Trowell, *Classical African Sculpture*, p. 65.

20. A good illustration of the sense of the concrete in traditional African art is furnished by recent census exercises in Nigeria. To give the whole affair an aura of honesty and objectivity, the federal government assigned enumerators to states other than those in which they belonged. Some of the female enumerators wore colorful hairstyles that had never before been seen in the communities to which they were assigned; before long the local hairdressers tried to reproduce these strange and fascinating styles on the heads of their local clients, and the new styles were called "census." It is worth noting that "census" in this case means not the entire counting exercise but the one concrete feature of it that has caught the interest of the local hair artist.

21. D. P. Kunene, *Heroic Poetry of the Basotho*, p. xvi.

22. "Le chanteur s'associe intimement avec son sujét et ses héros, à tel point, qu'il semble s'identifier à eux" D. Biebuyck and K. C. Mateene, "Chante Hunde," p. 158; cf. R. Finnegan, *Oral Literature in Africa*, pp. 383f.

23. *Mwindo* 144. Cf. *Sunjata* IV. 83f.

24. Niane notes, *ad loc.*: "The clear language *par excellence* is Mandingo. For the Mandingoes, their language is clear like their country of open savannas, which they often contrast with the dark forest—hence references to Mali as the 'Bright Country.'"

25. C. Bird et al., *The Song of Seydou Camara*; vol. 1, *Kambili*.

26. "Le texte reproduit est, à plusieurs égards, interessant et significatif. Il représente un texte chanté d'une longueur considerable pour cette région africaine, où la plupart des chants se réduisent à un simple proverbe." Biebuyck and Mateene, "Chant Hunde," p. 158.

27. An interesting relationship between landscape and art has been observed in modern African fiction by Gerald Moore, *The Chosen Tongue*, p. 158. Moore draws a contrast between the milieux of the novels of Chinua Achebe of Nigeria and James Ngugi of Kenya: he finds that Ngugi's characters are rather lonely, because they are cast against the background of the "vaster scenes" of the scanty Kikuyu grasslands or savannas, whereas Achebe's scenes teem with fellowship in the "crowded human landscape of the village," against the background of the "surrounding forest."

28. See Meauzé, *African Art*, p. 57. Nothing from further north would compare with such a mask, in girth or in sheer exuberance.

29. For interesting observations on the *ibeji* myth, see T. Mobolade, "Ibeji Custom in Yorubaland," and M. Hammersley Houlberg, "Ibeji Images of the Yoruba."

30. Because they are prepared to pay so much for the "real old stuff," tourists and collectors have encouraged the wildest swindles imaginable in art traffic. The story is well known in cultural circles around Ibadan, for instance, how "middlemen" would sponsor the mass production of *ibeji* or twin-baby figures from old or ailing wood (to ensure amputations here and there), have them buried in a garbage heap for a couple of weeks (to ensure the due layer of fungi on removal), and then pass them off on eager clients at strategic outlets!

31. Pp. 15–24.

32. A. B. Lord, *Singer of Tales*, p. 28.

33. Nketia notes that, among the Akan of Ghana, a drum musician (as an act of courtesy) tries to fit the name of a patron into the text of an old tune in his repertoire: thus "truth" is slightly readjusted to give a brand-new pleasure. See J. H. Nketia, "The Musician in Akan Society," p. 94. A classic example of this partisan element is provided by the griot Dembo Kanute, whose version of the Sunjata epic was sung in the presence of a Seni Darbo. In that version, the griot makes "the ancestor of the Darbos" the star of the final climax of the tale: the pursuit of the fleeing Sumanguru by the Sunjata party is led by that Darbo (*Sunjata* III.954ff.).

34. C. M. Bowra, *Heroic Poetry*, p. 369.

35. See Finnegan, *Oral Literature in Africa*, p. 126.

2. Resources of the Oral Epic

36. "Fait bien connu des spécialistes des traditions orales africaines: Le griot compose toujours sur un schème fixe et, selon son humeur et son public, développe tel ou tel épisode; si dans une même journée on fait répéter à un conteur la même histoire, on entendra chaque fois de nouvelles variantes. Le griot, en effet, répugne à conter cette histoire deux fois de suit dans le termes identiques. Il est avant tout un homme de lettres; la variét de son langage est sa coquetterie en même temps que la preuve de son talent et de sa virtuosité. A. H. Ba and L. Kesteloot, "Une éopée peule: 'Silamaka,' " p. 5. The motivation for variability is of course often mercenary. For the mercenary character of court minstrelsy, see D. Scharfe and Y. Aliyu, "Hausa Poetry," p. 35.

37. Lord, *Singer of Tales*, p. 28.

38. Babaloba, *Content and Form*, p. 45. Cf. Abraham, *Mind of Africa*, p. 91; H. F. Morris, *The Heroic Recitations of the Bahima of Ankole*, p. 25; J. H. Nketia, "Akan Poetry," p. 27.

39. S. Macebuh, "African Aesthetics in Traditional African Art," p. 22.

40. We may note here the endless harassment by that spectator in *Ozidi* who takes the bard to task for using the loan-word "tain" (*time*) instead of the Ijo equivalent: his atavism is clearly well in the way. For partisan interest, See Babalola, *Content and Form*, pp. 61–64.

41. G. S. Kirk, *Myth: Its Meaning and Functions*, p. 28. Kirk is trying to qualify his own "general theories."

2. THE RESOURCES OF THE ORAL EPIC

1. Cf. A. B. Lord, *Singer of Tales*, p. 5.

2. A. B. Lord, "Homer, Parry and Huso," p. 42; cf. Lord, "Homer's Originality: Oral Dictated Texts," p. 126f; and Lord, "Homer and Other Epic Poetry", p. 195.

3. Lord, *Singer of Tales*, p. 6.

4. For the varied repertoire of Seydou Camara, see *Kambili*, p. ix. Some of the chants in the story—e. g., the hunters' marriage song sung at the wedding of Kambili and Kumba and the song of praise for the killing of the lion—are, apparently, independent songs that have simply found fitting use in the story; see notes 157 and 164 to the text of *Kambili*. Cf. also *Mwindo* 14.

5. Something of a uniform pattern can indeed be seen in the following portraits of the singer-musician (in terms of training at least): Lord, *Singer of Tales*, pp. 20ff.; Babalola, *Content and Form*, pp. 40–55; D. W. Ames, "A Sociocultural View of Hausa Musical Activity"; and A. P. Merriam, "The Bala Musician." The last two studies are in W. L. d'Azevedo, ed., *The Traditional Artist in African Societies*.

6. Cf. Babalola, *Content and Form*, pp. vi, 23.

7. Nketia, "Musician in Akan Society," p. 88.

8. See R. Finnegan, *Oral Literature in Africa*, p. 116.

9. One suspects, though, that in many of these cases the bard simply accords the art to the hero as a way of glorifying it: it is the occupation even of kings and heroes!

10. C. M. Bowra, *Heroic Poetry*, p. 410. For the various instances in which traditional African poetry and song are practiced on a nonspecialist basis, see Finnegan, *Oral Literature*, p. 104. Sir Walter Scott has made perhaps the best comments on this issue of proliferation of poetical skill in a community: "It is indeed easily discovered, that the qualities necessary for composing such poems are not the portion of every man in the tribe; that the bard, to reach excellence in his art, must possess something more than a full command of words and phrases, and the knack of arranging them in such a form as ancient examples have fixed upon as the recognized structure of national verse. . ." (*Minstrelsy of the Scottish Border*, p. 3).

11. Nketia, "Musician in Akan Society," p. 83.

12. Merriam, "Bala Musician," p. 258; cf. D. Biebuyck, "The Epic as a Genre in Congo Oral Literature," p. 261.

13. Babalola, *Content and Form*, p. 41.

14. *SCHS*, pp. 59f., 225, 235, 263, and 289 respectively.

15. "Le récit du vieillard dan souligne la fonction primordiale du musicien attaché à la cour: augmenter le prestige du chef. Le texte indique aussi la position particulière du griot malinké: il sert de messager." H. Zemp, "Musiciens autochtones et griots malinke chez les Dan de Cote d'Ivoire," p. 377; cf. also p. 378 on professionalism. Gordon Innes has also argued, quite forcefully, that there is little support for the claim that griots held lofty positions in the courts of the old Mandingo kings: see *Sunjata: Three Mandinka Versions*, pp. 8-9. Indeed, in the version of the Sunjata legend by Banna Suso, griots appear occasionally to be grouped together with slaves: see *Sunjata* I. 65ff. (though here the bard awards greater wisdom to his mythic counterpart) and 1173.

16. Babalola, *Content and Form*, p. 47.

17. *Ibid.*, pp. 41f., 61f.. Dembo Kanute and his brother Banna, two of the griots of the Innes collection, prove that the student does not have to echo his teacher. Dembo was trained by their father and then trained Banna under their father's supervision (Innes, *Sunjata* p. 260); but their versions are thoroughly different. Not only are their temperaments evidently unalike but they have pursued their careers in different environments.

18. Cf. Nketia, "Musician in Akan Society," p. 87.

19. Babalola, *Content and Form*, p. 50.

20. Ames, "A Sociocultural View," p. 153.

21. H. M. Chadwick and N. K. Chadwick, *The Growth of Literature*, 1:603.

22. Cf. Lord, "Homer and Other Epic Poetry," p. 209.

23. *Odyssey*, 14.121, 17.541, and 14.13ff.

2. Resources of the Oral Epic

24. Among the Asaba Igbo of midwestern Nigeria, there is a traditional war dance called *egwu-ota*, a quite frightening affair. The young men clash their matchets against wicker shields and howl war cries as the dance proceeds in a phalanxlike movement.

25. Ames, "A Sociocultural View," p. 154.

26. Biebuyck, "The African Heroic Epic," p. 22.

27. Kirk thinks (wrongly, I believe) that this is simply a tourist pose and an evidence of "degeneracy" in the bardic tradition: see G. S. Kirk, *The Songs of Homer* plate 8c.

28. G. S. Kirk, "Homer and Modern Oral Poetry," p. 289. For the rhapsode's adornments, see Plato, *Ion* 530b, 535d.

29. Ames "A Sociocultural View," p. 144.

30. Merriam, "Bala Musician," p. 256.

31. Hymn to Apollo, pp. 166ff. Also, for the rhapsode's exaggerated claims, see Plato, *Ion* 530c, d, 533c, 541b.

32. "Les chanteurs sont des artistes, le fait qu'ils se monstrent extremement jaloux l'un de l'autre le prouve encore. Un jour, à Sarajévo, aprés avoir recueilli des phonogrammes de trois chanteurs, je donnai à tous trois la même recompense. L'un d'entre eux réfusa de l'accepter. Je flairai aussitôt que je l'avais froissé de quelque manière. Les personnes presentes me previnrent en effet qu'il se considérait comme un bien meilleur chanteur que les deux autres." M. Parry, "Studies in the Epic Technique of Oral Verse-Making II;" p. 15.

33. Babalola, *Content and Form*, p. 46.

34. H. Zemp, 'La légende des griots malinke," pp. 614ff.

35. J. P. Clark, "The Azudu Saga," p. 9. For the dream/vision, compare the story of Caedmon in Bede, *Hist. Eccles.* IV.24; also Ennius' vision of Homer, in Cicero, *Acad. Pr.* II.16.51.

36. See *Sunjata* IV.2f.; cf. N. Levtzion, *Ancient Ghana and Mali*, pp. 25f.; and C. Bird, "Heroic Songs of the Mande Hunters," *African Folklore*, p. 446.

37. J. H. K. Nketia, *Folk Songs of Ghana*, p. 154.

38. Zemp, "Musiciens autochtones," pp. 376f.

39. Ames, "A Sociocultural View," pp. 155f.

40. Bowra, *Heroic Poetry*, p. 428.

41. Merriam, "Bula Musician," pp. 262f.

42. Audience response cannot be taken lightly in a live performance of tales in Africa, and in this connection J. P. Clark's work on *The Ozidi Saga* is somewhat of a landmark in transcription. He has reproduced all those instances in which various native-speaking spectators interject questions and comments into the bard's narration. Some of these are positive, as they help promote the affective force of certain situations in the narrative: for instance, in two cases (*Ozidi* 179 and 304f.) a spectator's exclamation brings out effectively for the bard the horror and panic into

which Oreame is thrown as Ozidi faces destruction at the hands of the enemy. In some other cases, the audience simply responds to the antics of various characters in the tale (219, 234, etc.). But most other comments are a bit of a distraction and menace: the bard is frequently forced to take a defensive position when some of his details and usages are challenged as being ill chosen or out of place (94, 153, 262, 274, 284, 287, 331). On the whole, the fervor of the scene is unmistakable.

43. A. Parry, "Have We Homer's *Iliad*?" p. 185.

44. Clark, "The Azudu Saga," 9.

45. See Finnegan, *Oral Literature*, p. 6.

46. Lord, *Singer of Tales*, p. 68.

47. "Contrairement à l'amateur, qui gesticule du corps et de la voix, le récitant professionnel adopte une attitude impassible, un débit rapide et monotone. Lors d'une réaction admirative de l'auditoire, il suspend la voix avec détachement, jusqu'à ce que le silence se rétablisse." A. Coupex and Th. Kamanzi, *Littérature de cour au Rwanda*, p. 77.

48. J. H. K. Nketia, "Akan Poetry," p. 12.

49. Finnegan, *Oral Literature* p. 15. In this connection, J. P. Clark has done an excellent job in his transcription of *The Ozidi Saga*; he has indicated all those points in the narration–performance at which the audience (or perhaps the bard, expressively) bursts into laughter. In some cases it is not clear what has caused the laughter (e. g., *Ozidi* 114 and 124), and we can only conjecture a histrionic effort on the part of the bard that the text cannot adequately capture.

50. Zora Devrnja (in "The Functions of Metaphor in Traditional Serbian Narrative") points to this preference for recitation over singing (p. 12) and to the tendency of the audience to watch carefully for deviations from standard versions (p. 24).

51. See J. B. Obama, "La Musique africaine traditionelle: ses fonctions sociales et sa signification philosophique," p. 284.

52. C. M. Bowra, "Metre," p. 22.

53. A. B. Lord, "Homer and Other Epic Poetry," p. 182.

54. *De Musica* 1132b.

55. W. W. Merry, ed., *Homer: Odyssey 1-XII*, p. 308. The later (rhapsodic) tradition of heroic singing evidently explored to the full the histrionic resources of the Homeric songs: cf. Plato, *Ion* 535b, c.

56. See D. Biebuyck, "The African Heroic Epic," pp. 22-23; and *Ozidi*, 29-31.

57. Cf. *Ozidi* 30.

58. Ames, "A Sociocultural View," p. 148.

59. *De Musica* 1131.

60. *Laws* 656d.

61. "L'encouragement par le chant et la musique joue un rôle considérable dans le société dan . . . . Il ne s'agit pas seulement d'un encouragement banal par

251

2. Resources of the Oral Epic

des paroles flatteuses, mais d'une véritable transmission de force par la musique." "Musiciens autochtones," pp. 371f. For an interesting view of the socio-psychological role of music as a necessary complement in the life cycle (birth-growth-death) of the African, see Obama, "La Musique africaine traditionelle," p. 290.

62. Nettl, *Music in Primitive Culture*, p. 21.

63. J. A. Notopoulos, "Homer, Hesiod, and the Achaean Heritage of Oral Poetry," p. 192.

64. It is significant that the words were actually put into Sulejman's mouth by Nikola. That Nikola, who was assiduously trained by Milman Parry to take an intensive interest in the *epos*, should seem to maintain a partiality for the music says something, I think, for its importance in south Slavic heroic song.

65. A. Parry, *Making of Homeric Verse*, p. 442.

66. A bard's imagination strays, no doubt because it is overstrained; and very often music and chant are summoned to the relief of the bard when the job of narration has taken a toll of his energies. Thus in *Ozidi*, at the end of the fourth night of performance—about halfway through the arduous stretch of seven nights—the bard and his group go into an extended coda (203–5) of songs, some of which have nothing to do with the action of the tale. They are glad it's all over, for that night at least!

I have myself witnessed some performances in which the bard lost the trend of his tale; a tune is suddenly struck up, and while this is being sung, one of the accompanists whispers to the narrator the missing detail of the story.

67. Personal communication, March 10, 1975.

68. That the right sort and measure of music are needed to help the narration move effectively is demonstrated in *Ozidi* 220. The bard has just been narrating how Ozidi's hornblower blew endlessly for the hero to call off the fight with the Scrotum King. At this momentous point, the bard feels the need for the music to lend textural support to the detail of narration and calls his supporting orchestra: "Now let the things speak up!" Compare also Innes, *Sunjata*, p. 262.

69. Nettl, *Music in Primitive Culture*, p. 123; cf. Ames, "A Sociocultural View," pp. 150f. On polyrhythms, see further Obama, "La Musique africaine traditionelle," p. 300.

70. See K. Y. Daaku, "History in the Oral Traditions of the Akan," pp. 120f.

71. D. Biebuyck, "The Epic as a Genre in Congo Oral Literature," p. 263.

72. See G. Towo-Atangana, "Le Mvet: genre majeur de la littérateur orale des population Pahouines (Bulu, Beti, Fang-Ntumu)," pp. 163–66.

73. Called "phorminx" in Iliad 1.603, *Odyssey* 8.257, *Hymn to Apollo*, 183, etc.; "Kitharis" in *Iliad* 3.54. For a detailed discussion of musical instruments in Homer, see Max Wegner, *Musik und Tanz*, pp. 2ff. However, the discovery of "late-Geometric" Attic vases, showing the figure of a citharode flanked by rattlists (see Kirk, *Songs of Homer*, plate 7a), is significant: perhaps we have in them an indication of

the orchestral circumstances of *aoidoi* like Demodokos and the singer of the *Hymn to Apollo*. How Kirk gets the impression that the scene is "probably funerary" and that the minstrel "may be singing a dirge for the dead" is not quite clear.

74. For a more detailed treatment of prosody in African heroic songs, see Babalola, *Content and Form*, pp. 344ff.; Nketia, "Akan Poetry," pp. 8ff.; *Kambili*, pp. x-xi. Each of these discussions stresses the basic looseness of the metric pattern.

75. "Homer, Hesiod, and the Achaean Heritage," p. 196; cf. A. Parry, *Making of Homeric Verse*, pp. 323ff.; and R. Carpenter, *Folktakes, Fiction, and Saga in the Homeric Epics*, p. 7. The concept of "artificial" diction, for a bard who sings mostly for native consumption, is a hard proposition. However, there is an interesting phenomenon in midwestern Nigeria that may have a relation to the kind of dialectal potpourri (Arcado-Cypriot-Aeolic-Ionic) that has been claimed for Homer (see especially T. W. Allen, *Homer: The Origins and Transmission* pp. 98ff.). The village of Ebu is known to have been formed (sometime during the ancient Benin empire) almost exclusively by a division of the imperial army that had been disbanded after its campaigns. Soldiers were usually conscripted from various reaches of the empire; in this case they chose to settle in a new place—situated on the banks of the River Niger, Ebu has a lovely climate—rather than go back to their several homes. Today the language of Ebu is totally unlike any other around it: it contains just about every midwestern Nigerian dialect!

76. C. H. Whitman, *Homer and the Heroic Tradition*, p. 82, and Lord, *Singer of Tales* pp. 153–57; Kirk, "Homer and Modern Oral Poetry"; p. 278. Others, however, prefer to see Homer as a literate poet: see H. T. Wade-Gery, *The Poet of the Iliad*, p. 2.

77. Cf. Bowra, *Heroic Poetry*, pp. 240f. Consider the distinction, made by Sulejman Makić, between the sung (i. e., to the gusle) and the dictated texts (*SCHS* 263).

78. Bowra, *Heroic Poetry*, p. 39.

79. Nettl, *Music in Primitive Culture*, p. 25. For a more colorful statement on this issue, see Scott, *Minstrelsy of the Scottish Border*, pp. 4f.

80. Bowra, *Heroic Poetry*, p. 36; A. Parry, *Making of Homeric Verse*, p. 443; Lord, "Homer and Other Epic Poetry," p. 184.

81. *Oral Literature*, pp. 108ff.

82. Lord, "Homer and Other Epic Poetry," p. 200.

83. A. B. Lord, ed., *Slavic Folklore*, p. 125.

84. Nketia, "Musician in Akan Society," p. 74. That an occasion is a funeral does not necessarily mean that the bard is singing dirges. Heroic chants are mostly the business at the funeral of a famous hunter among the Yoruba and the Akan: cf. Babalola, *Content and Form*, pp. 15f.

85. P. Vivante, *The Homeric Imagination*, p. 75.

86. Babalola, *Content and Form*, p. 65; cf. Finnegan, *Oral Literature*, p. 9.

2. Resources of the Oral Epic

87. See V. Monteil, ed., *C. Monteil: Les Empires du Mali*, p. 74; M. Sidibe, "Soundiata Keita, héros historique et légendaire," p. 50.

88. The following verses from *Kambili* illustrate the "group" sensibility of the Mande of western Sudan:

All groups can be broken;
However, a killing group cannot be broken.
Should you leave it, you will befoul yourself.
Man, if you were to do that,
A bit would be trimmed off your height.
Master, that is never done.

(1614–19)

89. "Un souci de vérité qui est tout á l'honneur de la caste des griots." D. T. Niane, "Le Probléme de Soundiata," p. 123. For a detailed discussion of the causes of the war between Sunjata and Sumanguru, see A. Shelton, "The Problem of Griot Interpretation and the Actual Causes of War in *Soundiata*,"pp.146ff. Ba and Kesteboot make an equally interesting case about historical inexactitude in the oral epic. They state that the bard is scarcely interested in objectivity: it can only come by accident, and in any case the picture that emerges always carries a taint of partisanship. "The epic," they declare, "is not history, but the poetry of history" ("Une épopée peule: 'Silamaka,' " p. 9). For other cases of griots paying special court to earlier griots in their tales, see M. Konate, "Da Monzon de Segou," p. 177; and *Sunjata* I.71ff.

90. See L. R. Palmer, "The Language of Homer," p. 106; cf. J. A. Davison, "The Transmission of Text," p. 219.

91. See Wade-Gery, *Poet of the Iliad*, p. 62. For the simile as a reflection of Homeric, not Mycenaean, times, see G. P. Shipp, *Studies in the Language of Homer*, p. 79.

92. Lord, "Homer as Oral Poet," p. 6; cf. his *Singer of Tales*, p. 44.

93. Lord, "Homer and Other Epic Poetry," p. 208. For arguments for and against the historicity of the Trojan tale, see especially D. L. Page, *History and the Homeric Iliad*, and M. I. Finley, "The Trojan War," pp. 1–9.

94. For bards celebrating contemporary events with old lines, see A. Mafeje, "The Role of the Bard in a Contemporary African Community," pp. 193ff.; and J. Opland , "*Imbongi Nezibongo*;" pp. 194ff.

95. For a brief but relevant discussion of generosity and hospitality within the scheme of Mandinka etiquette, see Innes, *Sunjata*, p. 124.

96. *Beowulf* 1172, 1602; *Maldon* 196. For generosity as the most outstanding element in the image of the early Germanic king, see H. M. Chadwick, *The Heroic Age*, p. 348.

97. "Le même apprenti ira le matin cultiver le champ du maître, et sera le soir initie au arcanes du conte mystique ou de la généalogie des rois. . . . L'enseigne-

ment que le jeune Africain reçevait donc dans ces ateliers, était un enseignement complet et equilibre, visant á integrer parfaitement l'individu au groupe ... a l'occasion de telle technique agricole, ou de tel motif à tisser, le maitre peut expliquer le mythe d'origine; de même, l'épopée de Soundiata par exemple, sera interrompue pour une leçon de psychologie sociale sur l'état de perclus, ou une leçon de botanique sur l'utilisation des feuilles de baobab; tout sujét de conversation ou d'observation est prétexte à digression, et tout digression est prétexte à enseignement." L. Kestleloot, "Les Épopées de l'ouest africain," p. 207.

98. Cf. A. Parry, "Have We Homer's *Iliad?*," p. 192.

3. THE HERO: HIS IMAGE AND HIS RELEVANCE

1. C. H. Whitman, *Homer and the Heroic Tradition*, pp. 181ff.

2. Aristotle was, however, not ignorant of certain literate features akin to oral literature. Something of this awareness is reflected in his condemnation of what he calls the *eiromene lexis*, the continuous or "stringed" style of rhetoric (*Rhetorics* 1409a), of which he says: "The continuous style is the ancient one, as for instance, 'Here is the exposition of the investigation by Herodotus of Thurii.' This style used to be quite popular, but not many people use it nowadays. By 'continuous' I imply that the style serves no real purpose other than the exhaustion of detail. It is unpleasant, because there's no end to it." Yet the bard counts upon this exhaustion of detail for a full and successful evening of song. As Rhys Carpenter has put it, "Dwelling on detail for detail's sake is oral narrative's eternal prerogative" (*Folktale, Fiction, and Saga*, 78).

3. G. S. Kirk, *Myth: Its Meaning and Functions*, p. 135. Aristarchus' scalpel was quite severe. An interesting athetesis by him is of *Iliad* 20.180–86, which he condemns as "language unbefitting [ου πρεποντες] of the character of Achilles." For an angry Achilles, hell-bent on vengeance, nothing can be considered a cheap taunt so long as he draws his man on to a fight; and taunting and bragging are a standard habit of the Homeric hero. The concept of το πρεπον such as Aristarchus had must therefore be considered a questionable criterion for the oral art that the Homeric songs primarily are.

4. J. A. Notopoulos, "Parataxis in Homer."

5. *Ibid.*, p. 16.

6. Something of this is reflected in the concept of the "emotional core" of the narrative song as discussed by C. G. Zug, "The Ballad Editor as Antiquary."

7. See *Mwindo* 14; D. Biebuyck, "The Epic as a Genre in Congo Oral Literature," p. 263; G. Innes, *Sunjata: Three Mandinka Versions*, pp. 16, 19.

8. H. Zemp, "Musiciens autochtones et griots malinke chez les Dan de Côte d'Ivoire," p. 377.

3. The Hero: His Image and Relevance

9. Hesiod, *Theogony* 79f.

10. Cf. *Sunjata* I.29–32.

11. M. Sidibe, "Soundiata Keita, Héros historique et légendaire," p. 41. Compare also the warning given to Da Monzon on the birth of Silamaka (*Silamaka* II).

12. G. Towo-Atangana, "Le Mvet: genre majeur de la littérateur orale," p. 171.

13. This phenomenon is not unknown in Africa, especially where there is a cycle of tales. For instance, none of the published tales of the Monzon cycle talks about the birth of Monzon or his son Da.

14. For the progression from birth through development and manhood, cf. the medieval Greek epic *Digenes Akritas*, ed. J. Mavrogordata.

15. The other famed hero of African myth who destroys a wild beast in early youth is Chaka the Zulu. For his fight with the lion in his "uncircumcised youth," see Thomas Mofolo, *Chaka* pp. 18ff.

16. He tells Unferth that he and Breca "were both yet very young" (536f.).

17. A different picture of the physical personality is presented by *The Mwindo Epic*. The hero is a dazzling beauty—"the multiple rays of the rising sun and the moon. That is the beauty of the child Mwindo" (72). But he is also frightfully small and indeed remains rather a child all through his range of activities—so small indeed that at one point his aunt and his uncles "carried him on their fingertips" (114). Evidently, he has been kept small in the story so as to make his feats appear all the more wonderful, as his enemies are forced to observe (72). Something of the same order is seen in Odysseus. He is a bit stooped in figure and not eminently handsome (*Iliad* 3.193ff.); and though Polyphemos, a giant, is not the best judge of normal human size, his observation of Odysseus seems suggested by the *Iliad* picture. Of the man prophesied to rob him of his sight the Cyclops says:

> But always I was on the lookout for a man handsome
> and tall, with great endowment of strength upon him, to come here;
> but now the end of it is that a little man, niddering, feeble,
> has taken away the sight of my eye . . . .
>
> (*Odyssey* 9.513–16)

See also W. B. Stanford, *The Ulysses Theme*, p. 66f.

18. Achilles is the central personality in the *Iliad*, but Homer is by no means silent about the image and capabilities of the other notable figures. Indeed, so much attention is given to Hektor, Ajax, Diomedes, and others, that it is sensible to suggest that the Homeric "hero" is an aggregation of the several qualities revealed by these individual braves. It is a cardinal error of the organicist judgment that it attempts to suppress the merits of other heroes to the advantage of Achilles. This is a major flaw in Cedric Whitman's logic, particularly his understanding of Patroklos. Whitman (*Homer and the Heroic Tradition*, p. 194) considers him a "gentle person" suddenly turned bellicose ("equal to Ares," ισος 'Αρηι, 11.604) the moment he takes on a commission from Achilles to check on a wounded Achaean;

later, when Patroklos in his *aristeia* gloats over his fallen victims, Whitman (p. 345) thinks this "out of character." In the first instance, Whitman forgets that Homer has earlier prepared us for Patroklos' eminence. During the embassy of *Iliad* 9, while Achilles cuts up the meat to be roasted for the envoys, "the son of Menoitos kindled a huge fire, a man equal to a god" (ισοθεος φως, 9.211). It appears from the context that "equal to a god" is simply a variant for "equal to Ares," and perhaps that Patroklos is being complimented on a size of fire that only a god could have made. Secondly, gloating over a fallen enemy is a thing done by numerous warriors from either side who have nothing at all to do with Achilles.

19. For a good spate of proverbs as a mark of wisdom in courtly environment, see A. H. Ba and L. Kesteloot, "Da Monzon et Karta Thiema," pp. 187ff. Perhaps the most lucid statement (itself pithily framed) on the value of proverbs in African speech comes from the Nigerian novelist Chinua Achebe: "Proverbs are the palm-oil with which words are eaten" (*Things Fall Apart*, p. 10). For a detailed discussion of proverbs in the oral literature of Africa see R. Finnegan, *Oral Literature in Africa*, pp. 389ff.; cf. E. O. Arewa and A. Dundes, "Proverbs and the Ethnography of Speaking," pp. 70ff.

20. Whitman, *Homer and the Heroic Tradition*, p. 184. I find it difficult to agree with Werner Jaeger's judgment of the relative qualities in the *Iliad*: "The poet presents the eloquent Odysseus and Ajax the laconic man of action as contrasts to Achilles himself. By this contrast he emphasizes the highest ideal of developed humanity as personified in the greatest of the heroes—Achilles. . ." (*Paideia* trans. G. Highet, 1:8). There is here, to say the least, a considerable misevaluation of Odysseus: see *Iliad* 10.231f. and 243ff. for Diomedes' estimation of him.

21. In *Odyssey* 11.337, Arete, the wife of Alkinoos, applauds the physical appeal as well as mental balance in Odysseus. There is a very real temptation to deduce here a certain allegorical blessing on the personality of Odysseus, especially in view of the meaning of the word *arete*. Homer tells us in 7.54 that the word is a "nickname" for Alkinoos' wife, and Merry (*Odyssey, ad loc*) agrees that it has "a special significance"; the scholiast thinks it comes from her being born to nobility and wealth. Could "Arete" by any chance be the Greek image of "Culture," pointing to Odysseus as the picture of balanced human excellence?

22. Hrothgar (*Beowulf* 1844) credits the hero with "strength, and prudence, and wisdom of word." Quite possibly Gilgamesh is the ancient eastern world's supreme aggregation of heroic virtues: "He was wise, he saw mysteries and knew secret things . . . . When the gods created Gilgamesh they gave him a perfect body. Shamash the glorious sun endowed him with beauty, Adad the god of the storm endowed him with courage, the great gods made his beauty perfect, surpassing all others, terrifying like a great wild bull. Two thirds they made him god and one third man" (*Gilgamesh* 61).

3. The Hero: His Image and Relevance

23. Note that in 2115, shortly before he launches into his gnomic lines, the bard warns his accompanist to "pay attention to the rhythm."

24. *Nicomachean Ethics* 9.8.

25. On the public consciousness of the ancient Greeks, see Jaeger, *Paideia* I:9; cf. E. R. Dodds, *The Greeks and the Irrational*, pp. 17f.

26. Cf. Ogueren's self-admiration in *Ozidi* 121. Incidentally, we will recall that when the Achaean embassy visits Achilles in his tent, they find him holding a lyre with which "he cheered his heart and sang the glories of men" (9.186-89). There is in this a tempting analogy with the practice known among warrior-chiefs in old African communities; a good example is the sorcerer-king Sumanguru, who has a charmed harp-lute to which "after each victory he would come and sing his own praises" (*Sunjata* IV.39). What Achilles actually says in his lyrics, Homer doesn't tell us. But in view of the hero's superlative self-love it is not unlikely that he is the subject of his own song; in that case, the *klea andron* (glories of men) would simply be a formula equally usable in Achilles' peculiar circumstance. Whitman thinks roughly along the same lines: "Is it an over interpretation to see a symbol of. . .self-search in Achilles' song of 'the glories of men'? We are told that the passage indicates that in the heroic age warriors improvised epic lays, and this is doubtless true. But Achilles is the only one who actually does any singing in Homer, aside from the professional bards of the *Odyssey*, perhaps for the very reason that to Homer, the practice of epic singing was profoundly involved with the roots of early self-consciousness, the estimate of oneself in the light of the future's retrospect" (*Homer and the Heroic Tradition*, p. 193).

27. Cf. also his fateful wish for immortality and an honor equal to that of the gods (8.538ff.).

28. In the African heroic tradition, there are several varieties of the end of the hero's career. Chaka is speared to death by his brothers Dingana, Mhlangana, and Mopo. But at the point of death he regains his old splendor with such awesome effect that his assassins flee in terror. His body does not decay, and even the ravenous beasts and birds of prey are afraid to approach his body, which has turned "green like seaweed!" (See Mofolo's *Chaka*, pp. 197f.)

The Sunjata epic presents an interesting case. The historical Sunjata seems to have met a rather inglorious end. D. T. Niane (in his notes, pp. 95f.) mentions two versions. The first is that the emperor was killed by an arrow during a public protest in his capital; the second that he was drowned in the river Sankarani. M. Sidibe records a version close to the latter and which is equally unflattering: Sunjata made an unjust war against the Ouassoulou (Wasulu); in the decisive battle fought on the river Sankarani, Sunjata and his men were worsted, and he plunged into the floods with his favorite wife. At that moment, a hippopotamus surged up, and a cry was raised that the emperor had turned into a hippo rather than fall into the hands of his enemy! ("Soundiata Keita' héros historique et légendaire," pp. 46f.). A hippopotamus may be a fine way to end; but Djeli Mamoudou, the bard of Niane's edition, has maintained an absolutely tight lip on details of his hero's death and even discourages such inquiry (*Sunjata* IV.84).

Kambili and Mwindo survive; but such a romantic end is no less heroic than the tragic one. And I don't agree with C. M. Bowra's assessment of Odysseus that "to his heroic career the final fitting touch is lacking" simply because he is assured of "ever so gentle" an end (*Heroic Poetry*, p. 131). Odysseus happens to represent a different but not less heroic strand of Homeric heroism. Yet he has surmounted the wrath of Poseidon, has tamed the menace of the lawless princes in Ithaka, and to the end remains favored of Athene. It is significant that the *Iliad* we know does not leave Achilles dead. In spite of the charged denouement and the overhanging hand of destiny, U. von Wilamowitz's conclusion that the original *Iliad* ended with Achilles' death a day after that of Hektor (*Die Ilias Und Homer*, pp. 68ff.) remains only an intelligent conjecture.

29. For "play" used euphemistically to signify trouble, cf. *Kambili* 1937.

30. On the hero's fears, see A. S. Cook, *The Classic Line*, p. 86, and A. E. Youman, "Climactic Themes in the *Iliad*." Various African heroes are also seen to demonstrate a certain trepidation just before or during a major engagement. For instance, Sunjata earns a reproof from his griots when he seems to flinch before Sumanguru in their encounter (I.674ff.; III.772ff.), and Ozidi cries from fear of the headwalking ogre Tebekawene (332). But all this is simply set up to make the problem look insurmountable before the hero goes ahead and disposes of it.

31. This is a point not sufficiently appreciated by those who have stressed Achilles' love of life, such as W. Schadewaldt (*Von Homers Welt und Werk*, p. 369). The peace that Homer's hero understands comes only after action: "port after stormy seas," to borrow a phrase from Spenser.

32. See Bowra, *Heroic Poetry*, pp. 91ff.; cf. F. J. Oinas, "Folk Epic," p. 101.

33. In *Sunjata* IV.41, the hero's archenemy, Sumanguru, is said to be "the bulwark of fetishism against the word of Allah."

34. See *Sunjata* IV.2-3; cf. C. Bird, "Bambara Oral Prose and Verse Narratives Collected by Charles Bird," pp. 444ff.

35. Nilsson has, incidentally, an interesting interpretation of Athene's aid to Diomedes against Ares and Aphrodite: he thinks it "recalls the age when the prince set out with the goddess of his city and might meet in battle the protecting deities of another town." See M. P. Nilsson, *A History of Greek Religion*, p. 155.

36. B. Malinowski, *Magic, Science, and Religion and Other Essays*, p. 90.

37. On this confrontation between Islam and traditional African beliefs, see further M. Hisket, "The 'Song of Bagauda,' " pp. 382f.; cf. *Silamaka* 7.

38. Cf. Bowra, *Heroic Poetry*, p. 91: "Even when the hero has supernatural powers and is all the more formidable because of them, they do little more than supplement his essentiallly human gifts."

3. The Hero: His Image and Relevance

39. The sense of uncertainty is here conveyed by the particles κεν πως, which are even stronger than αι κε in Athene's statement above (1.207). Walter Leaf (*The Iliad*) considers Zeus's phrase "an expression of studied courtesy"; I think there is more to it, but even courtesy is a deference that only a personality like Achilles will compel.

40. See E. B. Idowu, *African Traditional Religion*, pp. 194f. Andrew Lang has a vivid description of this kind of magic in the phrase "the part influences the whole; you burn some of a man's hair, and so he catches a fever": see his *Magic and Religion*, p. 46.

41. The subject of totems in the western Sudan is usefully discussed by Spencer Trimingham in his book *Islam in West Africa*, pp. 131f.: cf. Idowu, *African Traditional Religion*, p. 177, and R. Pageard, "Soundiata Keita et la tradition orale." On the possibility that totemism may have its roots in the sanctification of the pastoral fauna, see A. H. Ba, "The Fulbe or Fulani of Mali and Their Culture." For a more detailed discussion on totems see especially S. Freud, *Totem and Taboo*, tr. J. Strachey; C. Lévi-Strauss, *Totemism*, and *The Savage Mind*.

42. This is the device that some scholars have called the "taboo of impurity," as for instance Trimingham, *Islam in West Africa*, p. 58. For a fairly detailed treatment of the subject as it relates to the rivalry between Sunjata and Sumanguru, see Pageard, "Soundiata Keita," pp. 66f., and Sidibe, "Soundiata Keita."

43. See Leaf, *The Iliad*, for classical references on the connections between magic and metallurgy. The old germanic equivalent of the smith-magician is Volund of the Norse Saga (Weyland in Anglo-Saxon): cf. *Beowulf* 455 and *Waldhere* 2.

44. Bowra, *Heroic Poetry*, p. 93.

45. Kirk, *Myth*, p. 38.

46. *Sunjata* IV.23, 35, 48. The connection with Alexander is an interesting one: he is said to have counted Achilles lucky in having a Homer to sing his glory (Arrian, *Anabasis* 1.12.1).

47. The affinity between the two tales is essentially one between the two careers of warfare and hunting. Hugo Zemp found that, among the Dan of the Ivory Coast, "la grande chasse est assimilée à la guerre. 'Le chasseur, c'est comme le guerrier, il ne sait jamais s'il reviendra.' " ("Musiciens autochtones," p. 372.).

48. Leaf's note on *meta kleos*, as implying "in the direction whence came the rumor of" the Achaeans, aptly describes Iphidamas' exuberant joy. An interesting parallel to this urge is seen in the Bahima praise line, "I who Am Quick was drawn from afar by lust for the fight. . .": see H. F. Morris, *Heroic Recitations of the Bahima of Ankole*, p. 42.

49. It has been suggested, again as proof of Sunjata's consideration, that he originally left home with his family to avoid the fierce fraternal rivalry (*fadenya*) which in the western Sudan (as in many other parts of Africa) is often a feature of life in the polygamous home: see Pageard, "Soundiata Keita," p. 61.

50. D. T. Niane, "Le Problème de Soundiata,"

51. See S. N. Kramer, *The Sumerians*, pp. 187ff.

52. See, for example, Jaeger, *Paideia* 1:11.

53. J. Campbell, *The Hero With a Thousand Faces*, p. 353.

54. See Leaf, *The Iliad*, II. 153.

55. See, for example S. A Babalola, *Content and Form*, p. 172.

56. Soyinka, *Idanre, and Other Poems* (London: Methuen, 1967), p. 72. It seems clear from *Kambili* that killing, far from being looked upon in the heroic society as objectionable is glorious—a sign of the killer's supremacy over his victim. The grim justice of Samory Toure, who systematically executes the experts who fail to solve the Kambili riddle, sustains the affective appeal of the tale to no small extent. What we have there is a case of the magnificent terror.

Charles Bird also has an interesting reading of the frequent formula, *The hero is welcome only on troubled days*: he thinks it means the hero "is an antisocial character, usually destructive to the social system, but in times of trouble it is only he who is capable of action necessary to save the society" (see *Kambili*, n. 63). Compare also the picture of Roland. He is the pride of French heroism, but Oliver makes a touching point when he chides him, "Your prowess, Roland, is a curse on our heads" (1731).

4. ON FORM AND STRUCTURE

1. For useful discussions on breaks in a singer's performance and the implications of these on the probable divisions of Homer's songs, see M. Parry, "Homer and Huso: 1. The Singer's Rests in Greek and Southslavic Heroic Songs"; A. B. Lord, "The Singer's Rests in Greek and Southslavic Heroic Songs"; J. A. Notopoulos, "Continuity and Interconnection in Homeric Oral Composition."

2. J. H. Nketia, "The Musician in Akan Society," p. 85. We will also recall that earlier in *The Mwindo Epic* the bard complains that he has been made to eat with everybody else and has not been treated with special hospitality (81, n. 148). The situation would seem to have been corrected in 101.

3. M. Parry, *Les Formules et la Metrique d'Homere*, p. 80.

4. "Studies in the Epic Technique of Oral Verse-making. I: Homer and Homeric Style," 81-83, 122, 124.

5. Some recent scholars have argued, often convincingly, for the aesthetic relevance of the formulaic epithets in Homer: see especially W. Whallon, *Formula, Character, and Content*.

6. For a description of the three basic types of formula in Homer, see C. M. Bowra, "The Comparative Study of Homer." Bowra's concept of the formula is generally more flexible than Parry's; see also his *Heroic Poetry* p. 222.

7. In *Sunjata* IV, Alexander the Great is called "king of gold and silver" three times (23, 32, 48), a combination analogous to "Agamemnon, king of men" or

4. On Form and Structure

"Hektor, tamer of horses," or (in Salih Uglijanin's "Song of Bagdad") "Sultan Selim, light of the world" (Parry and Lord, *Serbocrotian Heroic Songs*, pp. 68ff.). In *Mwindo*, we have the hero's untiring reference to himself as "Little one-just-born-he-walked."

8. A. Parry, *Making of Homeric Verse*, p. 446; cf. Babalola, *Content and Form*, p. 52.

9. An interesting variant of the *Ali mang a long* matrix occurs later on. Dembo confesses he has gone hoarse and allows his brother Banna (the bard of *Sunjata* II), who is present at the performance, to take over. Banna does a few lines of recitative in honor of Sunjata's ally Fakoli, and one of them is: "*Ali mang a long kuru dundungo fota a mama le ma*" (Don't you know that the drum to summon meetings was sounded for his grandfather) (811).

10. There are also numerous variations on this formula, consisting in a slight alteration of words, as in "He rose up, saying, 'Toure ni Manjun!' 'Yes!' (*Kambili* 455).

11. C. Bird, "Heroic Songs of the Mande Hunters," p. 283. Cf. Nketia, "Akan Poetry," pp. 8ff., and Babalola, *Content and Form*, pp. 344ff. The principle is particularly well illustrated in Babalola's collection. See for instance, the "Salute to My Ogun" (pp. 172ff.), where verses 2-4 are later packed into one flashing line (39).

12. The Fang has a parallel French translation, but I have turned the latter straight into English to save space.

13. See Parry and Lord, *Serbocroatian Heroic Songs*, p. 73; *Smailagic Meho* 167.

14. Lord, "Composition by Theme in Homer and Southslavic Epos." The origins of the concept of "theme" as the unit of epic composition can be seen in Parry's review of Walter Arend's *Die typischen Scenen bei Homer* (Berlin, 1933), and more specifically in his Yugoslav field notes (*Making of Homeric Verse*, p. 446).

15. Lord, "Composition by Theme," p. 73. Lord also describes the theme as "in reality protean" in *Singer of Tales*, p. 94.

16. *Akoma Mba* 59ff. = 190ff. = 364ff. = 526ff. = 704ff. = 946ff. = 2005ff.

17. *Ibid.*, 358ff. = 1064ff. = 1295ff.

18. *Odyssey* 1.136ff. = 4.52ff. = 7.172ff. = 10.368ff.

19. *Sunjata* II.277ff. = 332ff. = 496ff. = 637ff. = 1574ff.

20. There are analogous instances in the Homeric and Yugoslav epics. In *Iliad* 9, Agamemnon announces the numerous gifts he will give to Achilles if Achilles will rejoin the army; but then he says, less winningly,

Let him give way. For Hades gives not way, and is pitiless,
and therefore he among all the gods is most hateful to mortals.
And let him yield place to me, inasmuch as I am the kinglier
and inasmuch as I can call myself born the elder.

(158-61)

These words would make an angry Achilles all the more angry, so the wise Odysseus omits them when the embassy takes the message of Agamemnon's offer to the sulking hero. In *Smailagic Meho*, the hero Mehmed sulks at a party given by his father, Hadji Smail; Mehmed's uncle, Clifric Hasan, asks why; Mehmed replies that he is unhappy because, though he has reached the flower of his youth, he has not known any acts of heroism and therefore cannot brag the way that many young men at the party are doing; he then adds that he has a mind to run off to Emperor Peter of Bogdan and offer him his service. This last detail is something of an abomination: Emperor Peter is the sworn enemy of the Ottoman empire, and it would be utmost treachery for a Turk to be associated with him in any way. When, therefore, Cifric Hasan reports Mehmed's grievance to Hadji Smail, he carefully omits that outrageous detail about Peter by simply tellling Hadji Smail, "nor shall I tell you all he said" (96).

21. *Iliad* 11.794-803 = 16.36-45.

22. *Iliad* 24.147-58 = 176-87.

23. *Odyssey* 1.374-80 = 2.139-45.

24. That is, the essential message of ten lines (691-700) is blown out into twenty-four lines (713-36); the added material is taken from an earlier passage 665-79.

25. Lord, *Singer of Tales*, p. 67.

26. *Ibid.* pp. 66f.

27. For various observations on repetition see Bowra, *Heroic Poetry* pp. 255f.; A. Olrik, "Epic Laws of Folk Narrative," pp. 132f.; Babalola, *Content and Form*, pp. 65f.; D. P. Kunene, *Heroic Poetry of the Basotho*, pp. 68ff. Olrik's epic "law of repetition" stresses repetition of scenes. See also Parry and Lord, *Serbocroatian Heroic Songs*, p. 329, n. 9.

28. See, for instance, A. Parry, *Making of Homeric Verse*, p. 443; A. B. Lord, "Homer and Other Epic Poetry," p. 200.

29. On the difficult subject of African prosody, see especially R. Finnegan, *Oral Literature in Africa*, pp. 72-76. What she says (following Greenberg) about the Arabic or Islamic influence in quantitive verse is interesting. However, while there is notable Islamic influence in *Kambili* and *Sunjata*, the number of syllables to the line in either case is far from regular: see Bird, "Heroic Poetry of the Mande Hunters," pp. 283f.; and G. Innes, *Sunjata: Three Mandika Versions*, pp. 14 and 17; cf. M. Hiskett, "The 'Song of Bagauda,' " 370ff.

30. See Finnegan, *Oral Literature*, p. 75.

31. G. P. Lestrade, "Traditional Literature," p. 306.

32. *Mwindo* 45 (147); cf. 58 (151), 79 (162), 98 (173), 101 (175). (The enclosed numbers represent the corresponding pages in the original Nyanga text at the end of the book. This formula also appears several times in the choral chants.)

33. *Mwindo* 62 (152), 64 (153), 132 (193), 139 (197).

34. *Mwindo* 45 (147), 97 (173); cf. 120 (187).

4. On Form and Structure

35. The theme of cleavage by lightning in aid of Mwindo also occurs in 103.

36. I have noted at least twenty-four uses of this theme; for a random sampling, see *Ozidi* 54, 76, 92, 120, 168, 191, 253, 306, 355.

37. The following are some of the notable victims involved: *Ozidi* 70 (Agbagidi) = 99 (Azezabife) = 127 (Ogueren) = 142 (Akpobrisi) = 201f (Ofe).

38. *Ozidi* 63 = 84 = 127f = 158 = 317.

39. See Finnegan, *Oral Literature*, pp. 379ff.

40. Lord, *Singer of Tales*, p. 68.

41. See Bowra, *Heroic Poetry*, p. 222. Bowra's conception arises from his broad comparative study of the heroic epic from various traditions. Otherwise, perhaps the first serious challenge to Parry was by G. M. Calhoun, "The Art of Formula in Homer."

42. J. B. Hainsworth, *The Flexibility of the Homeric Formula*; A. Hoekstra, *Homeric Modifications of Formulaic Prototypes*; J. A. Russo, "The Structural Formula in Homeric Verse"; M. N. Nagler, *Spontaneity and Tradition*. For a somewhat similar work in Old English poetry, see F. P. Magoun, "Oral-Formulaic Character of Anglo-Saxon Poetry."

43. Nagler, *Spontaneity*, p. 74.

44. See T. W. Allen, *Homeri Ilias*, p. 206.

45. Lord, *Singer of Tales*, p. 94.

46. A term that Nagler has borrowed from Pindaric scholarship and uses frequently in his discussions: see *Spontaneity*, p. 8.

47. For an account of the various positions held on the subject, see J. J. Duggan, *The Song of Roland*, pp. 12-13.

48. Youman, "Climactic Themes in the *Iliad*."

49. My colleague, J. B. Egberike, has collected an epic from the same region as *Ozidi* and corroborates this gradation.

50. Youman, "Climactic Themes," p. 225.

51. Lord, *Singer of Tales*, pp. 94f. For a list of the major discussions on the subject of narrative inconsistency, see D. M. Gunn, "Narrative Inconsistency and the Oral Dictated Text in the Homeric Epic."

52. M. P. Nilsson, *A History of Greek Religion*, p. 140; cf. C. M. Bowra, *Tradition and Design in the Iliad*, p. 218.

53. Youman, "Climactic Themes in the *Iliad*," p. 225; cf. G. G. E. Mylonas, "Burial Customs," p. 480. For the disalignment between Greek religious beliefs and Homeric art, see the interesting discussion of Homer's portrait of Zeus in A. W. H. Adkins, *Merit and Responsibility*, pp. 11-23. For further observations on the dramatic environment of divine character, see Adkins, "Homeric Gods and the Values of Homeric Society."

54. Nagler, *Spontaneity*, p. 81.

55. *Ibid.*, pp. 8f. From his work on the oral poetry of the Scottish world, James Ross also talks about "conceptual formulas" whose variety of expression "shows

that what makes an idea useful to the oral poet is not its availability in a fixed verbal form or in a system of metrically similar statements": see his "Formulaic Composition in Gaelic Oral Poetry,"

56. With Nagler's "rhythmical groups," compare the concept of rhythm segments in Babalola, *Content and Form*, pp. 344ff., and breath groups in Innes, *Sunjata*, p. 17. Perhaps for a somewhat similar reason, we may take a look at R. A. Waldron's identification of the "rhythmic" uses of the formula in Middle English alliterative verse: "Oral-Formulaic Technique and Alliterative Poetry." We are here dealing with a literate tradition, but the conclusions are important for a reexamination of the old Parryan conceptions of formulaic composition.

57. The phenomenon is different, in spite of E. M. Forster's interesting observations on "rhythm" in his *Aspects of the Novel*, pp. 151-70.

58. Innes, *Sunjata*, p. 312.

59. Pindar, *Nemean* 2.1f.

60. *Mwindo* begins with a simple temporal formula, "Long ago. . . . " Some bards do not care for an extended preamble—I think this is a matter of choice. For such unpretentious beginnings, compare *SCHS* 122, 133, 269, etc.

61. The neatness of the conception can hardly be denied, in spite of the Joycean mode and the so-called movement "against closure" which critics seem to identify in the contemporary novel. On this movement, see for example Alan Friedman, *The Turn of the Novel*, pp. 179ff.

62. They have often been condemned as late Hesiodic interpolations on the original Homeric text. Such augustan views of a "detached" Homer are, to say the least, uncorroborated by all available field evidence.

63. See, for example, *Iliad* 2.196f., which bears a striking resemblance to Kalchas' words in 1.80.

64. See, for examples, *Beowulf* 1002ff.; 1724-68. The sentiments in the latter passage are amazingly Christian for a Hrothgar whose kingdom has earlier been condemned as a heathen land.

65. Compare with this the fierce owl-banter between Sunjata and Sumanguru in *Sunjata* IV.60f.

66. For the various attempts by scholars to reduce the three dirges to lyric meters, see W. Leaf, *The Iliad*. Leaf concedes that "the contents of the laments naturally give them something of a lyric character." Another famous lyrical lament in heroic song is that of Euphrosyne in *Igor* 691ff. For other examples of the song within a song, cf. the Finnsburg lay in *Beowulf*.

67. Rhys Carpenter (*Folktale, Fiction, and Saga*, pp. 78ff.) has an interesting view of the *Iliad* as drama, with observations on the "divertive interlude."

68. *Iliad* 11.547-55, 556-64. A. B. Lord may be right in his observation that "to the method of dictation one can also attribute the piling up of similes in Homer and the extended simile" ("Homer's Originality," p. 77). But *Kambili* shows clearly that the digressive chain of ideas and images is native to the overactive imagination

of the performing bard. It is likely that the well-manicured order and directness of the Homeric similes is the product of careful editing.

69. There is a subtle difference between the digressions here and the bard's plea for a substitute. The latter anticipates the detail about the hero's "fainting away" (in the drum), and the stresses felt by the bard simply find a fitting articulation in a line recalling the hero's experience. In the other case, however, the order is reversed: a detail in the story leads on to an external observation.

70. If it was ever true that the songs of Homer were put together from various pieces collected in the field, as ancient authority held (Plato, *Hipparchus* 228b; Cicero, *De Oratore* 3.137; Josephus, *Contra Apionem* 1.12), his editors must have been inclined to delete all these obtrusive details from the "variants" that they had before them. The poet's tribute to the choral maidens in *Hymn to Apollo* 166ff. (like Seydou Camara's salute to his accompanists and guests) seems, however, to suggest a tradition whereby the bard took some account of the environment of his song.

71. A Parry, *Making of Homeric Verse*, p. 454.

72. Cf. *Kambili* 494-500, where the enumeration is even less relevant.

73. *Rhetorics* 1409a.

74. J. Tate has given a useful summary of this theory as propounded by W. A. A. van Otterlo in his *De Ringcompositie als Opbouwprincipe in de Epische Gedichte van Homerus*. See alos Notopoulos, "Continuity and Interconnection," pp. 96ff.; C. H. Whitman, *Homer and the Heroic Tradition*, pp. 252ff.; and J. H. Gaisser, "A Structural Analysis of Digressions in the *Iliad* and the *Odyssey*."

75. Notopoulos, "Continuity," p. 98.

76. For various kinds of the "return"/"ring" device in Homer, see the impressive catalogue in Gaisser, "Structural Analysis," pp. 37-40.

77. Homer's verbs are ηρυγον (bellowed), ελκω (drag); and the word for the life-breath that is lost is Θυμος. The ring pattern therefrom is as follows: θυμον—ηργγεν—ηρυγεν—ελκομενος—ελκοντων—ερυγοντα—θυμος. Whether or not this is the order in which these words were sung orally, there is no doubt that the poet would have kept the ideas in some form of close association so as to reclaim his story line.

5. ELEMENTS OF THE ORAL NARRATIVE STYLE

1. Compare also the wild obscenities used by Tale of Orasac in *Smailagic Meho* 176ff. (see Lord's notes). The so-called Homeric laugh is a somewhat dry, grand, aristocratic haw-haw, but the Deceit of Zeus in *Iliad* 14, and the Ares-Aphrodite affair in *Odyssey* 8, are not without the pornographic interest of low comedy.

2. Notice the underlying histrionic touch in the text:

Ogueren remained there anchored—
> [*Laughter*]
His eyes rolled—
> [*Laughter*]
and rolled.

We can see a rhapsode making the same effort when he says of Patroklos: "his eyes spun . . . . Disaster caught his wits, and his shining body went nerveless. He stood stupidly . . . . "

3. M. Hiskett, "The 'Song of Baguda,' " p. 132.

4. Wande Abimbola, *Sixteen Great Poems of Ifa*, p. 61.

5. 11.218ff., 299ff.; 14.508ff. The last scene has been challenged by W. Leaf: "The appeal to the Muses is out of place, as there is no great crisis, but only a temporary reflux of the tide of battle." But the bloody career of the small group of heroes led by Ajax gives a fresh if momentary turn and interest to the progress of the war, and the bard takes due account of the development by jolting us anew.

6. For instance, there is a recitative chant at the point in Bamba Suso's version of *Sunjata*, where the hero threatens to kill his mother unless she tells him the circumstances of his birth (I.284ff.). G. Innes recognizes that it is "a point of extreme emotional tension" and suggests that the recitative "was introduced at this point to reduce the emotional temperature," giving "time for the audience to recover from the emotional shock" (notes, p. 110).

7. C. M. Bowra, *Tradition and Design*, pp. 112f.

8. *Ozidi* raises an interesting problem. The division into seven nights is, as my colleague Joseph Egberike confirms, conceived less in terms of time than conveniently spaced fight episodes. To take off successfully an episode is often introduced by a theme song. Perhaps the best example of this is in *Ozidi* 326, where Tebekawene's song is first rehearsed so that the bard can be worked up to the narration of the fight between Ozidi and Tebekawene.

What D. Biebuyck says of the program of *Mwindo* is also noteworthy: "The entire epic cannot, of course, be performed in a single evening or a single day. A series of consecutive evening performances may be scheduled, but a simple performance may also be limited to one evening and restricted to a couple of episodes. The bard is largely free to select whichever episode he wants, depending somewhat on his mood, inspiration, and sometimes on local social circumstances." ("The Epic as a Genre in Congo Oral Literature," p. 263). On the random choice of episodes, compare Odysseus' plea to Demodokos that the bard change his subject and "sing the making of the wooden horse" (*Odyssey* 8.492).

9. Other narrative inconsistencies, however, must be put down to sheer failure of skill or memory. We have one such glaring example in Banna Kanute's version of

5. Elements of the Oral Narrative Style

Sunjata. Sumanguru sends his griot Bala Faasigi Kuyate on a mission to Sunjata. Sunjata, impressed by the griot's musical excellence, cuts his Achilles tendons and forces him to leave Sumanguru's service and stay in his court (II.1552ff.). Later, Sunjata's sister, Nene Faamaga, comes over to Sumanguru, pretending to want to marry him; after the normal courtesies before the king, Nene is asked by Bala Fassiga what brings her to the court of Sumanguru! (1584ff.). This is somewhat of a Pylaimenes-type reappearance; but though we may defend Pylaimenes on the grounds that the two scenes (in *Iliad* 5 and 13) are far apart, the Bala Faasigi scenes are much too close in the same performance to be excused. Perhaps the singer is confusing his narration at this point with a different tradition (related by his brother Dembo, *Sunjata* III.270-325) which reverses the facts: the griot has been sent to Sumanguru, who, impressed by the griot's musical skill, cuts his heels to make him stay. This is the only acceptable excuse.

10. A. Parry, *Making of Homeric Verse*, p. 460.

11. For a useful case study, see Philip A. Noss, "Description in Gbaya Literary Art," pp. 73-101.

12. See C. Bird, introduction to *Kambili*, p. vi. There is some sense in what Ernst Cassirer has said in this regard: "The original bond between the linguistic and the mythico-religious consciousness is primarily expressed in the fact that all verbal structures appear as also mythical entities, endowed with certain mythical powers, that the Word, in fact, becomes a sort of primary force, in which all being and doing originate" (*Language and Myth*, pp. 44f).

13. Which, according to Innes in his notes (p. 121), means "jealousy"; "nooya" means "power."

14. Babalola, *Content and Form*, p. 182.

15. For assonance and alliteration in Homeric and Slavic epics, see A. B. Lord, "Homer and Other Epic Poetry," pp. 200f.

16. "N'Ko" is Mandingo for "I say."

17. Cf. *Iliad* 13.322; Hesiod, *Works and Days* 82, and *Catalogue of Women* 58.12.

18. M. P. Nilsson's attempt to uphold Homeric "anthropomorphism" against the "grotesque figures of deities from Africa and Polynesia" (*History of Greek Religion*, pp. 143ff.) is rather unnecessary. It is easy enough to point to several nonhuman epiphanies of divinities in Homer, or even to the general theriomorphic picture in the Mesopotamian "epics"; but what counts is not whether these figures look like human beings or like animals. We know they are not human, but the mythmaker has endowed them with enough human characteristics (speech, behavior) for us to admit them on equal terms with the human figures whose world they are shown to share. If we are impressed by their human qualities, we have taken them for granted as humans: that is the point of the realism. Nilsson's view of Skamandros is therefore gratuitous logic: "The power of the description of Achilles'

fight with Skamandros lies in the fact that the river is regarded as an element—an inundation, a torrent—to which the hero is nearly forced to yield, until he is saved by the sending of another element, fire, against it" (p. 144). How, if one may ask, does fire neutralize a torrent?

19. On such naming devices, see further P. A. Noss, "Description in Gbaya Literary Art," pp. 79-81, 99-101.

20. Aristarchus, for instance, rejects *Iliad* 1.195-96 as being wrongly anticipative of 208-9.

21. On *Iliad* 12.176.

22. The outlook in *Beowulf* oscillates between the traditional heroic and the Christian, but in the frequent authorial views we can see the bard's anxiety to be the real mouthpiece of whatever values emerge from the tale. Cf. also the author's apostrophe in *Igor* 491ff.

23. The authorial empathy is frequently used also in *Mwindo*; see, for example, the chants on pp. 79, 135, etc. Even the formulaic "Scribe, move on!" (uttered by Mwindo in the chants) is a mark of this happy confusion of the personae of the bard and the hero.

24. Bowra, *Heroic Poetry*, p. 32, where see comparative examples of the authorial empathy from Nordic and Slavic heroic songs.

25. Parry and Lord, *Serbocroatian Heroic Songs*, p. 421 (n. 28). Cf. *Smailagic Meho* 226, where Avdo's use of personal pronouns ("that we might know our debt and tell of it") somehow betrays his attachment to the Ottoman empire of which he sings.

6. CONCLUSION

1. M. N. Nagler, *Spontaneity and Tradition*, p. 199.

2. See R. Finnegan, *Oral Literature in Africa*, pp. 109-10.

3. J. B. Hainsworth, "The Criticism of an Oral Homer," pp. 91f.

4. Finnegan, *Oral Literature in Africa*, p. 518.

5. The old professionals are still very much active. I have been unable to get hold of Kesteloot's collection, *Da Monzon de Segou: Epopee Bambara* (Paris: Nathan, 1972), 4 vols., mentioned by her in her paper, "Un Épisode de l'épopée Bambara de Segou." There have been other collections from the Fang country: see D. Biebuyck, "The African Heroic Epic," p. 34. My students in oral literature here at Ibadan have also been active in field collections of epic tales, among other kinds of folklore. I feel proud to be associated with them, and would like to draw attention to two of them in particular: Paul O Akegwure's work on "The Ogiso Epic," from the Isoko clan of Bendel State, and John Edemode's on "The Agboghidi Epic" from the Etsako, also of the Bendel State of Nigeria. Both pieces are in the holdings of the English Department of Ibadan University.

6. Conclusion

6. "Le voix negres, parce que non domestiquées par l'école, épousent toutes les nuances des sentiments-idées; puisant librement dans le dictionnaire infini de la nature, elles lui empruntent ses expressions sonores, depuis les chants transparents des passereaux jusqu'aux sombres éclats du tonnerre." See J. B. Obama, "La Musique africaine traditionnelle," p. 276.

SELECTED BIBLIOGRAPHY

Please see pages xvi–xvii for the abbreviated forms used for some of the following works in the text and footnotes.

PRIMARY SOURCES

African

Abimbola, W. *Sixteen Great Poems of Ifa*. Paris: UNESCO, 1975.

Awona, S. "La Guerre d'Akoma Mba contre Abo Mama." *ABBIA* (1965), 9–10: 180–214; (1966), 12–13:109–209.

Ba, A. H. and L. Kesteloot. "Da Monzon et Karta Thiema." *ABBIA* (1966), 14–15:179–205.

—— "Une Epope Peule: 'Silamaka.' " *L'Homme* (1968), 8:5–36.

Biebuyck, D. and K. C. Mateene. *The Mwindo Epic from the Banyanga*. Berkeley and Los Angeles: University of California Press, 1969.

Bird, C. "Bambara Oral Prose and Verse Narratives." In R. M. Dorson, ed. *African Folklore*, pp. 441–77. New York: Doubleday, 1972.

Bird, C., with M. Koita and B. Soumaoro. *The Song of Seydou Camara Volume 1: Kambili*. Bloomington: African Studies Center, Indiana University, 1974.

Boelaert, P. "Nsong'a Lianja: L'Epopee nationale des Nkudo." *Aequatoria* (1949), 12:1–75.

Clark, J. P. *The Ozidi Saga*. Ibadan: Ibadan University Press and Oxford University Press, 1977.

Hisket, M. "The 'Song of Bagauda': A Hausa King List and Homily in Verse." *BSOAS* (1965), 28:112–35.

Selected Bibliography

Innes, G. *Sunjata: Three Mandinka Versions*. London: School of Oriental and African Studies, 1974.

Konate, M. "Da Monzon de segou." *ABBIA* (1966), 14–15: 171–78.

Mofolo, T. *Chaka*. Translated by F. H. Dutton. Oxford: Clarendon, 1931.

Niane, D. T. *Sundiata: An Epic of Old Mali*. Translated by G. D. Pickett. London: Longmans, 1965.

Homeric

Evelyn-White, H. G. *Hesiod, the Homeric Hymns, and Homerica*. London: Heinemann, 1959.

Lattimore, R. *The Iliad of Homer*. Chicago: University of Chicago Press, 1951.

——*The Odyssey of Homer*. New York: Harper, 1965.

Leaf, W. *The Iliad*. 2 vols. London: Macmillan, 1900–1902.

Merry, W. W. *Homer: The Odyssey I–XII*. Oxford: Clarendon, 1884.

Monro, D. B. *Homer: Iliad*. Oxford: Clarendon, 1903.

——*Homer: Odyssey XIII–XXIV*. Oxford: Clarendon, 1901.

Other

Bowra, C. M. *The Odes of Pindar*. Harmondsworth, U. K.: Penguin, 1969.

Gordon, E. V. *The Battle of Maldon*. New York: Appleton, 1966.

Kennedy, C. W. *Beowulf*. Oxford: Clarendon, 1940.

Mavrogordato, J. *Digenes Akritas*. Oxford: Clarendon, 1956.

Nabokov, V. *The Song of Igor's Campaign*. New York: Vintage Books, 1960.

Parry, M. and A. B. Lord. *Serbocroatian Heroic Songs*, vol 1. Cambridge, Mass: Harvard University Press, 1954.

Parry, M., A. B. Lord and D. Bynum. *Serbocroatian Heroic Songs*. Vol. 3: *The Wedding of Smailagic Meho by Avdo Mededovic*. Cambridge, Mass.: Harvard University Press, 1974.

Sandars, N. K. *The Epic of Gilgamesh*. Harmondsworth, U. K.: Penguin, 1960.

Sayers, D. L. *The Song of Roland*. Harmondsworth, U. K.: Penguin, 1937.

Wrenn, C. L. *Beowulf*. London: Harrap, 1958.

SECONDARY SOURCES

African Studies

Abraham, W. E. *The Mind of Africa*. Chicago: University of Chicago Press, 1962.

Ames, D. W. "A Sociocultural View of Hausa Musical Activity." In W. L. d'Azevedo, ed., *The Traditional Artist in African Societies*, pp. 128–61. Bloomington: Indiana University Press, 1973.

Arewa, E. O., and A. Dundes. "Proverbs and the Ethnography of Speaking Folklore." *American Anthropologist* (1964), 66:70.

Ba, A. H. "The Fulbe or Fulani of Mali and Their Culture." *ABBIA* (1966), 14–15:55–87.

Babalola, S. A. *The Content and Form of Yoruba Ijala*. Oxford: Clarendon, 1966.

Beier, U. *Contemporary Art in Africa*. London: Pall Mall, 1968.

Biebuyck, D. "The African Heroic Epic." *JFI* (1976), 13: 5–36.

—— "The Epic as a Genre in Congo Oral Literature." In R. M. Dorson, ed., *African Folklore*, pp. 257–73. New York: Doubleday, 1972.

Biebuyck, D. and K. C. Mateene. "Chante Hunde." *Afrika Und Ubersee* (1965), 49:157–69.

Bird, C. "Heroic Songs of the Mande Hunters." In R. M. Dorson, ed., *African Folklore*, pp. 275–93. New York: Doubleday, 1972.

Carnochan, J. " 'Nzeanzo and Won': A Bachama Folktale." *JFI* (1967), 4:230–39.

Clark, J. P. "The Azudu Saga." *African Notes* (1963), 1:8–9.

Coupez, A. and Th. Kamanzi. *Litterateur de cour au Rwanda*. Oxford: Clarendon, 1970.

Crowley, D. J. "The Uses of African Verbal Art." *JFI* (1969), 6:118–32.

Daaku, K. Y. "History in the Oral Traditions of the Akan." *JFI* (1971), 8:114–26.

Finnegan, R. *Oral Literature in Africa*. Oxford: Clarendon, 1970.

Idowu, E. B. *African Traditional Religion*. London: S. C. M. Press, 1973.

Kesteloot, L. "Les Epopées de l'ouest africain." *Presence Africaine* (1966), 58:204–9.

—— "Un Episode de l'épopée Bambara de Segou." *BIFAN* (1973), 35:881–902.

King, B., ed. *Introduction to Nigerian Literature*. Lagos: Evans Brothers, 1971.

Knappert, J. "The Epic in Africa." *JFI* (1967), 4:171–90.

Kunene, D. P. *Heroic Poetry of the Basotho*. Oxford: Clarendon, 1971.

Lestrade, G. P. "Traditional Literature." In I. Schapera, ed., *The Bantu-Speaking Tribes of South Africa*, pp. 291–308. London: Routledge, 1966.

Selected Bibliography

Leuzinger, E. *The Art of the Negro Peoples.* New York: Crown, 1967.

Levtzion, N. *Ancient Ghana and Mali.* London: Methuen, 1973.

Macebuh, S. "African Aesthetics in Traditional African Art." *Okike* (1974) 5:13–24.

Mafeje, A. "The Role of the Bard in a Contemporary African Community." *JAL* (1967), 6:193–223.

Meauzé, P. *African Art.* Cleveland: World, 1968.

Merriam, A. P. "The Bala Musician." In W. L. d'Azevedo, ed., *The Traditional Artist in African Societies,* pp. 250–81. Bloomington: Indiana University Press, 1973.

Monteil, V. ed. *C. Monteil: Les Empires du Mali.* Paris: n.p., n.d.

Moore, G. *The Chosen Tongue.* London: Longmans, 1969.

Morris, H. F. *Heroic Recitations of the Bahima of Ankole.* Oxford: Clarendon, 1964.

Niane, D. T. "La Problème de Soundiata." *Notes Africaines* (1960), 88:123–26.

Nketia, J. H. K. "Akan Poetry." *Black Orpheus* (1958), 3:3–21.

—— "The Musician in Akan Society." In W. L. d'Azevedo, ed., *The Traditional Artist in African Societies,* Bloomington: Indiana University Press, 1973.

Noss, P. A. "Description in Gbaya Literary Art." In R. M. Dorson, ed., *African Folklore,* pp. 73–101. New York: Doubleday, 1972.

Obama, J. B. "La Musique africaine traditionnelle: ses fonctions sociales et sa signification philosophique." *ABBIA* (1966), 12–13: 273–308.

Opland, J. "*Imbongi Nezibongo*; The Xhosa Tribal Poet and the Contemporary Poetic Tradition." *PMLA* (1975), 90: 185–208.

Pageard, R. "Soundiata Keita et la tradition orale." *Presence Africaine* (1961), 36:51–70.

Scharfe, D. and Y. Aliyu. "Hausa Poetry." In U. Beier, ed., *Introduction to African Literature,* pp. 34–40. London: Longmans, 1967.

Shelton, A. J. "The Problem of Griot Interpretation and the Actual Causes of War in *Soundjata.*" *Presence Africaine* (1968), 66:145–52.

Sidibe, M. "Soundiata Keita, héros historique et légendaire, empereur du Manding." *Notes Africaines* (1959), 81:41–51.

Towo-Atangana, G. "Le Mvet: genre majeur de la litterateur orale des populations Pahouines." *ABBIA* (1965), 9–10:163–79.

Trimingham, S. *Islam in West Africa.* Oxford: Clarendon, 1959.

Trowell, M. *Classical African Sculpture.* New York: Praeger, 1964.

Zemp, H. "La legende du griots malinke." *CEA* (1966), 6:611–42.

—— "Musiciens autochtones et griots malinke chez les Dan de Cote d'Ivoire." *CEA* (1964), 4:371:82.

Homeric Studies

Adkins, A. W. H. "Homeric Gods and the Values of Homeric Society." *JHS* (1972), 92:1–19.

Allen, T. W. *Homer: The Origins and Transmission*. Oxford: Clarendon, 1924.

—— *Homeri Ilias: Prolegomena*. Oxford: Clarendon, 1931.

Bowra, C. M. "Metre." In A. J. B. Wace and F. H. Stubbings, eds., *A Companion to Homer*, pp. 19–25. London: Macmillan, 1962.

—— "The Comparative Study of Homer." *AJA* (1950), 54:184–92.

—— *Tradition and Design in the Iliad*. Oxford: Clarendon, 1930.

Calhoun, G. M. "The Art of Formula in Homer." *CP* (1935), 30:215–27.

Carpenter, R. *Folktale, Fiction, and Saga in the Homeric Epics*. Berkeley and Los Angeles: University of California Press, 1962.

Davison, J. A. "The Transmission of the Text." In A. J. B. Wace and F. H. Stubbings, eds., *A Companion to Homer*, pp. 215–33. London: Macmillan, 1962.

Finley, M. "The Trojan War." *JHS* (1964), 84:1–9.

Gaisser, J. H. "A Structural Analysis of the Digressions in the *Iliad* and the *Odyssey*." *HSCP* (1969), 73:1–43.

Gunn, D. M. "Narrative Inconsistency and the Oral Dictated Text in the Homeric Epic." *AJP* (1970), 91:192–203.

Hainsworth, J. B. "The Criticism of an Oral Homer." *JHS* (1970), 90:90-98.

—— *The Flexibility of the Homeric Formula*. Oxford: Clarendon, 1968.

Hoekstra, A. *Homeric Modifications of Formulaic Prototypes*. Amsterdam: N-H.U.M., 1965.

Kirk, G. S. "Homer and Modern Oral Poetry: Some Confusions." *CQ*, n.s. (1960), 10:271–81.

—— *The Songs of Homer*. Cambridge: Cambridge University Press, 1962.

Lord, A. B. "Composition by Theme in Homer and Southslavic Epos." *TAPA* (1951), 82:71–80.

—— "Homer and Huso: II. Narrative Inconsistencies in Homer and Oral Poetry." *TAPA* (1938), 69:439–45.

Selected Bibliography

—— "Homer and Other Epic Poetry." In A. J. B. Wace and F. H. Stubbings, eds., *A Companion to Homer*, pp. 179–214. London: Macmillan, 1962.

—— "Homer as Oral Poet." *HSCP* (1968), 72:1–46.

—— "Homer, Parry, and Huso." *AJA* (1948), 52:34–44.

——"Homer's Originality: Oral Dictated Texts." *TAPA* (1953), 84:124–34.

—— *The Singer of Tales*. Cambridge, Mass.: Harvard University Press, 1960.

—— "The Singer's Rests in Greek and Southslavic Heroic Songs." *TAPA* (1936), 67:106–13.

Mylonas, G. E. "Burial Customs." In A. J. B. Wace and F. H. Stubbings, eds., *A Companion to Homer*, pp. 478–88. London: Macmillan, 1962.

Nagler, M. N. *Spontaneity and Tradition: A Study in the Oral Art of Homer*. Berkeley and Los Angeles: University of California Press, 1974.

Notopoulos, J. A. "Continuity and Interconnection in Homeric Oral Composition." *TAPA* (1951), 82:81–101.

—— "Homer, Hesiod, and the Achaean Heritage of Oral Poetry." *Hesperia* (1960), 29:177–97.

—— "Parataxis in Homer: A New Approach to Homeric Literary Criticism." *TAPA* (1949), 80:1–23.

Page, D. L. *History and the Homeric Iliad*. Berkeley and Los Angeles: University of California Press, 1959.

Palmer, L. R. "The Language of Homer." In A. J. B. Wace and F. H. Stubbings, eds., *A Companion to Homer*, pp. 75–178. London: Macmillan, 1962.

Parry, A. "Have We Homer's *Iliad?*" *YCS* (1966), 20:177–216.

Parry, A. ed. *The Making of Homeric Verse: The Collected Papers of Milman Parry*. Oxford: Clarendon, 1971.

Parry, M. "Homer and Huso: I. The Singer's Rests in Greek and Southslavic Heroic Songs." *TAPA* (1936), 66:xlvii.

—— *Les Formules et la metrique dans Homère*. Paris: Société des Belles Lettres, 1928.

—— "On Typical Scenes in Homer." *CP* (1936), 31;357–360.

—— "Studies in the Epic Technique of Oral Verse Making: I." *HSCP* (1930), 41:70–147.

—— "Studies in the Epic Technique of Oral Verse Making: II." *HSCP* (1932), 43:1–50.

Russo, J. A. "The Structural Formula in Homeric Verse." *YCS* (1966), 20:219–40.

Schadewaldt, W. *Von Homers Welt Und Werk.* Stuttgart: Koehler, 1959.

Shipp, G. P. *Studies in the Language of Homer.* Cambridge: Cambridge University Press, 1953.

Tate, J. Review of W. A. van Otterlo, *De Ringcompositie als Opbouwprincipe in de Epische Gedichte van Homerus* (Amsterdam, 1948). *CR* (1949), 63:137–38.

Vivante, P. *The Homeric Imagination.* Bloomington: Indiana University Press, 1970.

Wade-Gery, H. T. *The Poet of the Iliad.* Cambridge: Cambridge University Press, 1952.

Wegner, M. *Muzik Und Tanz.* Gottingen: Vandenhoeck, 1968.

Whitman, C. H. *Homer and the Heroic Tradition.* Cambridge, Mass.: Harvard University Press, 1958.

Wilamowitz-Moellendorff, U. von. *Die Ilias Und Homer.* Berlin: Weidemann, 1920.

Youman, A. E. "Climactic Themes in the *Iliad.*" *CJ* (1966), 61:222–28.

General

Adkins, A. W. H. *Merit and Responsibility.* Oxford: Clarendon, 1960.

Bowra, C. M. *Heroic Poetry.* London: Macmillan, 1952.

Campbell, J. *The Hero with a Thousand Faces.* Princeton: Princeton University Press, 1972.

Cassirer, E. *Language and Myth.* New York: Dover, 1953.

Chadwick, H. M. *The Heroic Age.* Cambridge: Cambridge University Press, 1912.

Chadwick, H. M. and N. K. Chadwick. *The Growth of Literature,* vol. 1. Cambridge: Cambridge University Press, 1932.

Cook, A. S. *The Classic Line.* Bloomington: Indiana University Press, 1966.

Dodds, E. R. *The Greeks and the Irrational.* Berkeley and Los Angeles: University of California Press, 1959.

Duggan, J. J. *The Song of Roland: Formulaic Style and Poetic Craft.* Berkeley and Los Angeles: University of California Press, 1973.

Forster, E. M. *Aspects of the Novel.* Harmondsworth, U. K.: Penguin, 1962.

Freud, S. *Totem and Taboo,* translated by J. Strachey. London: Hogarth Press, 1950.

Selected Bibliography

Friedman, A. *The Turn of the Novel*. New York: Oxford University Press, 1966.

Jaeger, W. *Paideia: The Ideals of Greek Culture*, vol. 1 Translated by G. Highet. New York: Oxford University Press, 1945.

Kirk, G. S. *Myth: Its Meaning and Functions*. Cambridge and Berkeley: Cambridge University Press and University of California Press, 1970.

Kramer, S. N. *The Sumerians*. Chicago: University of Chicago Press, 1963.

Lang, A. *Magic and Religion*. London: Longmans, 1901.

Lévi-Strauss, C. *The Raw and the Cooked*. New York: Harpers, 1969.

—— *The Savage Mind*. London: Weidenfeld and Nicolson, 1972.

—— *Totemism*. London: Merlin Press, 1964.

Lord, A. B., ed. *Slavic Folklore: A Symposium*. Philadelphia: American Folklore Society, 1956.

Magoun, F. P. "The Oral-Formulaic Character of Anglo-Saxon Narrative Poetry." *Speculum* (1953), 28:446–67.

Malinowski, B. *Magic, Science, and Religion and Other Essays*. New York: Doubleday, 1954.

Nettl, B. *Music in Primitive Culture*. Cambridge, Mass.: Harvard University Press, 1956.

Nilsson, M. P. *A History of Greek Religion*. Oxford: Clarendon, 1956.

Oinas, F. J. "Folk Epic." In R. M. Dorson, ed., *Folklore and Folklife*. Chicago: University of Chicago Press, 1972.

Olrik, A. "Epic Laws of Folk Narrative." *The Study of Folklore*. A. Dundes, ed. Englewood Cliffs: Prentice-Hall, 1965.

Ross, J. "Formulaic Composition in Gaelic Oral Poetry." *MP* (1959), 57:1-12.

Scott, W. *Minstrelsy of the Scottish Border*. Edited by E. F. Henderson. London: Oliver & Boyd, 1932.

Stanford, W. B. *The Ulysses Theme*. Oxford: Blackwell, 1954.

Waldron, R. A. "Oral-Formulaic Technique and Middle English Alliterative Poetry." *Speculum* (1957), 32:792–804.

Whallon, W. *Formula, Character, and Content*. Washington D. C.: Center for Hellenic Studies, 1969.

Zug, C. G. "The Ballad Editor as Antiquary." *JFI* (1976), 13:57–73.

Unpublished Works

Akegwure, P. O. "The Ogiso Epic." Collected and translated as part of term paper from field research. Department of English, University of Ibadan, Ibadan, Nigeria, 1977.

Devrnja, Z. "The Functions of Metaphor in Traditional Serbian Narrative." Dissertation, State University of New York at Buffalo, 1974.

Edemode, J. "The Agboghidi Epic." Collected and translated as part of term paper from field research. Department of English, University of Ibadan, Ibadan, Nigeria, 1977.

INDEX

Index

Index

Index